The
Narrative in Tabletop
Role-Playing Games

The Creation of Narrative in Tabletop Role-Playing Games

JENNIFER GROULING COVER

McFarland & Company, Inc., Publishers

Jefferson, North Carolina, and London

LIBRARY OF CONGRESS CATALOGUING-IN-PUBLICATION DATA

Cover, Jennifer Grouling.
    The creation of narrative in tabletop role-playing games /
Jennifer Grouling Cover.
       p.   cm.
    Includes bibliographical references and index.

    ISBN 978-0-7864-4451-9
    softcover : 50# alkaline paper ∞

    1. Fantasy games.   2. Board games.   3. Role playing —
Social aspects. I. Title.
GV1202.F35C68   2010
793.93'2 — dc22   2010016058

British Library cataloguing data are available

Cover imagery ©2010 Shutterstock

Manufactured in the United States of America

McFarland & Company, Inc., Publishers
  Box 611, Jefferson, North Carolina 28640
  www.mcfarlandpub.com

To my husband, Scott,
for introducing me to *D&D*
and to the wonderful worlds he creates.

Contents

Abbreviations, Terms, and Transcription Symbols

Gaming Terms

CRPG: computer role-playing game
D&D: *Dungeons and Dragons*
DM: dungeon master, the term for the gamemaster in *D&D*
DMG: *Dungeon Master's Guide*
GM: gamemaster, the one who runs a TRPG campaign
LARP: live action role-play
MMORPG: massively multiplayer online role-playing game
NPC: non-player character
RPGA: role-playing game association, an organization for *D&D*
  players
TRPG: tabletop role-playing game
XP: experience points

Terms from Possible-World Theory
(adapted from Ryan, Possible Worlds, *vii*)

APW: An *alternative possible world* in a different system of reality, a fiction
  that is accepted as true when the reader shifts to this world.
AW: The *actual world* is our reality.
NAW: The *narratorial actual* world is the world that the narrator presents
  to the narratee.
TAW: The *textual actual world* is the view of the text reference world that
  is presented by the author.

TRW: The *textual reference world* is the world that the text claims as factual. It is the alternative possible world that the text refers to.

Transcription Symbols

[overlapping utterances
(#) length of pause in seconds, noted if 3+
: extension of sound or syllable
/ rise in intonation
CAPS loud and emphasized utterance
(laughter) general laughter in the group
(laugh) laughter by participant indicated
... speaker trails off
--- speaker self-corrects

Preface and Acknowledgments

It was the fall of 2003, and my first semester of graduate school. I signed up for a course called "Discourse Analysis," thinking it had something to do with Foucault. As it turned out, it was really a methods course in linguistics, and when my professor — David Herman — told us we needed to tape record a conversation, I had the perfect idea: I would record part of a session from my *Dungeons and Dragons (D&D)* group. I signed up to present to the class under the unit called "narrative analysis," thinking my recording would be a perfect fit. I quickly came up against the traditional linguistic definitions of narrative — that it was a story, told about an event in the past by a narrator to a narratee. "Maybe it's not a narrative," David Herman said in reference to my *D&D* transcript. But as I sat there week after week engrossed in the story of Whisper and her companions in the world of Sorpraedor, I knew that at least part of what kept me interested was the story I was experiencing. And thus, I continued to attempt to reconcile my personal experience with the narrative theory that drew my academic attention.

My course project turned into other course projects, including a seminar paper for Carolyn Miller's rhetorical criticism class where I first tested out some of my ideas on the rhetoric exigence behind the tabletop roleplaying game. These course projects turned into a thesis, under the direction of David Herman, David Rieder, and Mike Carter. I can not thank my committee enough for their input in this process. It was one the most rewarding writing experiences, and when David Herman suggested that my thesis had the potential for a book, I was floored. After my defense, I went out and bought some shiny new dice for my *D&D* game.

At times, I wished that, like my sorceress Whisper, I could have summoned some magic energies, perhaps a polymorph spell, to magically transform the thesis into a book length project. Of course, I found it wasn't that simple. However, with the help of many people, I was able to complete what really is a transformation. I added massive amounts of research to this book project, I completely rewrote nearly everything, and I even changed some of my ideas.

I would first and foremost like to thank my research participants. From those anonymous gamers who completed a survey to my long-time gaming companions, this book is about you and in many ways by you. Even if your names do not appear here, your words and your stories do. I hope I have represented you well.

Then there were those who accompanied me on my writing journey. Like in *D&D*, some companions were with me all the way, while others came and went. My officemate Dan Lawson was rather like an oracle, who I consulted multiple times over the course of the book in times of need. We talked about ideas, and he directed me to several key sources.

Patrick Johnson was the equivalent of the fellow adventurer met in a tavern in the *D&D* world, who says, "what is your quest?" And when you tell him, responds, "Cool. Can I come along?" I met Pat in line for lunch at the Writing Program Administrators (WPA) conference in July 2009 as I was finishing this book, and our conversation quickly turned to my research and *D&D*. Pat kindly volunteered to provide additional feedback on one of my revised chapters.

There were others who helped me out along the way, from Professor Brian Epstein, who fielded my questions about possible-worlds theory to my many professors at Virginia Tech who were flexible with my Ph.D. work while I was writing and who answered any number of questions on publishing and book writing. There are my parents, who raised me to be an academic and a writer, and my husband who is the backbone of this book. Scott not only got me interested in *D&D*, but also pushed me to continue my academic work on the topic. He has held my hand when I was frustrated, and celebrated with me when I was excited, and is the main reason this book exists. Without the support of these people, I could not have completed this project.

Finally, there are those who would be considered members of my adventuring party, had this book been a *D&D* campaign. Dean Browell and Tim Lockridge are two of the smartest, most talented people I know, and I was extremely fortunate to have their feedback through the entire course of writing this book. Dean, who wrote a dissertation on *World of Warcraft*, served as my "MMORPG police," helping me see beyond *D&D*

to where my book might interact with videogame research. Tim is everything one could ask for in a reader — he is the type of guy that finds the loose thread in your writing, pulls on it just hard enough that everything starts to fall apart, and then hands you what you need to sew it back up again. This book is inordinately better because of his feedback.

However, all of these efforts would be in vain if it weren't for you — my reader. Whether you are a gamer, a researcher, or just a curious onlooker, I invite you to take an active role as you read this book. I have tried here to write a book that will be useful in multiple disciplines, and it is my hope that it will help spur discussion about tabletop role-playing in multiple forums. Whatever your position in relation to this text, I hope that I have shown here that your voice counts. I have been told multiple times by multiple people that I'm not supposed to write a book yet, that as a graduate student I "don't have a book in me." As the physical artifact in your hand proves — I did. Likewise, I believe that you, my reader, has something to say, and I, for one, would like to hear it.

Introduction: Defining the Tabletop Role-Playing Game

You approach the Blaze Arrow outpost. The bastion that guards the frontier of the city of Gateway is silent except for the distant cry of gathering carrion birds. You notice that the ground around the outpost has been scarred by the hobnailed feet of dozens of invaders. The three-story tower is surrounded by a now broken gate. The smell of burning orcish flesh, the smell of death, profanes the air. As you enter the gate, you find the remains of a ballista that once defended the outpost. Another rests farther in, still fully loaded, its human operator dead beside it. All in all, twelve human bodies lie around, evidence of the attack that took place only hours ago. It appears the victors have suffered losses as well, but their dead have undergone the cremation rituals known to exist in orcish societies. There are also orc bodies piled up and smoldering. Yet the process seems to have been done quickly and was perhaps not completed. Some remains of orcish clothing and some shields have been left behind. They are marked with the symbol of a bloody hand, which you recognize as the sign of the Blood Fist tribe of orcs.

What do you do?

The passage above is very similar to one that was told on a Sunday afternoon around a kitchen table during a session of the Sorpraedor *Dungeons and Dragons (D&D)* role-playing campaign. Yet, it fails to represent the complexity of tabletop role-playing games (TRPGs). No one passage can represent the complexity of player interaction, textual manipulation, or cultural significance of the TRPG. For those of you who are familiar with the game, this passage might bring up memories of your own gaming session. For those who are less familiar with gaming, you may be wondering how this story is different from any other story told in any other medium. Whatever your relationship to the game, this book is intended

5

offer a scholarly look at TRPGs that highlights both their complex narrative and social structure.

If you are unfamiliar with TRPGs, you may first be wondering what exactly happens in a gaming session. As the book progresses, we will see that the answer is more complex than it first appears; however, I offer a brief introduction here. As suggested by the name, TRPGs are played face-to-face (around a table, most likely), and involve players "acting out" a role. This acting is not always literal. Players do not arrive in costume or speak exclusively in-character — something that differentiates TRPGs from live-action role-playing games (LARPs). Instead, players develop characters based on certain rules and are responsible for deciding what those characters do over the course of the game. The DM, or dungeon master — now called the gamemaster (GM) in some TRPGs — develops a setting where the game takes place, a basic storyline, and any characters not being represented by the players of the game. The DM presents the players with situations, such as the one above, and asks the players, "What do you do?" at which point the players offer up actions for their characters. Many of these situations, referred to as *encounters*, involve fighting a monster or an evil villain. Most TRPGs also involve rolling dice to see whether certain actions succeed, and some involve positioning miniature figures on a battle map. Games may be played over the course of years, where a group continually meets to extend the same story with the same characters time after time, or they can be played over a few hours (usually at least four) as a one time endeavor. There is no "winning" in a TRPG, although characters do gain experience points for completing certain challenges, and in an ongoing game, these experience points allow the player to continue building his or her character. However, these challenges are met as a group, not as individuals.

TRPGs were introduced in 1974, and by the year 2000 they comprised a two billion-dollar industry (Dancey 2000). In addition, they have influenced countless other enterprises from other games to novels and movies. Despite their widely recognized influence, there is limited scholarship specifically on TRPGs. Gary Fine's ethnographic study *Shared Fantasy* (1983) lays a useful foundation for studying the TRPG and gaming culture, but is now outdated. In the past 27 years, there have been changes to both the *D&D* game itself as well as the community of gamers. Daniel Mackay builds on Fine's study in his 2001 book, *The Fantasy Role-Playing Game*, and shifts to view the TRPG as performance art. Mackay's study is useful in terms of looking at the TRPG as an aesthetic text and as a process-performance but does not include a specific discussion of the

TRPG as a genre or relate it to other games. More recent work has continued to place the TRPG alongside other fantasy games in terms of cultural significance. *Gaming as Culture: Essays on Reality, Identity and Experience in Fantasy Games* (Williams et al., 2006) features several essays that focus on aspects of the TRPG from gender and identity issues[1] to specific linguistic analysis.[2]

These texts can be said to be foundational; however, with *games studies* (not to be confused with *game theory*) emerging as its own discipline, more work clearly needs to be done on such a fundamental game as *D&D*. Some have called this new discipline *ludology*, but have limited it to the study of videogames rather than all games; not only has scholarship left TRPGs in the dust, but so have those seeking to define the boundaries of games studies as a discipline. Furthermore, the study of TRPGs serves an important role in the context of other scholarship as these games are highly complex, both in terms of narrative structure and their social interaction. Fine's book focuses on sociology, and Mackay's on performance studies. I engage with narrative, linguistic, cultural, and writing studies in this book, although, as a scholar I primarily identify with the disciplines of rhetoric and composition. The breadth of scholarly attention to the TRPG makes this project both exciting and challenging. In this book, I seek to explore multiple frameworks for the study of the TRPG rather than limit it to the purview of any one discipline. Thus, a central concern of this text is developing a way of talking about the TRPG that transcends disciplinary lines by seeing where disciplinary frameworks are useful, and where they are not.

In particular, I am concerned with the concept of genre and medium in relation to TRPGs and other games. Because so much scholarly attention has been given to videogames, I look at the differences between TRPGs and other games. Do theories about computer role-playing apply to the TRPG or should these texts be studied separately? How do we define genres for texts that function on multiple levels? What counts as a narrative when stories operate in different media? What might draw a person to a certain genre or medium over another? While my own study must be limited in scope, I suggest a possible framework for future study of TRPGs, and possibly other games, as rhetoric. Rhetorical study has so far not figured prominently in game studies; however, I believe it offers a way to meld semiotic and social issues currently being discussed in the field and thus opens the boundaries of this work in a meaningful way.

Situating the TRPG

In order to further understand the differences and connections between TRPGs and other games and also other types of texts, it is important to look in greater depth at the origins of the TRPG. It all started with the release of *Dungeons and Dragons* in 1974. The idea for *D&D* began when Dave Arneson, a fan of the *Lord of the Rings* fantasy novels, introduced Tolkien-like fantasy elements into his war games and shifted the focus from controlling entire armies to controlling a single character (Mackay, 2001, p. 15). Mackay's account of *D&D*'s origins clearly aligns the text with two different traditions: a gaming tradition and a literary tradition. In terms of antecedent genres to the TRPG, then, we have both war-gaming and fantasy novels.

If we look at the gaming tradition, it is clear that *D&D* emerged from war games, which involve enacting battles between armies, usually with a large battle map and many miniature figures. According to Mackay (2001), the first war game evolved from *War Chess* in 1811. Herr von Reiswitz created a war-strategy game called *Kriegspiel* with the purpose of educating Prussian military officers. In this game, miniature battlefields showed the terrain and counters represented troops; dice rolls added a degree of random chance in determining the way in which the battle progressed (Mackay, 2001, p. 13). War games moved from military use into the popular sphere in the late–Victorian era, when H.G. Wells created a popular game called *Little Wars*. *Little Wars* replaced counters with miniature figures to represent soldiers (Mackay, 2001, p. 13). War games are still popular today, particularly Games Workshop's Warhammer series.[3] *D&D* did not replace war games any more than computer games have replaced TRPGs, yet we can see that the optional use of battle map, miniatures, and dice reflect the war gaming side of TRPGs' history.

In addition to being fascinated with medieval war gaming, co-creator of *D&D* Dave Arneson was fascinated by the fantasy worlds created in J.R.R. Tolkien's *Lord of the Rings* trilogy (Mackay, 2001, p. 15). Although its creators later denied the direct influence of Tolkien's work, the *D&D* world consists of character classes similar to those found in Tolkien such as a fighter, a wizard, and a rogue. The character races include humans, elves, and halflings (which were originally called hobbits but had to be changed to avoid copyright infringement). By incorporating the fantasy of Tolkien into these gaming worlds, Arneson also made significant changes in the relationship between gaming and literature. TRPGs became, in many ways, a response to literature and a way of interacting in literary worlds. The characters that resulted from Arneson's initial attempt at role-playing were endowed with magical weapons and spell-casting abilities, and their enemies evolved into "mythical creatures such as dragons" much like the characters found in fantasy novels (Mackay, 2001, p. 15). Thus, players were given a way to interact with fantasy worlds by playing their own heroes in those worlds. Soon after incorporating these elements of fantasy into his war gaming, Arneson teamed up with fellow war-gamer and fantasy buff Gary Gygax. In 1974 they published the first copy of the *Dungeons and Dragons* rule book (Mackay, 2001, p. 15).

Acknowledging both the antecedent game genre (war games) and the antecedent literary genre (fantasy) is important to showing the dual nature of the TRPG. As I will argue later, TRPGs are difficult to categorize because they are both games and narratives, thus breaking down a binary that both narrative theorists and ludologists often cling to. Perhaps one of the most significant advances that *D&D* made possible was a reimagining of the ways that stories and games interact. While *D&D* was the first of its kind, similar games (often also based on fantasy or science fiction literature) emerged as TRPGs. Among these are *Vampire the Masquerade*, based on the vampire mythos; *Call of Cthulhu*, based on H.P. Lovecraft; *Babylon5* and *Star Trek* TRPGs, based on the sci-fi television series; and *Champions*, based on comic book characters.

Defining the TRPG isn't easy, but let's start by looking more specifically at the rather uncontroversial notion that the TRPG is a type of game. What does it mean to classify something as a game? Ludwig Wittgenstein (1958) asks,

> What is common to them all? — Don't say: "There *must* be something in common, or they would not be called games" — but *look and see* whether there is anything common to all. — For if you look at them you will not see something that is common to *all*, but similarities, relationships, and a whole series of them at that [p. 31].

These similarities, which Wittgenstein goes on to describe as "family resemblances" (p. 32), offer a good starting point for defining the TRPG. Often when studying games, or the even a narrower category such as role-playing games, it is difficult to find one thread that connects them all. While looking for connections is admirable and necessary, in terms of genre studies the lack of differentiation made by scholars is sometimes troubling.

A good example of this may be found in some of the early work on computer games. In his book *Cybertext* (1997), Espen Aarseth comments that many MUDs (Multi User Dungeons) facilitate *"Dungeons and Dragons* style gaming" (p. 146). Yet, he never explains what "the *Dungeons and*

Dragons style" is, and gamers are quick to recognize that even within a single game it is difficult to pinpoint one particular style. In addition, Aarseth calls *D&D* a "board game" (p. 98). Some board games may have a similar structure to TRPGs, but they have more static game mechanics and always include a physical component such as a board and figures.[4] The use of a battle map and miniature figures might be seen as a connection to board games; however, these are not mandatory features of TRPGs as they are for board games. Thus, *D&D* cannot be considered a board game. In fact, the use of a battle map and figures is actually more in line with war games than board games, a distinction that is important when looking back to the history of TRPGs. Scholars, in general, have been guilty of evoking gaming terms without acknowledging the history of individual games or the differences between them.

Although games have a lot of differences, we can continue to look for the resemblances that Wittgenstein calls for. One might say that one such resemblance is an element of chance; another that all games follow a set of rules. Indeed, an element of chance is often added to role-playing through the use of dice rolls. However, like miniature figures, dice are also optional in the TRPG. The *Adventure Game Industry Market Research Summary* (*RPGs*) showed that 76 percent of gamers used some sort of detailed chart, though not necessarily a battle map; only 56 percent used miniatures; and 33 percent of TRPGs were dice-less. Furthermore, as many as 80 percent of those surveyed said their gaming group followed house rules (Dancey 2000). Simply trying to link together all TRPGs, let alone all games, is problematic. Gamers who play in their home rather than at official tournaments may alter rules and often gamers continue to play with older versions of the rules even when new rule books are released. These variations make it difficult to establish the relationship between TRPGs and more traditional, tightly rule-bound, games.[5] How, then, do we define the TRPG? If we can't link it closely with other games, what is it that makes one TRPG resemble another?

Mackay (2001) defines the *tabletop* role-playing game as

> an *episodic* and *participatory* story-creation *system* that includes a set of quantified *rules* that assist a group of *players* and a *gamemaster* in determining how their fictional *characters'* spontaneous interactions are resolved [pp. 4–5].

This definition further defines the TRPG within the broader category of RPGs. For example, most CRPGs do not include the gamemaster, which is key to Mackay's definition.[6] Although they can be played in a single session, TRPGs are often played by a group of participants who meet on a regular basis. In this case, TRPGs are *episodic* because each session can be seen as an episode in a story that continues to develop. Even when a game consists of a single session, there are often multiple tasks, or episodes, that lead up to the climax of the story. In this story, each player *participates* by controlling the *character* that he or she has created. The *gamemaster* (GM) also participates in the creation of the story by setting up the storyworld and the situations that these characters encounter, as well as controlling any non-player characters (NPCs). Rule books such as *The Player's Handbook* and *The Dungeon Master's Guide* (for *D&D*) provide *rules* that assist participants in creating and controlling their storyworld. These books create the *system* that is used to structure the game.

Naturally, this explanation is somewhat oversimplified. The dungeon master (DM) or gamemaster,[7] for example, might not create the storyworld but might use a pre-prepared module or setting published by Wizards of the Coast or another gaming company. Likewise, an adventure module might even come with pre-made characters rather than having players generate them. However, a gamemaster still participates by adapting that setting to the players and situations presented in that gaming session, and the players still participate by controlling the actions of their characters. As previously mentioned, home rules may be instituted in a particular game; however, rules continue to exist and guide players and DMs. In subsequent chapters, I will explore some of the differences in authorship and participation among different types of TRPG sessions; however, I maintain that Mackay's definition is broad enough to encompass these variations.

Looking at this definition of the TRPG enables us to situate it in relation to other texts. TRPGs are *episodic*, but so are television shows and many computer games. They are *participatory*, but again, so are computer games. Pretty much every game, whether computerized or not, can be considered a *system* that uses *rules*, although those rules may vary from game to game or even player to player. *Characters* are present in nearly every kind of narrative. From this definition alone, we can see that TRPGs overlap with several different categories, including both narrative and game. However, it is the interaction between the *players* and the *gamemaster* that sets this form apart.

Game designer Andrew Rilstone also sees the interaction between player and DM, and the goal of that interaction, as the defining characteristics of the TRPG. In his 1994 introductory essay for the *Inter*action* magazine, "Role-Playing Games: An Overview," Rilstone defines the

TRPG as "a formalized verbal interaction between a referee and a player or players, with the intention of producing a narrative." The DM, which Rilstone calls the *referee*, sets up the story and the world that the game will focus on. Often times this setting is as basic as a dungeon populated with monsters, but it can be as complex as a complete world. The DM presents a situation, such as the one presented in the epigraph, and asks the players "what do you do?" The players, who create and manage characters in the world, respond with "I do [such and such]." For Rilstone, this form of interaction and its goal of producing a narrative is what sets TRPGs apart as a distinct form. Even still, this definition seems rather tentative as the interaction between a DM and a player may vary considerably depending on the individual group and game, just as the interaction between a teacher and student may vary greatly depending on the classroom.

To what degree is definition and classification a necessary prerequisite to studying games and to what extent must our definitions and classifications come from our studies? Although I have cited previous definitions of TRPGs that I believe to be valid, I don't believe that they alone explain the complexities of TRPGs. Therefore, one aim of this book is to further define and categorize the TRPG. In addition, I believe the struggle to define a text such as this may pose questions for methods of defining and categorizing other texts as well, particularly other games. Thus, I also aim to address larger issues surrounding the nature of texts and the way we define them, particularly in terms of narrative, genre, and rhetorical studies.

Research Samples

Many previous studies on gaming are ethnographic in nature. Although traditionally ethnography has involved a researcher looking at an unfamiliar culture, it seems to be more common in the field of game studies that researchers analyze cultures that they are already a part of. Mackay (2001) analyzes his own role-playing group as do many of the authors in the *Gaming as Culture* (2006) essay compilation. There are several reasons for this trend. In many cases, a great deal of "insider" knowledge is needed not only to play these games but also to analyze them. Therefore, it is advantageous to have a researcher who is familiar with both the rules and norms of game play and the gaming subculture. In addition, while a computer game can easily be purchased and played alone or with others online, TRPGs often involve groups that develop over time and are by invitation only.[8] Thus, researchers who have experience with a gaming community are in a better position to conduct studies than those who are not. In keeping with previous research I, too, base my study on examples from my own gaming experience.

However, as with ethnography in general, one experience may prove idiosyncratic and not generalizable, and thus not particularly useful for answering definitional questions. Therefore, I draw on multiple gaming experiences, both mine and others, as well as textual analysis for this book. As a result, I am more familiar with some of my research participants than others. The home game of Sorpraedor, which I draw on heavily in this book, consisted of friends and my spouse, who was the DM in charge of the game. Although it would be naïve to call such methods completely objective, I believe the advantage gained by this insider knowledge outweighs any bias that may be present in this study. In contrast, I had never met any of the gamers I worked with at the *D&D* Experience tournament, Worldwide *D&D* Game Day, and NC State Game Day, and these multiple experiences add balance to the current study. While each of these experiences is unique, I seek to present a comparison that will be more applicable to future studies than a single case study would be.

A common way to play TRPGs is to organize a gaming group, a number of people who meet on a regular basis to advance the same TRPG adventure. Such adventures are referred to as *campaigns*, and the characters, known as *player characters*, form a *party*. My first research sample comes from the Sorpraedor campaign, which began in the spring of 2002 and continued until 2006. The world of Sorpraedor was created by DM Scott Cover and has involved various players, though a stable group of five played twice a month from January 2003 through September 2004. In September 2004, one player moved away and in February 2005 two other players left the game. While new players replaced them, with new characters, the overall story arc remained continuous for the entire four years. In addition to some variation in players, when a character in the story dies, the corresponding player often continues playing with a new character. This has happened several times in the Sorpraedor world. In fact only one character, Whisper (my character), remained stable in the game world from its creation in 2002 to the end of the campaign in 2006.

While I draw on my experiences throughout the Sorpraedor campaign, I offer several specific samples as representative of our game play. The first of these is the narrative of Blaze Arrow that spanned several gaming sessions from the end of January to the end of February 2003. The appendix includes the full written story of this episode as I composed it after the gaming sessions. This narrative was originally written to report events in the Sorpraedor world for a player who had not been able to attend a gaming session, and was written before I began this research project. As such, I leave it in the original form as a research sample from the Sorpraedor campaign. For the second sample, I recorded and analyzed several hours from a session in October 2003, and snippets of this transcript serve as data in chapter 5. Even before I began officially gathering data as a researcher I was the group note-taker and had compiled detailed notes from most of our gaming sessions, which were useful to me as both a gamer and a researcher. In addition to these notes, I draw on notes that Scott took as the DM and email conversations saved between Scott and other players. Finally, I include interviews with several members of the gaming group to ask specific questions about their experiences.

Throughout my analysis I refer to both characters and players in the game, depending on whether the situation involved the character or the player. Note that other than myself and Scott (the DM) the names of my fellow players are pseudonyms. Because of my familiarity with these players and characters from years of campaigning, I often refer to them by name and thus offer an introduction to them here. When I refer to both player and character at the same time, I include the player name followed by the character name. The characters in the campaign at the time of the sample were as follows:

- Whisper (played by myself): a 17-year-old human sorceress whose mother is a dragon. Her magical powers are innate, and as she grows older she develops more magical powers and more dragon-like features and abilities.
- Maureen (played by Mary): a human thief who led a hard life, but is always open for more adventures.
- David (played by Alex): a halfling ranger; a creature of the woods who believes strongly in his principles.
- Cuthalion (played by Mark): an elven ranger; who is extremely talented with a bow and arrow.
- Fletch (played by Nick): a human fighter; the strong silent type.
- Gareth (played by Mary): a bard with an intelligent viola who replaced Maureen as Mary's character.

The sample adventure in which the party encountered the orcs at Blaze Arrow was one of the first for this group of party members, whereas the transcripts from the adventure at the Foppish Wererat come later in the campaign. Often the entrance or exit of characters can be seen as beginnings or endings to narratives within the overarching narrative of the campaign. David, Cuthalion, and Fletch were all new characters at the time of the Blaze Arrow adventure, and Maureen had only been adventuring with Whisper for a few weeks. By the time of the Foppish Wererat adventure, the players had been together for approximately 9 months, and Mary's character of Maureen had met a tragic end and been replaced with Gareth, who is featured prominently in this second story. I also analyze other shorter narratives from the Sorpraedor game, including the story of the confrontation between Whisper and David, and individual stories about Maureen.

In order to show how the Blaze Arrow story fit within the larger Sorpraedor narrative I recount it briefly here, but a full version can be found in the appendix. At the point of this adventure, Whisper and Maureen had been working to uncover a subversive agency that had infiltrated the hierarchy of the town of Gateway. They had established themselves as heroes in the town and were working closely with the town's magistrate to assist in any difficulties. When this group of players came together, the new characters were immediately associated with Whisper and the reputation she had created for herself. This story begins after the magistrate has asked the group to go to the outpost, Blaze Arrow, that has not reported in with the main city of Gateway as scheduled. Maureen, a character who often likes to go off on her own, joins the group later in the journey, while they are camped for the night. Immediately, chaos ensues as a threat and two severed heads are thrown into the camp. A mysterious tattoo makes the party wonder if Maureen is being watched, and she is sent back to town. In reality Maureen's player, Mary, was not able to attend a gaming session. Therefore, the narrative was altered to reflect this choice.

Meanwhile, the rest of the party continues on to Blaze Arrow where they find the scene as conveyed in the epigraph of this chapter. Orcs have attacked the tower. However, the party manages to capture some of the orcs and finds out that their real target was the Skullbash, another orcish tribe. Cuthalion gives a rousing speech to the leader of the orc tribe, Grumbach, who agrees to leave the human town out of his conquest. This story ends when the party returns to Gateway and a new story picks up from there.

An overarching narrative spans across individual stories like this one, just as the world of Sorpraedor exists outside of any particular tale. The party has larger quests that continue from session to session and each smaller story adds to the larger narrative. If you read the story of Blaze

Arrow carefully, you will see references to these larger quests. For example, Whisper asks the prisoner if he was sent by Thaddeus, who was a recurring villain in the campaign. In addition, individual characters have their own overarching narratives and as we will see in chapter 8; the beginning of the Blaze Arrow story takes on new meaning when we know Maureen's history. In each session some plot points in the larger story are resolved, but they are intertwined with new ones; much the way chapters of a novel consist of individual threads that make up a whole work.

Unlike the examples from the Sorpraedor campaign, my other examples are more self-contained. In addition to home campaigns such as Sorpraedor, gamers often meet up at conventions or gaming stores for one-time sessions (sometimes called *one-shots*). The Role-Playing Game Association (RPGA) is a worldwide organization of players that connects those wishing to play *D&D* with others. Pre-made adventures are released specifically for the RPGA, and players create characters that they run in multiple RPGA adventures. However, these episodes are more isolated than the episodes in the world of Sorpraedor and may involve different characters and a different DM each session. I observed an RPGA game at *D&D* Experience, an annual convention for RPGA players. The characters in the game I observed were high-level indicating that players had been building these characters in multiple adventures. However, they had not played them together continually the way the party in Sorpraedor had continued together. Instead, these players came from different areas of the country to meet at *D&D* Experience and game together. There were many games going continually at the convention, each lasting approximately six hours. When one game concluded, gamers would take their characters and join a new adventure or switch to a new DM.

The pre-made adventure, or *module*, that I observed being played at *D&D* Experience had not been available outside of the convention and is not available to members outside the RPGA. It belonged to a larger campaign setting of the *Forgotten Realms*. This setting is published through rule books published by Wizards of the Coast and many gamers use it as a world for their adventures, both in home adventures and pre-made modules. However, the players indicated that the RPGA added some consistency to this world and that modules often built on each other to create a fuller world view. Thus, some players knew interesting facts about other areas of the *Forgotten Realms* because of previous adventuring experiences. Because of their lack of previous relationships, the characters and players in this adventure remained far more anonymous than in the Sorpraedor campaign. Often, they were referred to only by character class or category.

For example, the DM might ask what the dwarf would do next rather than naming the character, with whom he might not be familiar. Thus, I will not list character and player names for this adventure as I have for those in the ongoing Sorpraedor campaign.

While I could not participate in the *D&D* Experience game because I was not an RPGA member, I did participate in several other one-time games for comparison. At both NC State Game Day in 2004 and at World-wide *D&D* Game Day in May 2009, I played a pre-generated character in a pre-made adventure. I also attempted to DM a pre-made, one-shot adventure in a home setting in order to more successfully compare the experience of playing versus running a game. These diverse experiences allow me to comment further on the commonalities and differences between playing and running *D&D* in an ongoing homebrew campaign and in a pre-made, one-time adventure. However, as I elaborate on further, the distinctions are not always as clear cut, particularly when ongoing campaigns incorporate pre-made adventures as well.

To go beyond my own experiences I also frequented online gaming forums and distributed an online survey, which was made available through several of these forums. The forums that I observed were not specific to *D&D* and thus allowed me to gain the perspective of gamers who might be more involved with a different TRPG or even a different type of role-playing. My survey asked participants to specify which types of role-playing they participated in and to further identify what they saw as the differences between computer role-playing and tabletop role-playing. Interestingly, 97 percent of the respondents participated in TRPGs, leading me to believe that forums designed for "role-playing games" were designed more for TRPG players than for other types of role-players (an assumption that was confirmed by the content of the postings in these communities). Because my focus here is on the TRPG, I did not distribute the survey to members of other communities that focused more on online or computer role-playing; however, 45 percent of my respondents also played computer role-playing games (CRPGs) and 28 percent played massive multiplayer online role-playing games (MMORPGs). Interestingly, 22 percent played RPGs online but through email or blogs. The smallest category was those who participated in live-action role-play (LARP), at only 12 percent of my survey respondents.

In addition to asking about their role-playing habits, I asked participants if they were familiar with the classic *D&D* story *The Temple of Elemental Evil,* and, if so, asked them to recall the story. To these qualitative samples I add textual analysis of this well-known *D&D* adventure in chapter 3. *The Temple of Elemental Evil* is a name commonly recognized among gamers as a famous adventure and, in fact, only 6 percent of my respondents had never heard of it. Thus I sought out the many different versions of this adventure in different mediums to see how the text changed over its many iterations. I look at the original adventure by Gary Gygax, co-creator of *D&D*, as well as the videogames and novel versions of *The Temple of Elemental Evil*. This type of textual comparison mixed with accounts from actual gamers allows me to comment on narrative and genre across media as well as in different types of gaming interactions.

My aim with multiple samples and methods is to allow for a more complete overview of TRPGs and the way that they compare with other texts. However, no analysis can be complete. This study focuses primarily on *D&D*. Looking at other RPGs such as the White Wolf series may illuminate additional difference between games. Nevertheless, as the origin of the TRPG, a focus on *D&D* is foundational to our understanding of the genre.

Methods of Analysis and Overview

Just as multiple research samples are important to gain a broader view of TRPGs and how they are played, I believe that multiple methods of analysis are useful for looking at this complex subject. As I have mentioned, no one discipline has claimed the TRPG as an object of study and even many of those who research games wish to limit that study to videogames. Thus, part of my aim in producing this book is to test which methods of analysis prove useful when studying the TRPG.

I begin historically by looking at the rise of interactive narrative in the 1970s. I use comparative analysis to show the similarities and differences among these early models for interactive storytelling. Chapter 1 compares the gamebook, text-based adventure game, and TRPG. In chapter 2, I employ genre theory to discuss the way that the TRPG functions as an antecedent genre to computer games that have followed from this initial push for interactive storytelling. I take my definition of genre from rhetorical studies (Miller, 1984; Swales, 1990; Russell, 1997) and argue that in order for a text to represent a new genre, it must serve a new rhetorical purpose. This chapter gives an overview of the rhetorical approach to the RPG genre and explains the exigency of narrative agency that is present in the TRPG. I argue here for a distinction between TRPGs and CRPGs on the basis of rhetorical need rather than formal structure.

In chapter 3, rather than looking at the influence of *D&D* as a whole on other genres, I turn to one specific *D&D* adventure — *The Temple of Elemental Evil* and follow this story through its multiple versions. I use textual analysis as well as survey data to look at how this adventure started as a *D&D* module and became a videogame and novel. I hereby engage not only with the definition of a *genre*, but with the definition of a *medium*, as well as the interaction between these two terms.

After establishing the importance of studying the TRPG as a different kind of text from other games, I turn more closely to developing a model for studying it. I turn here to narrative theory. In particular, I look at narratology as employed by linguists and media scholars. Chapter 4 engages with the debate between narratologists and ludologists over whether or not games should be studied within the framework of narratives or whether their unique form necessitates new methods of analysis. Because this debate has largely focused on videogames, I here suggest a return to questions of narrative with the TRPG in mind. I continue to analyze the ways in which *D&D* players and characters develop and draw on larger storyworlds and what this means for viewing TRPGs through either the narratology or ludology lens.

In chapter 5, I shift to linguistic analysis, including both narratology and possible-world theory as a framework. Using Ryan's (1991) possible-world terminology and Jenny Cook-Gumperz's (1992) study of children's make-believe games, I present a model that explains the levels of communication involved in the RPG in terms of their degrees of narrativity. This model is important for showing the complexity of the TRPG and breaking down the binaries between narrative and non-narrative so often drawn upon by ludologists and narratologists alike.

In chapter 6, I discuss the ways in which the TRPG is an immersive text and the importance of this immersion in creating a narrative experience that fulfils a rhetorical purpose for gamers. I use specific examples from the Sorpraedor campaign to explain the multiple ways that immersion functions in the TRPG genre.

The final section of this book shifts even farther from the structure of the TRPG to look at the social and cultural influence of *D&D*, and the way that players interact with multiple texts. Chapter 7 provides a detailed analysis of the way gamers interact with other texts, drawing specifically from examples in the Sorpraedor campaign. Using both textual analysis and interviews, I look at the way the players and the DM engage with texts outside of the gaming session and with each other, and how that interaction might constitute degrees of authorship.

In chapter 8, I move to look at TRPGs within the larger cultural frame. I outline theories from sociology, cultural studies, and media studies that look at fan cultures. I draw heavily on Henry Jenkins's (1992) study of fandom in *Textual Poachers* to describe the relationship between gamers and texts. I outline here several different characteristics of fans that are relevant to gamers. These characteristics show the varied rather than static relationship that gamers have with texts and thus challenge the notion that even within one genre or medium all audience members respond the same way.

Finally, I conclude the book with my own theory and definition of the TRPG. This definition calls into question not only traditional definitions of game and narrative, but also notions of authorship and audience. Chapter 9 explores the implications of this definition for the study of the TRPG under multiple frameworks including narrative studies, game studies, genre and media studies, and rhetoric and composition. It poses questions for future research in these areas in light of the current study.

Together, the chapters of this book work to challenge the way scholars typically study games by combining views from multiple disciplines. In particular, I reject the notion that videogames are the only games worthy of study and that the TRPG represents a former and inferior genre. Rather, I will argue that the TRPG and its complexities allow us to critique perceptions of narrative and authorship in ways that computer games are only beginning to allow.

1

Early Models of
Interactive Narrative

You are Omina, stepchild of the great Wizard Alcazar, and your efforts to rescue your stepfather and free your land from the icy spell of Warzen, the Winter Wizard, have led you straight into danger. Pursued by vicious, man-eating quagbeasts, you have taken refuge atop a snowy dune beside a clear pond. One of the huge-headed beasts is so close you can feel its foul breath hot on your skin! You must do something immediately [Lowery, 1983, p. 1].

At first glance, the passage above may not seem very different from the passage that opened the introduction to this book. Both address the audience in second person, and both lead to the point where that audience must take action. However, there are also some key differences — the former passage addresses a larger audience and *you* is multiple and undefined; the latter addresses one reader, and that reader's role is defined as the character of Omina. These two stories come from different, but related genres — tabletop role-playing and gamebooks. Both genres emerged around the same time in the 1970s, a key time in the development of interactive fiction. The drive to create interactive fiction began well before the Internet or videogames became mainstream. In their historical accounts of the development of interactive fiction, both Jay David Bolter (1991) and Damien Katz (2004) look as far back as the 1941 text "Garden of Forking Paths" by Jorge Luis Borges. As early as this, we see a frustration with the limits of print media. Bolter (1991) explains, "For Borges literature is exhausted because it is committed to a conclusive ending, to a single storyline and denouement" (p. 139). To be renewed, literature must embrace possibilities rather than shut them off (Bolter, 1991, p. 139). For some, this possibility of renewal existed in digital and electronic writing, which appeared to offer a flexibility that written prose did not. However, the rise of interactive fiction is not limited to the development of any one media.

What is interactive fiction and how does it operate? The term *interactive fiction* has been used to refer to a variety of texts from more standard literary works with interactive qualities, to hypertext, to adventure games, to role-playing games (RPGs). Although all fiction requires some participation of readers as they form the story in their minds, interactive fiction is more actively produced or navigated by the audience. Scholars have used a variety of concepts to highlight this difference from traditional texts, including terms such as *emergent stories*, *ergodic texts*, and *cybertexts*. Ryan (2003) defines an emergent story as one "that is produced dynamically in the interaction between the text and the reader" (p. 258). Following Genette and Chatman, Aarseth (1997) uses the term "erogodic" to describe texts which require "nontrivial effort" to navigate (p. 1). Ryan (2003) explains that ergodic texts create a feedback loop in which the user can go back and forth experiencing the story in a different sequence (p. 206). Aarseth goes on to favor the term cybertext as a medium that allows for texts that have both ergodic and narrative elements. Cybertext is not a genre, but a "broad textual media category" (Aarseth, 1997, p. 5). All of these models for interactive texts are helpful in defining interactive fiction, yet the differences among them highlight the fact that there are multiple types of interactivity.

A key difference is that when Ryan (2003) talks about emergent stories, she talks about the sort of interactivity that is productive. She defines *productive action* as anything "that leaves a durable mark on the textual world, either by adding objects to its landscape or by writing its history" (Ryan, 2003, p. 205). Examples of productive interactivity include such texts as amusement park rides, children's make-believe games, interactive drama, and MUD (Multi-User Domain) (Ryan, 2003, p. 287–331). These interactive genres blur the boundaries between authors and audiences, allowing those who participate in the interaction to help add to the world of the story.

In contrast, Aarseth (1997) shows how the user of text-based adventure games is separated from the author or narrator or creator[1] through interactive negotiation with the computer interface (pp. 111–114). Interactivity here is selective. In the model of cybertext, the event and the progression of the events is separated by the negotiation between user and interface (Aarseth, 1997, p. 126). The reader must solve the puzzle in order to access the story. There is a correct choice that must be selected to open the right path to reach the story. In this process, Aarseth (1997) sees that the idea of a traditional story does not hold up, and that "instead of a narrated plot, cybertext produces a sequence of oscillating activities effectuated (but certainly not controlled) by the user" (p. 112). Unlike Ryan's (2003) model, Aarseth's cybertext model does not allow for users to directly affect the story or storyworld, only to uncover it.

Despite the lack of research on *Dungeons and Dragons (D&D)* itself, scholars are quick to note that *D&D* has been foundational to the development of other interactive texts. In fact, Aarseth (1997) states that "the *Dungeons and Dragons* genre might be regarded as an oral cybertext, the oral predecessor to computerized written adventure games" (p. 98). Ryan (2003) does not specifically discuss RPGs, but she does mention that "a genealogy of interactive genres leads from ... *Dungeons and Dragons*" (p. 310). Both Aarseth (1997) and Murray (1998) specifically credit *D&D* as the inspiration for adventure games. Murray (1998) discusses that the adventure game *Zork* is based on *D&D* (p. 77). That both Aarseth and Murray acknowledge *D&D* as a foundational text to the development of adventure games points to the importance of *D&D* as a specific text, and tabletop role-playing games (TRPGs) as a generic text in the development of interactive fiction. However, neither of these scholars discusses *D&D* or TRPGs in any detail or traces their specific influence on other genres and, ultimately, the same models may not hold true. Just as *D&D* has roots both in literature and games (fantasy novels and wargaming), it has also been influential in both realms. In order to see the important role that *D&D* has played in the development of interactive fiction, we must look more closely at the structure of the narrative itself, as well as at some narrative forms that are commonly thought of as descendants to the TRPG. In this chapter I analyze the relationship between pick-a-path gamebooks and text-based adventure games, and the TRPG and its role in the historical rise of interactive fiction in the late 1970s and early 1980s.

Pick-a-Path: Selective Interactivity of Gamebooks

Very little has been written about the history of gamebooks. However, both Nick Montfort (2003) and Demian Katz (2004) credit Queneaus's 1967 short story as the first in the gamebook format. Montfort describes this work as having 21 possible segments that the reader may encounter as he or she makes choices in the story (p. 71). In his unpublished piece on the history of gamebooks, Katz also gives credit to Hildick's

Lucky Les: The Adventures of a Cat of Five Tales as the first full-fledged, published gamebook. Hildick's book was also published in 1967, yet the concept did not take off for another several years. While gamebooks technically started before TRPGs, *D&D* was, nevertheless, influential on their development. Katz explains that while *D&D* is played with a group, gamebooks allowed for solitary play, and gamebooks began to be marketed with this in mind. *Buffalo Castle*, released in 1976, was the first of a series of books called *Tunnels and Trolls*, and an obvious parallel to *Dungeons and Dragons*. According to Katz, the more well-known *Choose Your Own Adventure* series came out soon thereafter, in 1979, and lasted until 1998. Although there are accounts of gamebooks that predate *D&D*, it seems clear that subsequent iterations of the genre were highly influenced by the game. Furthermore, the gamebooks that followed more closely from *D&D* championed greater success.

In fact, Tactical Studies Rules (TSR), the gaming company that originally owned *D&D*, came out with a line of pick-a-path books designed to be a version of the game in novel form. This series of books is based in the same fantasy setting as *D&D*; however, their structure differs somewhat from the game itself. In these books, after several pages of story, the reader is asked to make a choice. For example, in the TSR, Inc. gamebook *Spell of the Winter Wizard* (1983), the reader is addressed in the second person and takes on the role of a wizard's child, Omina. The wizard has been kidnapped and the goal is to follow the path of the story so that it reaches the positive conclusion of the father-figure being rescued. At the end of the first section the reader is offered a choice:

1. You can try to destroy Warzen [an evil wizard] first, then save Alcazar before he freezes. Turn to page 65.
2. You can seek out the Druids, find the Crimson Flame Mushroom [a powerful magical item], and take it to Alcazar. Turn to page 21 [Lowery, 1983, p. 10].

The book offers similar choices throughout, some of which lead the reader to a happy ending, some of which do not. For example, if the reader follows the path that leads to page 188, she ends up being chased by a ghost: "You run and scream and hope that someone will hear you — hope that this is not ... THE END" (Lowery, 1983, p. 118).

Katz (2004) notes that these books came from a type of writing called "tree literature." Similarly, in her chapter titled "The Structures of Interactive Narrativity," Ryan (2003) maps out the tree structure to represent the form of the *Choose Your Own Adventure* book. This structure starts from a common point but branches out to multiple nodes. As Ryan (2003) points out, in order to avoid an unmanageable number of pathways, paths often merge (p. 249). Multiple endings are possible and the story continues to branch out until one of these endings is reached.

In order to get a better idea of the way interactivity is structured in gamebooks, I have mapped out the choices in *The Spell of the Winter Wizard* starting from one of the initial choices listed above. Figure 1 gives a more specific representation of the narrative structure of an example gamebook. My diagram comes very close to Ryan's (2003) generic tree diagram. However, a couple of interesting patterns come to light. As Ryan noted, certain pages are used multiple times, accessed through a variety of paths. I call these pages "nodes." When we look closely at these nodes, we find that there are, perhaps, far fewer paths than it initially seems. There are also pages that either redirect to a single page only or that ask the reader to turn back to the previous page and make another choice. This feature was not accounted for in Ryan's tree model. Thus, "real" choices are even more limited. For example, at one point your character meets an alchemist who offers to help in your quest. From the passage that begins on p. 97, it looks like the reader has three choices:

1. You ask the alchemist to make a potion for you and take it directly to Warzen's Castle. Turn to page 77.
2. You can have the alchemist make you disappear, then reappear with Cornelius in the Ice Cavern. Turn to page 35.
3. Or you can thank the alchemist for his offer but refuse his services. Turn to page 43

[Lowery, 1983, p. 101].

If the reader chooses to ask the alchemist for a potion and turns to p. 77, the next choice involves either trying that potion or leaving the alchemist. If you choose to try the potion, you turn into a cockroach and reach the unsatisfying ending on pp. 95–96. If you leave, you go to p. 43, the same node you would have reached had you rejected the potion in the first place. The potion, a supposed remedy, never shows up in the story again. Thus, the section of text on p. 77 proves to be a diversion from one carefully steered plot and not actually a new plot. The only real alternative to this line is p. 35, the choice to disappear and reappear in the Ice Cavern. This choice leads to the node on p. 28, which is also reached from the decision point prior to this one. As seen in figure 1, the only difference in how page 28 is reached is whether the character takes a magic potion or blows a magic whistle to reach it. Thus, a more limited number of

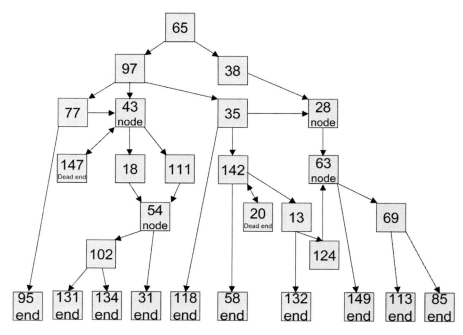

Figure 1: Narrative Structure of *Spell of the Winter Wizard* (Lowery, 1983).

options are really available from those that initially appear. If the story continues "successfully"—that is to a satisfactory rather than unsatisfactory ending—the reader must progress either through page 43 or 28.

One way that the text steers the reader toward these nodes is through dead ends. These dead ends are not unsatisfactory endings but instead direct the reader to return to a previous choice. The text from p. 147 is one of several dead ends. This section concludes thusly: "You have a split second to make another choice. Please go back to page 46 and make another choice" (p. 148). These dead ends are not common, but even a few of them will narrow the choices ultimately available to the reader. Ryan's (2003) tree diagram accounts for the branch-like structure of the *Choose Your Own Adventure* book, but it does not account for the types of backtracking I found in *Winter Wizard*. In Ryan's (2003) diagram, "once a branch has been taken, there is no possible return to the decision point" (p. 248). However, we see not only decisions that lead back to paths that were previous options, but also several dead ends where the reader is actually directed to turn back and choose again. In addition, it is unlikely that a reader who makes an unsatisfactory ending will put down the book and not return. If all endings were equally satisfying, then this sort of backtracking might not occur, but in actuality, only a handful of endings pass as satisfactory. Others, such as the ghost or the cockroach, clearly indicate that the reader has taken a wrong turn from the correct storyline.

The interactivity seen in gamebooks is clearly selective rather than productive. The reader does not actually affect the world of the story in a meaningful way, but simply navigates through the text. In fact, the selection of choices gives the illusion of more interactivity than is actually present. Although there proved to be a good number of endings in *Winter Wizard*, only a few of these were satisfactory. In addition, the pathways to these choices were limited by steering the reader through certain nodes. This early model for interactivity within the print media proves to be less interactive than it may at first seem.

Cybertext: A Model for Adventure Games

Text-based adventure games offer another model for interactive fiction that also emerged in the early 1970s. These games involve a computer database of commands and possible plotlines that the user attempts to access (Aarseth, 1997, p. 100). In these text-based games the user enters textual commands and receives a response, in text, that describes the resulting action in the story. As in the *Choose Your Own Adventure* books, adventure game players' decisions lead to certain predetermined outcomes but involve more activity on the part of the player to reach these outcomes. Rather than simply choosing one path or the other, the player must solve the puzzle in order to proceed.

The most often recognized first in text-based adventure games is *Adventure*, which was completed in 1975 (Montfort, 2003, p. 86). However, Montfort (2003) argues that SHRDLU, developed at MIT from 1968–1970 should instead be conferred this honor (p. 83). Again, we see that this form of interactivity existed before the TRPG, yet *D&D* still had an influence on adventure games. David Keller (2007), still credits *D&D* for the origin of interactive fiction because he explains that text-based adventure games developed before *D&D* were very basic (p. 280). While *Adventure* came first and was in development at the same time as *D&D*, *Zork*, released in 1979, became far more popular (Keller, 2007, p. 280). The influence of *D&D* in *Zork* cannot be denied. In fact, a leaflet from 1978–1979 directly says that the game was inspired by *D&D* (Montfort, 2003, p. 99). *Zork* was also named *Dungeon* for a while, but this caused concerns with copyright infringement and, according to Montfort (2003), also led to a change in the text of the leaflet which, after 1981, ceased to mention *D&D* specifically (p. 100).

Aarseth (1997) focuses one chapter of his book *Cybertext* on text-based adventure games. Aarseth's model for cybertext works to explain the structure of this particular type of interactive fiction, but is also intended to be representative of a larger group of texts, including TRPGs. He explains that in a traditional narrative there are two planes: the *event plane*, where events of the plot are narrated, and the *progression plane*, where the events are unfolded by the reader (Aarseth, 1997, p. 125). In traditional narratives, these planes must be connected because the reader follows the order of events as the narrator presents them. For Aarseth, hypertext is one step away from this traditional model. In hypertext the event progression planes are disconnected as the reader may vary the order in which the events are narrated (Aarseth, 1997, p. 125). However, there is no "wrong" outcome in hypertext, merely different ways to progress through the events.

Cybertext, however, involves the addition of another plane: that of *negotiation*. In cybertext the reader must negotiate with an intermediary in order to unfold the plot (Aarseth, 1997, p. 125). The gamer in a text-based adventure game may have to work with the computer to find the right language to progress through the text — this is negotiation. Aarseth (1997) explains that the gaps in adventure games are "not used to complement the written parts in a game of imagination; rather, they are used as a filter, in which only the 'correct' response lets the user proceed through the text" (p. 111). This extra level of effort to traverse the text sets cybertexts apart from traditional narratives as well as from hypertext (p. 110).

Negotiation in Aarseth's model does not change the actual events in the narrative. Negotiation is merely a means of puzzle solving. In fact, we might say that this sort of interactivity is neither selective nor productive. Readers ultimately have no choice at all in the actual textual events, only in how they get access to them and even that choice is not unlimited. In adventure games, there are only certain commands that are recognized by the "voice," which is the computer system. For example, in the game *Deadline*, if the player gives the command "stroll around," the computer responds, "The word 'stroll' isn't in your vocabulary" (Aarseth, 1997, p. 116).[2] Likewise, if the user enters in an action that is not expected by the computer, such as "hit Leslie with roses," the computer responds with the script for a losing ending in which Leslie falls dead and the character's avatar is arrested (Aarseth, 1997, p. 121). This ending may be analogous to one of the many unsatisfactory endings in the pick-a-path books. Yet, rather than selecting a pre-scripted action and turning to the correct page, the user of the adventure game must try to figure out the command that the computer is looking for in order to proceed. Leslie dying from being hit by roses is not a pre-scripted choice that the reader willingly followed; it is a mistake, a miscommunication between user and interface.

Interactivity in the TRPG

While gamebooks were attempting to create interactivity in print form, and adventure games in digital form, the TRPG emerged and made use of a combination of print and face-to-face interaction. Thus, the interactive possibilities in TRPGs have always been significantly different from these other genres. These differences may help account for the historical difference between the TRPG and these other forms of interactive narrative that emerged at the same time. While *D&D* is often credited as a foundational text, references to influential gamebooks or text-based adventure games are rare, and they continue to be distributed only within extremely niche markets. Their fan-bases have dwindled to near extinction, while TRPGs have continued to grow and recruit new audiences, even beyond the original *D&D* game.

The structure of interactivity in the TRPG may depend on the particular TRPG being played and whether or not that game is a part of a larger campaign created by a GM or DM or whether it is based on a pre-printed module. For example, the plot layout of a *D&D* module might look similar to a pick-a-path gamebook, particularly one like *Winter Wizard* that is marketed as "A *Dungeons and Dragons* Adventure Book." In the module *Speaker in Dreams* (Wyatt, 2001), which I ran as a DM, there is a flowchart in the back that resembles the narrative structure of *Winter Wizard*. Many such modules are organized around "encounters" or locations where the player will encounter some sort of action — whether that involves fighting a monster or talking to a non-player character (NPC) to obtain a clue. This organization was used in *Speaker in Dreams* and the included flowchart shows the progression from one encounter to the next. Sometimes an encounter can be reached from multiple points, such as the nodes in the gamebook. For example, "The Bell Tower," which is a key location according to the flowchart, can be reached from encounters six, seven, or eight. Other parts of the flowchart are extremely linear, though. Encounter three leads to four, then to five, and then to six, with no other listed way to progress through the story (Wyatt, 2001, p. 32).

However, I found that in practice the flowchart was easily set aside. The players in my game did not pick up on any of the clues from encounters three and four and were unable to proceed directly to encounters five and six, as shown in the flowchart. However, as the DM, I had added a little twist in the beginning that allowed the players to skip way ahead to encounter 14. The beginning of most modules lists adventure hooks, which are ways to get the party interested in the current adventure. One of the hooks listed in *Speaker in Dreams* was that one of the character's mentors was from the town where the adventure took place. I made this mentor, Alein, one of the NPCs in the adventure who had been kidnapped. This twist to the adventure hook gave the party reason to look immediately for Alein and thus go directly to encounter 14, her last known location. Unlike the gamebook, even in a fairly scripted module, the DM and players can subvert the intended narrative structure. It all depends on the way the game is run. In other cases, a *D&D* adventure may indeed be run in a way that is similar to the pick-a-path tree structure. For example, the players might reach a dead end. They might walk in a room, fight a bunch of rats (not exactly an exciting plot point), find no treasure and no exit other than the one they came from. This predicament seems quite similar to the gamebook reader who chooses the next page, only to find that after a bit of unsubstantial plot they are instructed to "return to the previous page and make another choice."

If we used a tree-like structure to represent the *D&D* module we would see that, like the gamebook, there are different endings depending on the actions of the players. What such a model doesn't account for is that unlike a gamebook, one very rarely encounters an unsatisfactory ending. In fact, in the episodic structure of the campaign setting, a final ending may never actually be reached, rather only partial endings to individual episodes. The group structure, along with the DM, usually prevents unsatisfactory endings from happening. It may be that one particular character meets an unfortunate and untimely end, that their story does not continue, but the story does not end there for the player. If the session is a part of a larger campaign, the player will usually draw up another character and continue. Even if the player ends playing the game at that point, the narrative continues with other characters and other players. A good DM will not only compensate for situations like this, but he or she will let players add to the world and story that surrounds them, something that is impossible in a pick-a-path story. Ultimately, the structure is similar in that both stories involve decision points, but in TRPGs the number of decision points or the direction they lead are not pre-determined.

Another key difference between TRPGs and gamebooks is that players not only have the ability to make a choice at decision points but also the opportunity to come up with what those choices may be. The pathways in *D&D* continually expand outward rather than having overlapping points in order to connect to pre-determined endings. When players are posed with the question "what do you do?" they are given the opportunity not only to make decisions but also to build their own pathways. This is especially true of home games and longer running campaigns. Although Scott did have several possible endings for the orc adventure (see appendix) in mind, no pre-set pathways existed to reach these endings, and any other endings that might have evolved from the players' actions would have also been acceptable. He had planned what would happen if we defeated the orcs through battle and what would happen if the orcs were allowed to pass, but the actual pathways in the adventure were left up to the party. For example, when our party first encountered the orcs rather than ask "Do you fight?" or "Do you negotiate?" the DM simply poses the question "What do you do?" We decided to carefully sneak up and assess the situation upon which David entangled the orcs, and we interrogated them. However, we could have attacked, returned to Gateway with the information that the orcs had invaded, made a treaty with the orcs or done pretty much anything we could imagine and justify a course of action to the other players. In the case of the TRPG, the diagram of the plot may end up looking similar to Ryan's (2003) tree diagram and my chart from the *Winter Wizard,* but there is nothing in the chart to account for who creates the possible choices. Like the narrative writeup in the appendix, an attempt to chart the TRPG session would erase the signs of the negotiation that took place between players and the DM.

Interestingly, while there is more freedom in the TRPG to come up with possible choices, there is sometimes less freedom when it actually comes to deciding which path is followed. This is another factor that is simply not accounted for in the tree structure of interactivity. Players often suggest an action that they would like their character to take, but that action will then need to be confirmed by rolling the dice. Dice rolls are made in either/or decisions where an action either succeeds or fails. The player may be able to propose any action, but the factor of chance contributes to whether or not the player is allowed to progress down that chosen path. Not only did Cuthalion need to give a good speech to convince Grumbach to withdraw his army, but Mark also had to make a successful diplomacy skill check on his twenty-sided die. In other words, he rolled a die, added the number of points he had given his character in the skill of diplomacy, and the DM decided if the combined number was enough to succeed. When dice rolls are included there is interactivity, but the choice comes from creating possible pathways rather than deciding which one to follow.

Finally, multiple pathways can simultaneously be pursued in *D&D* by different players. When Mary could not attend the Blaze Arrow session she decided that her character, Maureen, would go back to town. At this point her character entered an alternate plotline that none of the other characters had access to. Scott talked with Mary separately to work out the details of what happened to Maureen in town while the rest of us were dealing with the orcs. This example of a completely alternate pathway is rather extreme and does not happen often, yet smaller examples of the phenomenon can be found within the story of the orcs. The reason that Cuthalion's speech to Grumach, despite its success, is not fully reported in the writeup in the appendix is that Whisper and Fletch were not present for the speech, and the story is written from Whisper's point of view. At a decision point these characters chose to stay in the town while Cuthalion and David chose to confront Grumbach. Thus, the two plotlines were able to happen simultaneously, though neither decision was reversible. Depending on the situation, the player may remain and listen to what happens in a passive role as audience, but not as an active participant. I remained to hear Cuthalion's speech, though I could not affect its outcome because my character was not present. On the other hand, Maureen's adventures in Gateway were done behind closed doors and I was not allowed to find out the results. Thus, the model of narrative possibilities is complicated because, as Mackay (2001) also notes, each player's experience is different due to his or her character's position within the story (p. 86). To really create a diagram of the plot structure of a *D&D* game, it would have to be done separately for separate characters.

Ultimately, then, it is the collaborative nature of the TRPG that allows for its narrative structure to be different from something like the gamebook. Both structures could be represented in a tree-like form with starting points that branch out into nodes. There is so much in the TRPG that can not be seen on a model like this. If we were to map out only the dice rolls in a *D&D* game, we might see the either/or decision points like this. Yet, the player has no real control over how these dice rolls go and which path is followed. In addition, there are multiple decision points that simply cannot be represented as nodes — ones where the players themselves come up with the possible options and plan the narrative by working collaboratively.

In some ways it seems that Aarseth's (1997) cybertext model fits more clearly with the structure of TRPGs. In particular, *negotiation* describes the way the group uses social interaction to decide how the events will progress in the narrative. In the case of the TRPG the player states a proposed action aloud to the group, while in the text-based adventure game it is typed as a command on the computer. In both cases, there is a measure of success. Is the action allowed to proceed by the DM? Is a dice roll successful? Does the computer recognize the prompt and proceed with the story? In this way, the plot is decidedly more linear than in the gamebook in that once an action is attempted there is success or failure with no turning back. That physical ability to turn back the page and pick another option does not exist.[3] Thus, negotiation is a process of reaching a point that successfully lets the story progress.

However, negotiation in the TRPG is far more interactive than in the adventure game because of its social nature. An actual person has greater capacity for interpreting actions that may not be standard. Also, the complex game mechanics and the player and DM's ability to question and change those rules allows for more flexibility. If, to use Aarseth's (1997) example from *Deadline,* a player in *D&D* said, "I hit Leslie with the roses," the process to determine the result of this action would be more complex than in the text-based adventure game. The DM might not see this as a legitimate attack action and might interpret it as a joke instead. If the DM did consider that the player was serious when declaring this action, he or she might turn to the rule book for guidance. However, like in the computer game, roses would not be listed in the rules as weapon with statistics on how much damage they would do. Rather than this leading to failure, if the group decided this was a legitimate action, they would need to negotiate what such an attack would mean. Would the thorns do some damage or would the only injury be to Leslie's wounded ego as her gift was thrown in her face? The computer seems only to have recognized "hit" as an attack and calculated the only ending it knew as a result of the action "hit"—the death of Leslie. The difference between the computer and the live DM is especially pronounced here due to the nature of these very early text-based games, but serves to show that the structure of interactivity and the nature of negotiation vary between these two media. Again, a quick look at Aarseth's (1997) model for cybertext appears to apply to the structure of the TRPG, but it can not account for these differences.

Narrative Reward and Punishment

Much of the difference between TRPGs and gamebooks or adventure games comes down to a system of reward and punishment. In *D&D*, veering off the expected path is often rewarded with a more interesting story, but doing this in an adventure game is either impossible or results in narrative punishment. Aarseth (1997) finds that in adventure games, "noncooperation and free play result in narrative punishment, which equals the end, death" (p. 121). We have seen examples of narrative punishment in both gamebooks and adventure games. When the reader of *Winter Wizard* takes the potion and is turned into an insect or when one hits Leslie with roses in *Deadline*, the narrative comes to an illogical and unsatisfying end. Even if the player does not activate an ending that is unsatisfactory, the negotiation in the text-based adventure game can become so frustrating to the user that he or she may opt to quit playing rather than continue the narrative.[4]

Similarly, if we return to the structure of the gamebook, we see that the most satisfying endings also come after a long series of choices. One does not simply jump ahead to the happy ending, but must sustain a series of correct choices to get there. As seen in figure 1, in *Winter Wizard*, the reader has to make at least five and as many as seven choices to reach p. 69, which then leads to two satisfactory endings. One ending is violent, while the other is peaceful (Lowery, 1983, pp. 85–89, pp. 113–116). Both endings last for several pages (unlike the short, unsatisfactory endings) and both result in the safe return of the wizard Alcazar, which was the goal set out at the beginning of the book. However, the reader who chooses p. 85 is scolded for the choice of violence, and their character is told to remain a student until he or she has learned more peaceful methods (Lowery, 1983, p. 88). This ending is thus less satisfactory than the peaceful ending where the protagonist is reunited with Alcazar and championed for choosing peaceful methods over violence. The best choice results in the best ending.

Sometimes modules in *D&D* may also lead to narrative punishment or reward. However, that is rarely the point of a TRPG. Monte Cook explained to me that in his module *The Return to the Temple of Elemental Evil*, it was sometimes possible for creative players to get to an island that should have been unattainable until they were higher level (personal communication, June 30, 2009). Unfortunately, this could lead to character death or (at the very least) player frustration at not being able to meet the objectives on the island. Cook listed this as a limitation of the module because he noted that players should instead be rewarded for ingenuity and creativity. He also noted that skilled DMs would be more likely to adjust the module as needed to avoid punishing players for reaching what was intended to be an unattainable goal at that point in the game.

Interestingly, rewards and punishments in TRPGs are more likely to surround characters, which varies from either the gamebook or cybertext adventure game. As previously mentioned, unsatisfactory endings may come in the form of character deaths, but the game will still go on. Likewise, there may be consequences if a player does not play a character true to form, particularly in groups where character acting is an emphasis. Scott recalled an example later in the Sorpraedor campaign when a player was not very true to his character. This particular player was in charge of a cleric, Wrestfur, who stood for all things good and righteous. Clerics have spells in *D&D* that they learn through prayer. However, this particular character, through poor management by the player, committed a series of evil doings. For this, Scott orchestrated a storyline where another member of the same church sought out Wrestfur in the game in order to relieve him of his priestly duties. In addition, there were days when the cleric's prayers to his god for spells were unsuccessful, something that does not usually require a dice roll or even DM approval to succeed. Thus, the player was punished for veering too far from the role that he had laid out for his character within the narrative.

This sort of punishment, however, is more likely to be carried out in the social interaction of the game rather than in the story. If a player is not contributing to the story in a manner that is acceptable to the DM and other players, that player may not be invited to return, or social pressure may be applied to change the behavior. More often than not, a suggestion to do something that is out-of-character may come up when players are negotiating which actions to take next. Other players are likely to articulate questions such as "would your character really do that?" Likewise, players who apply their own knowledge to their characters, often called *meta-gaming*, are likely to be called out in the social sphere. For example, a long-standing *D&D* player may know exactly how to defeat the monster that his character has never seen before. If the player takes full advantage of that knowledge, either the DM or other players may question whether or not that character would act as the player intends and the result would be negotiated. In fact, it was only when Wrestfur's player did not respond to these social pressures that the DM resorted to narrative punishment.

In terms of rewards, Mark was rewarded by extra experience points for Cuthalion's expertly crafted speech to the orcs. Experience points and treasure are the biggest rewards in *D&D*. When players complete quests or defeat enemies, they receive experience points that allow their characters to go up in level and gain additional skills and abilities. They also are often rewarded with treasure that includes items for their characters or gold that is used to buy items for their characters. Characters in gamebooks and text-based adventure games are merely rewarded in terms of uncovering the story, not by advancing their characters. Because the reader expects to navigate a satisfactory outcome to the story, this hardly seems to be a reward at all.

The Continuation of Interactive Narrative

The 1970s was a key time in the development of interactive narrative. As authors sought to break free from the traditional constraints of the print medium, they experimented with genres such as gamebooks, adventure games, and TRPGs. However, the type of interactivity that proved to be the most influential in the long run was more productive than selective. It was also collaborative and revolved around character, in addition to plot. Finally, it allowed for tangible rewards, such as experience points, for the reader's interactive efforts. As interactive narrative grew, we discovered that it is not enough to uncover the story; the reader must be able to shape that story.

The genres of the gamebook and the text-based adventure game have waned in their popularity to the point of near extinction, yet TRPGs have continued to experience success. As the first of this genre, *D&D* is not only significant because of its influence on new types of texts, but also because the original game continues to be played. Wizards of the Coast estimates that an average of 2.5 million people play *D&D* each month (Dancey 2000), which shows that neither new literary or game genres have replaced traditional TRPGs.[5] Yet, text-based adventure games have generally been replaced by other forms of computer games that rely heavily on visual cues rather than requiring the user to enter only textual commands. Likewise, gamebooks seem to have been replaced, to a large extent, by new media alternatives. Hypertext, which has garnered far more scholarly attention, is now heralded as the medium for interactive literature. Much of the success of TRPGs may be to due to the affordances of the social medium, and as digital texts have continued to evolve they, too, have sought this social interaction. Massively multiplayer online role-playing games (MMORPGs), for example, involve textual negotiation similar to that engaged in by the players of a TRPG.

Why have TRPGs persisted when their generic cousins have been replaced by new media? Although the technology is quickly heading in that direction, the digital medium can not yet afford the same structure of interactivity as the social medium of the TRPG. The flexibility I have outlined here is very much an advantage of a face-to-face medium. Players are more often than not rewarded rather than punished for creativity, and the social structure of the game allows for flexibility that is simply not possible in even the best new media texts. In the the next chapter, I will continue to explore the way that *D&D* has influenced current games and establish that one of the primary reasons that players are drawn to TRPGs is this sense of narrative agency. They have control over the story that develops from their game play. This sort of productive interactivity is lacking in both the textual adventure game and the gamebook, both of which furnish "correct" paths for the story being told. The player in a TRPG is not out to discover the secret to the DM's story but to help create that story through active participation; thus this medium meets the need of readers to break from their traditional relationship with texts.

2

Role-Playing Game Genres

Although it would be a stretch to say that *Dungeons and Dragons (D&D)* is directly responsible for the development of computer games, its influence on early games in undeniable. As noted in chapter 1, early text-based games, such as *Zork*, were clearly influenced by *D&D*. Since then, more direct attempts to port the face-to-face game system to a digital medium have continued with varying degrees of success. As of *D&D*'s 25th anniversary, *Gamespot* reporters Allen Park and Elliot Chin (1999) counted more than twenty computer games based on *D&D*. Five years later (2004), *GameSpy*'s Allen Rausch added to the list in his extended "A History of *D&D* Videogames." While Rausch (2004) notes that some of these games are great videogames, he also comments that "they have yet to capture the open-ended magic of a simple *D&D* session with a creative Dungeon Master." The chase to capture some of the same type of interactivity afforded by the face-to-face medium continues. *Dungeons & Dragons Online (DDO)*, a Massively Multiplayer Online Role-Playing Game (MMORPG), was released on September 9, 2009, at the time of this writing. It is still too early to tell what influence this will have on the gaming industry, and the 2006 version of the MMORPG has not proved to be overly revolutionary. However, the 2009 *DDO* release operates on a new business model, with the basic game being offered to users for free. It is also a part of larger changes within the *D&D* community and follows the new fourth edition rules (4.0), released in 2008. Although change is occurring quickly in both computer and tabletop games, earlier versions of both games continue to be played. Single-player computer role-playing games (CRPGs), for example, may not necessarily be representative of the cutting edge of the gaming industry, but like the tabletop role-playing games (TRPG), should be studied on their own merits in terms of current and historical importance. Scholarship can not hope to keep up with the speed at which these genres are changing, but it can look back at the way these genres have influenced each other.

Genres have increasingly been recognized as "forms of action or modes of activity" (Jasinski, 2001, p. 275). As forms of activity, current rhetorical theory has come to recognize that genres are not stable forms, but living entities that change over time. They spawn new genres. They die out. They shift in purpose and in form; all of which makes the study of genre infinitely more complex. This definition of genre raises a number of questions which the study of the TRPG, as a genre, may prove useful in addressing. These shifts in genre can be seen in both *D&D* as a pen and paper game and in the videogame genres it has influenced. What happens when a text like *D&D* is ported to a new medium? When does that text become a new genre, and when does it merely shift? In this chapter, I address the relationship between *D&D* as a tabletop game and *D&D* as the basis for some computer role-playing games (CRPGs). A look at the tabletop game as an antecedent genre for later computer versions proves useful in explicating the relationship between these two forms. These games often draw on the same basic rules and settings; however, I argue that, rhetorically speaking, they represent not only different media, but different genres.

The TRPG as an Antecedent Genre

Genre affects both the author and the audience's expectations; our experiences with other genres will influence how we approach a new text. Kathleen Jamieson (1975) first used the term *antecedent genre* to note that a speaker will "draw on his past experience and on genres formed by others in response to similar situations" (p. 408). Thus, the notion of an antecedent genre shows the way that genres influence each other. Each time a speaker or a writer goes to produce text, that text is influenced by their prior notion of texts that already exist in that genre or in closely related genres. Specifically, antecedent genres come into play when new genres are created and draw heavily upon older genres. The act to use older genres as the foundation for new types of texts may be intentional or unintentional. For example, Jamieson (1975) analyzes how the State of the Union address and the response given by Congress used many of the same features as the king's speech to Parliament and Parliament's traditional response (pp. 411–13). Even when the situation seems to differ quite a bit, as it did when the United States formed its own union, Jamieson shows that speakers fall back on familiar genres. Despite wanting to create something new for a new country, the first authors of the State of the Union address fell into old patterns — knowingly or unknowingly, they drew on a powerful antecedent genre. Likewise, Anis Bawarshi (2003) notes that "as antecedent forms, genres constitute the ways we perceive situations" and our positions in relation to those situations (p. 94). We come to expect certain things from a genre, whether that genre is a political speech or a form of entertainment, like a game. When we create new genres we use those expectations, and if a genre does not meet those expectations we will likely be disappointed.

The resemblance of computer games to *D&D* has, for the most part, been a conscious choice of applying characteristics of an antecedent genre to a new text in a new medium. In the late 1980s, TSR, Inc. offered the license for *Advanced D&D*[1] to Strategic Simulations, Inc. (SSI), who used the original tabletop game rules to produce a series of CRPGs (Park & Chin, 1999). *Pool of Radiance* was released in 1988 (first for the Commodore 64 and then for the home PC), and this game even used images of monsters directly from the *D&D Monster Manual* book (Rausch 2004). SSI continued to produce games of this nature, but none were as successful as this first attempt. According to Rausch (2004), the release of *Baldur's Gate* (1998) represents another significant success in the quest to put *D&D* in CRPG form. He states that this game "capture(d) the *D&D* magic in a way that gamers hadn't experienced since the *Pool of Radiance* days" (Rausch, 2004).

Rausch (2004) explains that *Baldur's Gate* was more successful in capturing some of the more nuanced aspects of the tabletop game, such as character alignment. However, not all agree that the conversion to a CRPG was a complete success. Carr (2006) explains the lack of flexibility often found in CRPGs with a specific example about character alignment in *Baldur's Gate*. She attempted to play an evil character in order to test the limits of the game, but found that she was quickly thwarted by either direct interference (where a more powerful non-player character [NPCs] would destroy her character as punishment for her action) or by being unable to open up new areas of the narrative as NPCs became uncooperative. Thus, she found that to actually play the game, she needed to take the attitude that she was following the prescribed measures in the game only to manipulate the NPCs for her own nefarious goals. Carr (2006) explains that this means her character's "dominant trait (evil) would reside solely in the perceptions of her user" (p. 51).

The use of character alignment in *Baldur's Gate* comes directly from *D&D*. In the original tabletop game, players choose their character alignment on two scales: (1) whether their characters will be good, evil, or neutral and (2) whether they will be lawful, chaotic or neutral. Because computer game designers attempted to draw on the characteristics of the antecedent genre, the notion of alignment remains even when it cannot be truly realized due to the constraints of the medium. Yet, because players also have expectations based on the antecedent genre of the TRPG, they are able to see their characters as evil, even when the actual potential for evil action is limited by the CRPG form. Thus, we see the power of the antecedent genre in shaping both the author and audience's view of this new text.

Not all computer games have drawn as deliberately or directly on *D&D*, however, the power of the antecedent genre still remains. J. C. Herz (as cited in Rausch 2004) comments that a high number of computer game designers are tabletop gamers, usually *D&D* players. Likewise, David Kushner's (2003) *Masters of Doom* tells the story of two influential videogame designers, co-creators of *Doom* and *Quake*—John Carmack and John Romero — starting from their days as *D&D* players in the 70s and 80s. While the goal of these games was not to bring *D&D* to the digital medium, Burn and Carr (2006) argue that contemporary action adventure games also share characteristics with RPGs such as rules that "govern timing and turn taking, combat outcomes, character creation, and the kinds of weapons and magic on offer to different character types" (p. 17). Even some computer games that would be not be considered RPGs draw on some of these key features.

However, the history of CRPGs is complex; *D&D* is not the only influential text. Nor is it necessary for a new genre to draw only upon one antecedent genre. *Final Fantasy*, for example, comes from the Japanese tradition of console games rather than the Western tradition that influenced *Baldur's Gate* (Carr et al., 2006, p. 24). Still, it appears that *D&D* left its mark. Burn and Carr (2006) note that *D&D* had a presence in Japan in the 1980s — one that they believe to have been influential to early game designers there. Although games developed in Japan took on a different style from Western games, drawing on other antecedent genres, they still used similar game and narrative features to *D&D*, such as the use of monsters and combat to propel the story, avatars that gain experience, and generic fantasy settings (Carr et al., 2006, pp. 24–25).

In some cases, then, the use of *D&D* and the TRPG as an antecedent genre was quite deliberate, while in other cases it was only one of many influences. To what degree, though, do writers and game designers have choice over what genres influence their new creations? While Jamieson's

(1975) view of genre seems quite constraining, Devitt (2004) acknowledges more agency on the part of the rhetor. Jamieson (1975) uses such phrases as "bound by the manacles of the antecedent genre" to show the strength of the traditional speech form on the new Congress (p. 413). Devitt (2004) notes that the role of context is important in determining genre, but the role of the individual should not be discounted (p. 134). In other words, strong social and formal constraints do exist when talking about genre, but that does not mean that an individual is unable to break those constraints to reshape a genre or create a new one. One might say that Dave Arneson was such an individual who was able to break free of the genre conventions of war gaming to create role-playing games. Nevertheless, the social situation had to be right for others to accept this new genre. Gary Gygax's development and marketing of *D&D* lead to its widespread adoption, and he is more often recognized among gamers as the father of *D&D*. Arneson initiated the new game, but it was Gygax who really turned that game into a genre that was repeated time and time again in different settings. It is not only the author or rhetor that must break free of generic constraint for change to occur; an audience must be able to accept that change and adopt the new genre.

Similarly, lack of knowledge of an antecedent genre and how genres change may lead to misconceptions on the part of audience members and even scholars. Murray (1998), for example, expresses a common misconception that *D&D* is played by pre-teens, assuming that the antecedent genre will be less complex and evolved than the following genres. Genre change shakes us of this notion, for while new genres are emerging, genres also change within themselves. *D&D* may have initially appealed to a younger crowd, but that group has continued to be invested in the game. The Wizards of the Coast 2000 market survey found that 25–35 was the largest age group of TRPG players at 34 percent (Dancey 2000). Although the number of young players, ages 12–15 is also high (23 percent), they are no longer the largest age group playing TRPGs. Likewise, Wizards of the Coast now recognizes the importance of the growing female market (Dancey 2000), while Fine (1983) noted that women rarely engaged in the hobby.

In addition to the changes in the demographic, the original game created by Arneson and Gygax has gone through multiple editions and changes. *Advanced Dungeons and Dragons* (1978) was released not long after the original *D&D* game, and entered its second edition in 1988 (Park and Chin, 1999). Wizards of the Coast released *Dungeons and Dragons* 3rd edition in 2000, followed up by *Dungeons and Dragons* 3.5 in 2003. At the time of this writing, *D&D* has just entered edition 4.0. When I asked game designer Monte Cook (personal communication) if the differences in editions changed the narrative of the game, he said that he did not believe so. He noted that there were many minor changes between editions, but in terms of changing a tale like *The Temple of Elemental Evil* between editions, he did not see major changes to the story. However, Cook has continued to release game products that are compatible with the 3.5 rather than the 4.0 edition. Even when editions change, gamers may still prefer older forms. Particularly in times when genres are changing, we see that older forms continue to be used because the changes in the genre may not fit with previous expectations. If they are powerful enough, the older form may persist, as tabletop games have done despite efforts to make similar computer games. So far, it seems that none of the new *D&D* editions has instituted changes so significant as to create a new genre, but they show that the genre has continued to change throughout time. One significant change that came with edition 3.0 was the switch to a d20 System where many key dice rolls would use a twenty-sided die. This shift simplified what were seen as overly complex rules in 2nd edition, and also mainstreamed the tabletop gaming industry. Through the Open-Game License, Wizards invited other gaming companies to also use the d20 System. Certainly, another significant change in the genre of the TRPG is the expansion of the genre away from just *D&D* to include role-playing in other settings. It may no longer be a 12-year-old male playing *D&D* (if it ever was), but a 40-year-old female playing *Vampire, the Masquerade*. The demographics have changed and so has the genre.

D&D has been key to the development of computer games, particularly computer role-playing games, but the original game has also continued to change. With these changes, the question remains of how to recognize a new genre when we see it. When does the new form separate itself enough from the antecedent form to be considered something new? For example, is *D&D Online* a change within the larger genre of role-playing, or is it a different genre altogether? Does shifting to a different medium automatically mean a shift in genre? As I continue to explore these questions in the next section, I move from a formal to a rhetorical definition of genre.

Toward a Rhetorical Definition of Genre

It seems clear that the texts discussed in chapter 1 that tabletop games, gamebooks, and text-based adventure games, all represent different genres. All three exist in different media, and follow different forms. While gamebooks and text-based adventure games were influenced by TRPGs, they are referred to by separate terms and are not similar enough to be considered the same genre. Yet, not everyone would separate out the TRPG and the CRPG as different genres. Hammer (2007), for instance, includes all kinds of role-playing, even freeform role-play in her study of RPGs. She argues that they all share some common features, such as narration, collaboration, and improvisation in all their forms (Hammer, 2007, p. 70). However, I consider the TRPG to be distinct from other types of RPGs. Thus, the question of whether or not the TRPG and the CRPG are both members of the RPG genre depends on how genre is defined.

Burn and Carr (2006) explain that genre is a tricky word to get a handle on when talking about games:

> A game can simultaneously be classified according to the platform on which it is played (PC, mobile phone, XBox), the style of play it affords (multiplayer, networked, or single user, for instance), the manner in which it positions the player in relation to the game world (first person, third person, "god"), the kind of rules and goals that make up its game-play (racing game, action adventure), or its representational aspects (science fiction, high fantasy, urban realism) [Carr et al., 2006, p. 16].

The TRPG clearly operates on a different system than other TRPGs, using pen and paper rather than a computer platform. It favors collaborative play, but those within the game shift between first person and other positions in relation to the game world. A player may have a first person relationship to the story, but the DM may be seen more as a "god." Finally, there are TRPGs in all of the settings that Burn and Carr mention, just as there are CRPGs in these same sorts of settings. Burn and Carr (2006) argue that genre classification that looks at only one of these features is limited. However, they see the style of game play as the most important factor in determining game genre (Carr et al., 2006, p. 16).

In particular, they argue that it is a set of common ludic characteristics not a common type of setting that defines a game as a CRPG. These characteristics include the use of a character over which the gamer is given some choice, the ability of that avatar to gain experience points and skills as the player progresses through the game, the use of a team rather than a single avatar to complete challenges, and "long, journey-based narratives set within detailed and crowded worlds" (Carr et al., 2006, pp. 20–21). These elements of RPGs hold true for both computer and tabletop games and for games that are either collaborative or played alone. Even when a CRPG is played alone, that player often is responsible for multiple avatars or companions, thus meeting the criteria Burr and Carr set for focusing on a team. In addition, they note that "RPGs tend to prioritize reflection, reading and strategy over pace or spectacle" (Carr et al., 2006, p. 21). The features laid out by Burn and Carr do appear to be the sort of "family resemblances" that link together RPGs of all sorts.

However, Burn and Carr's (2006) definition of the RPG genre does not account for one very important factor — why people play the game. Current theories of genre, particularly within the field of rhetoric, have focused on purpose over form. According to Jonathan Swales (1990), "a genre comprises a class of communicative events, the members of which share some set of communicative purposes" (p. 58). When I posed a question on a role-players' blog asking the differences between computer and tabletop RPGs, the fifteen users who responded agreed that there were major differences between the two forms and that playing both met different needs. One user directly states "different needs are fulfilled by each." Another agrees that "you play each one for different reasons." For Swales, purpose is "the principal criterial feature that turns a collection of communication events into a genre" (Swales 46), and the users' comments above seem to indicate that the TRPG does indeed fulfill a different purpose than the CRPG.

In order to assess what that purpose might be, I continued by asking the members of the role-playing forum what kept them playing both games. I repeated this question in an online survey completed by 65 role-players. Participants who left written comments reinforced the idea that TRPGs met different needs from CRPGs. They pointed to flexibility as the main need that CRPGs could not fulfill in the same way as TRPGs. One user states that tabletop TRPGs are important because of their "unlimited choices" and "complete freedom in creating your own character." Another mentions that "without the social interaction with other players, complex character development, long term effect on the game world setting, and wide variety of choices in situations, I really don't classify a game a role-playing game." He continues by explaining that "there isn't a computer game in the world that can give me the chance to play all the options I want in a situation that I get in a role-playing game."

In addition, the social setting is a key reason that gamers give for wanting to play a TRPG. One participant says, "I play tabletop for the interaction with actual people. To laugh with them and pig out together on chips and soda. I do tabletop to feel the dice in my hand when I make a roll, to scribble down notes and stats for my character. I play tabletop for all the things that I can do that I can't with a computer RPG." This participant draws on the physical aspect of TRPGs that isn't present in CRGPs. Other users agreed that social interaction is important when they choose to play a TRPG over a CRPG. Yet, online games (particularly MMORPGs) have begun to change the shape of social interaction as players form tight-knit online groups that can chat and work together in real time. Furthermore, several respondents also pointed out the disadvantages to in-person social interaction. In particular, they commented on the difficulty of meeting people and coordinating schedules to game together regularly.

An important distinction that came up in the responses was the difference between games that are controlled by the computer (CRPGs) and the use of computers for role-playing games. Several respondents mentioned that in addition to tabletop games, they had participated in role-playing via email, Multi-User Shared Hallucination (MUSH), or another type of online forum. These games do not involve a pre-programmed interface the way many CRPGs do, but are instead built by the players as the game progresses. The new movement toward open-source MMORPGs may fall into this category as well, although it was not commented on by the participants in the current study. Several respondents mentioned that they felt these online games allowed them to exercise their creativity, while in contrast, they played CRPGs to "waste time." A detailed analysis of these texts falls outside the scope of my current study; however, a preliminary assertion is that they should be excluded from the CRPG genre despite the use of their use of a computer interface. If we define genre in terms of purpose, one could argue that these types of human-moderated text-based forums are more closely related to the TRPG generically.

A key difference here is the difference between *interactivity* and *agency*. Both the adventure game and the gamebook had interactivity, but interactivity (even productive interactivity) does not necessarily imply agency. Players can, in a sense, leave a mark on the storyworld by creating their own character in a CRPG; which is productive, rather than selective interactivity. However, the degree of control the player has over that character and his or her actions is a matter of agency, not interactivity. CRPGs are always limited by the code inherent in the computer programming. A gamer who responded to my survey explains why he or she prefers TRPG to computer games:

> There's no hard-coded limitation on what can and can't be in the game; it's all up to whatever your players are willing to roll with. If someone doesn't like the direction the story's going, they can act to change it ... and they have opportunities to do so in ways that make the audience participation in "American Idol" feel like scraps thrown to dogs.

Even in the best computer games, at this point there are areas that cannot be explored, plotlines that cannot be realized, and character traits that simply cannot be maintained. Buckingham (2006) also argues that while computer game users do have power over their gaming experience, "this power is bounded by the constraints of the game system and of the representational possibilities of the game" (Carr et al., 2006, p. 188). He goes on to say that "activity on the part of the players — or even of the most creative fans — should not be confused with agency, that is, the power to define the dominant parameters for cultural production" (p. 188). For players to truly have agency, they must shape the system itself.

Narrative Agency

This notion of agency is also key to making the connection between the structure and purpose of the TRPG and thus defining it as its own genre. Jessica Hammer (2007) defines several types of agency including textual, narrative, psychological, and cultural agency (p. 73). While any interactive text may give the feeling of agency (psychological agency), the TRPG affords real narrative agency, which Hammer (2007) defines as control over the story (p. 73). This agency is built into the way the game is designed. A player in a computer game can subvert the structure of the narrative by hacking the code or using cheats. Yet, this subversion is outside the scope of the intended use of the game; like Carr's evil avatar, it exists only in the realm of the reader. In contrast, the TPRG not only allows for, but encourages such subversion in its very structure.

For one, exploration of space in the TRPG is more malleable. In CRPGs, spaces must be laid out and programmed in advance. Even games with randomly created spaces already have coded in them the types of spaces and items that will appear in those spaces. In most games, there are spots where the user simply can't click to go any farther — space is finite. Furthermore, there are often areas of the map that don't open up until the player has completed certain quests or levels. In some CRPGs, a player might even find the location of another area of the map, but if he or she attempts to go there too soon, chances for survival aren't good. Failure means re-starting the game from a saved point; the story can only progress through success. The challenges in different parts of the game are more difficult and, without the character gaining additional skills through going up a level, they may prove too much, causing a re-start. In games that generate content more randomly as players progress, challenge levels may adjust depending on the level of the player character; however, these adjustments are made only on character level not player ability. The player may choose an ability level at the beginning of the game (easy or hard, for example), but will usually need to start the game over to adjust that level. In both CRPGs and TRPGs, characters improve as they meet challenges by gaining experience points; this is one of the direct influences TRPGs had as an antecedent genre on CRPGs. Thus, a challenge that may be unbeatable at first will become more doable as the character advances; however, the player's ability is separate from the character's ability. Some challenges in TRPG may also be designed for higher level characters. However, a DM can easily adjust the difficulty of an adventure or direct players a different way. A DM in a continuing home game will have a pretty good idea whether or not the players in that game are capable of handling the challenge at level 10 that the rule book says they should be able to handle. Furthermore, he or she might decide that the players who are level five should go ahead and take on the level 10 challenge because their failure will be key to building the story he or she wants to tell. Thus, the DM is an essential element of the tabletop game. The DM, as a role (whether that role is called a DM, a storyteller, a Gamemaster [GM], or another name), is a key feature of the TRPG that allows for narrative agency.

Much of a computer game designer's job involves placing clues in the gaming world to direct the player down a certain path (Lewis et al., 2004). DMs may do the same thing, but players have the narrative agency to determine which clues to follow, if any. For example, in a dungeon setting one door may be locked or have unbeatable monsters hiding behind it. However, a computer game may simply not allow the player to go a certain way. The directional mouse button may disappear, or the user may be unable to interact with certain characters or objects in the gaming world. In TRPGs such boundaries do not exist. The players may make a high enough roll to pick the lock on that door, or run back to town and hire more allies to beat that previously unbeatable monster. Whatever the obstacle, tabletop gamers can (and often do) find a way around it, at times to the chagrin of the DM who tried so hard to steer them in a certain direction.[2]

I argue that the key difference between the TRPG and the CRPG is not that the TRPG involves social contact (as that is becoming more common in computer games as well), but that the *nature* of that social contact is one that involves a high degree of agency. In the TRPG there are really two levels of game designers. There are those who write the rule books and campaign modules, and those who DM. At times (such as in the Sorpraedor campaign) the DM creates a campaign world, thus acting more as a game designer. In other instances the DM may build only on published materials, acting more as a player than a designer. CRPGs do not often have these varying levels, and players are removed from the game designers who write the code and story of the game. They may be able to write to the gaming company with ideas for future games or complaints about current game mechanics, or they may even be able to hack the code and create game "cheats." However, the average player is not able to interact with a game designer as a standard part of the game play the way that a player interacts with the DM. In addition, the DM may switch between running a game and playing a character in a game someone else runs. In the Role-Playing Gamers Association (RPGA) game that I observed, the majority of the players also ran games as DMs at other RPGA events. Computer game designers are often also gamers themselves; however, the chances of an average player gaming with a game designer are far more rare. While the DM may have ultimate control over a particular campaign or adventure, he or she is more of an equal within the community. Game designers, such as Monte Cook, do often run games at large conventions such as GenCon. Yet, these game designers do not have exclusive control over the direction of the game. All the rule books are clear — it is the DM's word that is final, not the written rules.

Having the DM's ear is thus an important influence in *D&D*. Being able to negotiate face-to-face allows players actual narrative agency, not just the chance for interaction. In fact, the DM often has to adapt the narrative to follow what the players decide. Scott found that he made up a great deal of the Sorpraedor world and story on the fly, in response to what the players decided to pursue. In this way, he was subject to the story that the players wanted to hear and obligated to take it in the direction they wanted to go. This obligation can be true when running a module as well. When my players did not follow the obvious plot points in *Speaker in Dreams*, I had to think on my feet and skip ahead in the module to where the players led me. While the DM can limit players' actions, in reality, the players have a great deal of agency in creating the story of the TRPG. Even if this action takes place via a computer-mediated environment, this interaction directly with the DM is important. In MMORPGs, players may still interact with other players in order to determine a course of action; yet, the decisions that the players make are still bounded by the constraints of the pre-programmed world. Players can determine how they will work to defeat a certain monster in the game, but they will not directly be able to interact with the person responsible for the creation of that monster. It is only when this interaction exists that players have true narrative agency.

Although TRPGs have been highly influential in the form of CRPGs, if we base our definition of genre on purpose as well as form, we see that the TRPG still represents a separate genre from its computer counterparts. Traces of the TRPG genre remain as game designers drew on their previous genre knowledge, but in creating the CRPG a new genre has evolved with a separate purpose from its antecedent. Perhaps this is the best way to tell the difference between a current genre undergoing change and a new genre emerging. While the new genre may have some commonalities with its antecedent, it will serve a different purpose for the audience. In the case of the CRPG, the switch in medium did not allow for the purpose of the TRPG to remain intact. However, it brought new qualities that were simply not possible in face-to-face interaction. Just as the gamebook tried to create a place where *D&D* could be played alone, the single-player CRPGs offers a great chance for gamers to play an avatar and engage with fantasy worlds without having to juggle the burdens of coordinating social schedules and meeting new people. Even as social interaction becomes more common in computer games, the accessibility as well as the visual and auditory power are advantages of these games for most players. Clearly, these factors can also exclude those without access to technology, or who have limitations in how they can use the technology. Yet, these are challenges that can be addressed as the technology continues to advance. In addition, as open source games become more of a reality, we may again see the split between the two genres narrow. As we continue to classify new games, however, I suggest a model that accounts for not only new forms, but new rhetorical purposes.

Advantages and Limitations of Genre Study

Carolyn Miller (1984) argues that "a rhetorically sound definition of genre must be centered not on the substance or the form of discourse but on the action it is used to accomplish" (p. 151). David Russell (1997) draws on Miller to propose that "a genre is the ongoing use of certain material tools in a certain way that worked once and might work again; a typified tool-mediated response to conditions recognized by participants as recurring" (p. 515). The early CRPG designers attempted to apply the tools of the TRPG to the digital medium, but the medium has so far proved too constraining to capture the purpose of the TRPG. Yet, if this quest had been a failure, the popularity of TRPGs would outweigh that of CRPGs, and this is not the case. Instead, we see that both continue to be played, often by the same gamers depending on what action they are seeking to accomplish. The new genre of the CRPG has offered greater affordances in terms of visual design and graphic representation. It has also allowed for game play without the presence of a DM, a quality some gamers may prefer to the constant social negotiation of the TRPG. They may sacrifice greater narrative agency for faster game play with fewer social constraints. A rhetorical definition of genre allows us to see why a gamer might engage with both genres rather than choosing one.

While a detailed analysis of purpose signals to authors that two texts are functioning as different genres, another important clue in separating one genre from another is found in the language of the communities using the genre. In the rhetorical view, for a text or a "communicative event" to constitute a new genre it must belong to a different community, involve different tools, or respond to a different rhetorical need than other genres. When texts move from one system to another, there is often a shift in terminology. Both Miller (1984) and Swales (1990) point out that those actively engaged in a community give names to types of communicative events that continually occur as a part of this community. Specifically, Miller and Shepherd (2004) note that "when a type of discourse or communicative action acquires a common name within a given context or community, that's a good sign that it's functioning as a genre."

In light of the aforementioned scholars' practice of defining genres based on common terminology, the names used in the history of the RPG become significant. The distinction between TRPGs and CRPGs does not come from scholarship, but from the gaming community itself. The term *role-playing* is used by both computer and tabletop gamers alike, but when communities do intersect and a distinction is necessary, the RPG label is most commonly reserved for the tabletop gamers. For example, conventions often separate their gaming schedules into "computer games," "Live Action Role Plays (LARPs)" and "RPGs." Not only do gamers acknowledge that they have different purposes in mind when playing TRPGs than when playing other games, but they refer to their activities by different names. Because the community of gamers recognizes the TRPG as a distinct genre that both uses different tools and has a different desired outcome from computer games, it would be irresponsible for scholars not to respect this differentiation.

However, one danger with genre theory is the tendency to universalize what may not be universal. It is difficult to say that the purpose of every gamer who plays in a TRPG is to gain a sense of narrative agency. Different types of gamers exist who prefer to focus on different aspects of the game. This issue of compatibility is one that participants in my survey brought up as a difficulty when finding people to play with face-to-face. In this way, the very concept of a genre becomes problematic because individual users' experiences may be quite different from one another.[3] Burn and Carr (2006) recognize that player expectations often determine the style of play. They note that the CRPG *Anarchy Online* served as a means of role-play for some audiences, but others outright rejected the possibilities for role-play and preferred to focus on the features of the game that resembled first person shooters (p. 28). Murray (1998) also notes that the same game can serve different purposes depending on the point of view of the player. She explains that the computer game *SimCity*, a simulation game in which users create and maintain their own city, was viewed very differently by a couple who both played it. The husband saw it as an engineering problem while the wife saw a narrative emerging in the lives of the townspeople in her city (Murray, 1998, p. 88). The husband and the wife imposed different generic conceptions on the text in order to achieve different purposes; perhaps because they drew on their knowledge of different antecedent genres.

Nevertheless, I maintain that the common purpose of narrative agency frees us from the trap that this audience-focused approach throws us. Not only do players have narrative agency to change the story, but they have textual agency; what Hammer (2007) defines as control over the text (p. 73). In the case of the TRPG, the text can be seen as both the rule books and other printed materials, and the text of the face-to-face gaming session. Players can adjust the text, even the rules, to fit their expectations. This agency allows a group that prefers to delve into character interaction, such as the Sorpraedor group, to do so. Meanwhile, a group such as the RPGA group I witnessed, can focus on conflict resolution and combat. Certain social situations may be more likely to elicit certain types of play. For example, modules may lend themselves more easily to combat and tactical oriented play, but the flexibility is there for the group to take advantage of. Diametrically opposed players may not function well together, but the truth is that most players fall in the middle of the spectrum in terms of preferred style, and that negotiation in the TRPG allows for game play that meets a variety of interests. The TRPG as a generic form gives players agency to define the form of their game, their social interaction, and the narrative that results.

Whether or not the players take full advantage of this agency depends on the group. However, it is arguable that the feeling of narrative agency remains in players' minds, even when not fully realized in action. The purpose of the TRPG, as a communicative act, is to foster this sense of agency over narrative. Although technology has not yet been able to provide this same type of agency in a computer mediated environment, this purpose is not necessarily bound to the medium of pen and paper games. The gamers who responded to my survey seem to indicate that the key to creating an environment for agency is the ability for human interaction to shape that environment. Currently they find that some online formats, such as writing to other people via email or blogs, lend themselves to more flexibility in this way even though most CRPGs do not.

What is valuable to take from rhetorical theory is the focus on genres as defined by purpose rather than form or medium. We can thus separate the TRPG from other genres that might maintain many of the same formulaic aspects. Although the TRPG has played an important role as an antecedent genre to many computer games, it should not be considered the same genre because it ultimately fulfills a different purpose for the audience. Furthermore, looking at genres as forms that meet different needs helps us explain why a genre persists. Because TRPGs currently fulfill the need for agency that other interactive texts do not, they are able to maintain popularity despite the emergence of other forms of role-playing. While it lends much to other genres in terms of both style and form, no other genre currently meets the same purpose as the TRPG.

3

A Transmedia Tale —
The Temple of Elemental Evil

"Well, as most of you know ten years ago a blight of evil assailed these parts, a festering sore in the form of a foul temple dedicated to the worship of things dark and elemental." An uncomfortable murmur rose up, and it was obvious to Shanhaevel that this discussion did not set well with some in the room. "The marshal of Furyondy, Prince Thrommel, raised an army to destroy this temple. Burne, Lanithaine, and I, among others, rode with the prince. At the Battle of Emridy Meadows, we scattered the forces of the temple. Most of their leadership was slain or captured, although a few managed to escape." Melias paused at this point, obviously troubled by this fact. Clenching both his fists and his jaw, he took a deep breath and continued, "The temple itself was thrown down. The prince's company, of which we were a part, was there to seal the place. However, recent activity in the area suggests that something may be stirring in or near the temple once again" [Reid, 2001, p. 36].

There is an ancient temple where evil forces were once defeated, and now ... they are on the rise again. Just as *The Temple of Elemental Evil* continues to rise time and time again, the story by that name also keeps reappearing — it has continually been re-invented in multiple genres and media. In the previous two chapters, I have looked at the tabletop role-playing game (TRPG) as a genre that is unique from but has also influenced other genres of interactive storytelling. A question that I have not yet addressed is the relationship between genre and media, a relationship that has long been problematic for scholars. While the TRPG fits with the concept of a genre as a text that fulfils a particular rhetorical purpose by giving its participants narrative agency, it also exists in a different medium from other role-playing games. A related question that scholars have long debated is the degree to which a certain story can be transported to different media. In this chapter, I explore the connection between genre and media, and look specifically at how one specific TRPG text has been transformed through a variety of media.

Temple is one of the best known *Dungeons & Dragons (D&D)* adventures. In the edition marking the 30th anniversary of *D&D, Dungeon* magazine ranked *Temple* the fourth greatest *D&D* adventure of all time (Mona & Jacobs, 2004). The original module by Gary Gygax (co-creator of *D&D*) and Frank Mentzer was published by TSR, Inc. in 1985, but it included Gygax's earlier module *The Village of Hommlet* from 1979. As the rules for *D&D* went through further editions, the module was re-done, this time by Monte Cook in 2001. Cook's *Return to the Temple of Elemental Evil* uses the same setting as the original story but is intended to be more of a sequel. In addition, the original *Temple* story was published as a novel by Thomas Reid in 2001 and became a computer game in 2003. In order to explore the relationship between genre and medium, I trace *Temple* as it has evolved and changed in its many iterations. I focus primarily on the printed texts of the original module, the computer game, and the novel, but also use comments from players on their experiences with *Temple* in its many different forms.

Genre and Medium

We have seen how the TRPG functions as a genre, but part of the reason that it differs from computer role-playing games (CRPGs) as well as novels is a difference in medium. The relationship between genre and medium is a problematic one. Ryan (2005a) notes that it is often difficult to classify texts as either a genre or a medium. She uses the example of hypertext, which she says "is a genre if we view it as a type of text, but it is a (sub)medium if we regard it as an electronic tool for the organization of text" (Ryan, 2005a, p. 290). Likewise, we could say that the TRPG is a medium in that it is a tool for creating and telling stories. To return to Mackay's (2001) definition, though, we see that the TRPG is more than a tool, it is a system — "an *episodic* and *participatory* story-creation *system*" (p. 4). As a system, the TRPG draws on multiple texts from multiple media. The oral text of the gaming session is the core of the genre, but it is supported by written text of the rule books and modules. The TRPG can thus be seen as a multimedia text. These media combine to meet a particular rhetorical need — that of narrative agency.

Based on player experiences, we can say that CRPGs fit a different rhetorical purpose than TRPGs, but the question of *how* they do so is a question more related to medium. Both genres and media appear to exercise control over the shape and form of texts, yet Ryan (2005a) sees genres as more malleable than media. She writes that "genre is defined by more or less freely adopted conventions chosen for both personal and cultural reasons, medium imposes its possibilities and limitations on the user" (Ryan, 2005a, p. 290). Miller and Shepherd (2009) define the difference in rhetorical terms referring to the relationship between medium and genre as "the way that the suasory aspects of affordances 'fit' rhetorical form to recurrent exigence." In other words, media offer affordances that allow for (or perhaps require) different forms in order to respond to exigencies or needs, which define different genres. It seems that for Miller and Shepherd (2009), as well as Ryan (2005a), media are less under our control than genres. The notion of affordance is key in both of these definitions.

Affordances are the physical aspects of a medium that allow for certain types of discourse to develop while constraining others. For example, if we look at the medium used for the TRPG, we could see the live Dungeon Master (DM) as an affordance of the face-to-face interaction that allows the TRPG more flexibility than the computer-mediated CRPG. However, visual design might be an affordance of the digital medium of the CRPG that is not found in the TRPG. While Aarseth (1997) argues that his notion of cybertext stretches across media, we can't deny that the negotiation the user engages in to access the narrative is decidedly different in the face-to-face oral storytelling medium of the TRPG than it is in the computer-mediated text-adventure game. There are clearly affordances of these two media that affect the way that a text is both created by an author-like figure[1] and navigated by an audience. When the concept of role-playing games emerged, they constituted a new genre of gaming. They were distinct from war games and board games in both their style of play and their rhetorical function. As we've seen, the rules and style of the game were extremely influential in the development of other texts. These texts, however, made use of different media than the original TRPG. Because of the affordances of these media, they were not able to maintain the same rhetorical purpose as the TRPG. The flexibility of the *medium* is key to meeting the need of the TRPG and thus key to the functioning of the TRPG as a *genre*.

This account of the relationship between genre and media means that when *Temple* is adapted for several different media, the rhetorical purpose also shifts. Of the gamers I surveyed, approximately half of those who had played *Temple* had played more than one version. In fact, all of the participants who had read the novel had also played one of the game versions — either one of the TRPG modules or the CRPG. Again, this seems to indicate that players engage with multiple versions of a text in different genre and media because those versions serve different purposes and allow them to experience the text in multiple ways. It also indicates that players may build their view of a particular story based on multiple experiences and media rather than just one. Let us turn, then, to the question of what happens to a particular story as it shifts between media.

Stories Across Media

The problem of storytelling across media is hardly a problem at all for structuralist narratology because of the clear separation between story and discourse. The distinction between these two concepts can be traced back to the Russian formalists. In his introduction to narrative theory, Michael Toolan (2001) notes that the terms *fabula* and *sjuzhet* (from Russian formalism); *histoire* and *discours* (from Barthes and Benveniste); and *story* and *discourse* (from Chatman) all represent similar concepts. The first term in each set, according to Toolan, "is meant [as] a basic description of the events of a story, in their natural chronological order, with an accompanying and equally skeletal inventory of the roles of the characters in that story" (p. 10). The second word in each binary "denotes all the techniques that authors bring to bear in their varying manner of presentation of the basic story" (Toolan, 2001, p. 11). Thus, there is a distinction made between the actual events occurring in the storyworld and the way those events are relayed through narration. The first of the terms is traditionally seen as transferable between mediums whereas the second is seen as dependant on the narrator and the medium of a particular telling of a story (Herman, 2004, p. 51).

Like most binaries, this one has come under question. Specifically, the move has been to divide discourse into text and narration (Toolan, 2001, p. 11). Shlomith Rimmon-Kenan (2002) explains this distinction clearly: "Whereas 'story' is a succession of events, 'text' is a spoken or written discourse which undertakes their telling" (p. 3). Some scholars might add visual or digital discourse to this definition. By this definition, texts are tied to media but stories are not. The third aspect, narration, pertains to "the act or process of production" (Rimmon-Kenan, 2002, p. 3). This distinction clearly separates the text as artifact from the text as production. In other words, narration involves the actual process by which the story is told rather than its physical form.

However, one wonders how these distinctions hold up in light of post-structural theory. As David Herman (2004) explains, the outcome of this structuralist approach has been a lack of attentiveness to "origin, medium, theme, reputation, or genre" without clear justification for generalization (p. 47). How does the medium or the genre affect the narrative? Herman (2004) notes that a more post-structural school of scholars has come out in opposition to the idea that "narrative is medium-independent" to argue that stories are "radically dependent on their media" (p. 50). However, he sees problems with both the structuralist and post-structural schools of thought. The first does not account for differences that do exist when stories transfer between media, while the second does not account for the similarities (Herman, 2004, p. 54). Instead, he offers a synthesis — the view that "stories are shaped but not determined by their presentational formats" (Herman, 2004, p. 54). Ryan (2004) agrees that a compromise is needed between "the 'hollow pipe' interpretation and the unconditional rejection of the conduit metaphor" (p. 17).

While compromise is certainly appealing, it doesn't immediately solve all of the problems with looking at stories across media. Walsh (2007) argues that anything other than the semiotic view of narrative implies that "narrative structure can be conceived in the absence of representation, or that representation can be conceived in the absence of any medium" (p. 104). When we shift our view from an audience receiving a message (which is problematic to begin with) to an author writing, it seems clear that all narratives are initially constructed within a medium. If stories are shaped but not determined by their media, what, exactly, does determine them? Where do they begin?

I agree with Walsh (2007) that every story is conceived within a particular media, and thus can never be "media-independent," particularly when we work from Walsh's perception of media as including both technological and mental frameworks. Nevertheless, we cannot deny that authors and readers have attempted to transfer stories between media and that there is often something we can recognize as common across these attempts. So, how do we account for these commonalities while still recognizing the dependence of texts on the affordances of media? What, exactly, did the game developers making *Temple* computer game take from *Temple* module that allows us to recognize this story as similar, if not the same, to the favorite classic? I will attempt to address that question in this chapter, but rather than reconciliation between the structuralist and post-structuralist views, I argue that any given story is shaped in the mind of the reader through their own transmedia experiences and associations. In other words, it is not that one story of *Temple* is transported into different media, but that by interacting with multiple media, gamers come to form one story of *Temple*.

Stories from The Temple of Elemental Evil

It seems that the next move to make would be to introduce the story of *Temple*. Yet, doing so implicates me immediately in the school of thought that says that the story can be separated from its medium. If I retell it here in an academic book, what does that do to the genre or the medium? What can possibly remain intact from the experience of playing the tabletop module, the computer game, or reading the novel? Thus, I am presented with a conundrum. In articulating the story, I already make judgments about which parts of it are key and translatable across media. Yet, some articulation of the story is necessary in order to analyze it. Therefore, rather than tell the story myself, I turn to the results of a survey in which I asked participants to recall for me the story of *Temple*.

Interestingly, not all participants responded to my request to "please briefly explain the story in your own words." Instead, they apologized for not remembering the story or explained other aspects of the game that they could recall. This may be because the majority of those who responded to the survey had not played the game, or had not done so in many years. Of 65 participants, 20 had played the initial module, 13 had played the sequel, and 16 the computer game. Only three had read the novel. Yet, 45 participants responded that they heard other gamers talk about their experiences with *Temple* and only four said they had never heard of it. Whether or not they had played it themselves, it seems participants knew *Temple* by reputation.

Several participants who had experience with multiple versions of *Temple* agreed to tell their versions of the story. One respondent who had played both modules and the computer game recalls:

> A group of greedy itinerant mercenaries (the player characters) are looking for monsters to kill so that they can take their stuff. Arriving in the tiny village of Hommlet, they find that a small job (clearing bandits out of an old abandoned moathouse) is only the tip of a much larger problem. Clues lead the mercenaries to an old temple dedicated to evil, long

thought abandoned but now teeming with activity. Infiltrating the temple, the mercenaries find a lot of monsters and evil cultists, a lot of treasure, and a lot of death.

Several things stand out about this entry. The first is the motivation of the player characters as greedy mercenaries only looking for treasure. As I will later explain, both the module and the computer game give multiple motivations for characters, so this part does not seem universal by any means. Another key feature of this response is the focus on location — the village of Hommlet, the moathouse, and the temple are all settings that remain constant in the multiple versions of the text, and here they seem linked to narrative progress. The story, as told by this participant, progresses by moving from one locale to another.

Another participant who played both the original module and the computer game explains the story in a very different way:

> Long ago, a demoness (Zuggtmoy, the Demon Queen of Fungi) was sealed away in the temple by a coalition of forces including adventurers, soldiers, and a council of wizards. Now, evil once again stirs in the temple, taking the form of bandits and evil humanoids stalking the surrounding countryside. When the heroes investigate, they find a vast tunnel complex beneath the temple, inhabited by priests of various elements, all ostensibly worshiping the same deity, but pitted against themselves to weed out the weak. Eventually the heroes discover that the servants of other gods — Iuz, I think, and/or Lolth — have been duping the lower-ranking priests and using the energy from their worship to make the deceptive gods stronger.

This telling differs significantly from the one above, despite this participant having experienced the same texts. Instead of focusing on location, this respondent focused more on plot and character. The plot relayed here is the general background story present in all versions of *Temple*— the sealing of Zuggtmoy in the temple and the rise of evil under Iuz. The names mentioned here, though, are not the player characters. The player characters are referred to more generically as "the heroes," a different take from the greedy mercenaries in the previous response. The names mentioned are key non-player characters (NPCs), mostly deities who are the ultimate powers behind the adventure. Zuggtmoy, Iuz, and Lolth appear in all versions of *Temple* while player characters are obviously more variable across versions.

Several players who had only played the videogame were also able to give a report that included details about *Temple*. One might suppose that having been written by participants who only experienced the story in the computer game format, these accounts might have more in common than the two accounts above, yet that is not the case. One participant tells the story this way:

> To the best of my understanding ... The temple, located in Emridy Meadows, once was a location where Zuggtmoy (the demon queen of fungi) attempted an attack on the material plane. The temple was sealed and Zuggtmoy imprisoned in the temple. Years later Zuggtmoy attempted another escape. Also in the temple were elemental nodes; points of power being used by cultists of Thurizden (an imprisoned ancient deity of wanton destruction sealed away by the other gods for the protection of the world). It is my understanding that the character Lareth the Beautiful was partially behind both incidents, and the hero, Robilar, was at the original battle of Emridy Meadows where the temple was first sealed.

Several key locations, such as Emridy Meadows and the temple come up in this account as well as key characters — Zuggtmoy and Lareth. Although this respondent had only played the computer version, these locations and characters are ones that repeat in the multiple versions of the text.

Another computer game player articulates the story in these terms:

> *The Temple of Elemental Evil* is a story in three parts. The first part is when the party arrives at this town marauded upon by bandits. The bandits, it turns out, are minions who are working for this cult, who are raising missing people into zombies. The party explores and defeats the bandits in the ruins of a castle and discovers a link to an ancient temple. This temple is the nexus point of the next story. The players travel into the swamps where they find a town full of corruption that they can rest in when not adventuring inside the temple. The temple itself is a multilayer death trap filled with bandits and unique monsters, and is gathering energies from four separate groups of cultist all worshiping the promise of power that a demon in its depths brings. The party eventually defeats the cultists, but in doing so, they accidentally unleash the demon. In order to stop the demon they must travel to four pockets of elemental evils to gather the items that can rebind and destroy the demon forever. And really, that's it in a nutshell.

Despite both of these participants having played the CRPG version of *Temple*, these accounts seem to have little in common with each other. The first focuses almost entirely on the back-story of Zuggtmoy's capture and the evil forces of the temple regaining power. The second entry begins with the player character's entrance and follows their progression through the events that happen in the videogame from the bandits in the moathouse, to the temple itself, and on to the exploration of the four elemental nodes that leads to the defeat of Zuggtmoy. Yet, both bring up key locations and characters that repeat through the *Temple* texts. Interestingly, none of the accounts point to the possibility of multiple endings. In the computer game, for example, the player has the choice to join Zuggtmoy rather than defeat her. In the re-telling, all accounts erase the traces of interactivity and the choices involved.

Although not all players could relate the story of *Temple,* only a few had never heard of it. Since my survey did not target *D&D* players specifically, but role-players in general, it may be that these players were more familiar with alternative TRPGs. Even so, it was a small percentage. In the world of *D&D* players, it could be said that knowing *Temple* carries a certain amount of social capital. It signals gamers who have been around awhile, since the original module was released nearly twenty-five years ago, and those who are familiar with the lore of the *D&D* universe. Being familiar with *Temple* does not necessarily equate to a nostalgic view of a great legendary story, though. Multiple survey participants expressed a dislike for the early module, and some for *D&D* in general. A participant who had only heard about *Temple* states, "My fellow told me horror stories about the excruciating deaths that happened as he played through the *Temple* module. I have no desire to play it." Another player who had only heard of it, says, "It's just Gygax being the party-killing GM he's always reported as being." Another, who had played both modules and the computer game, goes so far as to say, "It was *D&D*—a mechanics hackfest, not role-playing." Even some who refer to it in more positive terms seem to emphasize the combat aspects over the narrative. A player who was familiar with both modules and the computer version called *Temple* "a multi-part adventure that culminated in one of the best dungeon crawls ever." *Temple* seems legendary for the challenges it presented in terms of game combat, perhaps even to the point of being the type of adventure where survival of a character is a legendary accomplishment in itself.

Nevertheless, the survey shows a variety of responses, some of which do focus more on plot, characters or setting. One participant who had not played *Temple* in at least 20 years did not recall the overarching story, but did recall losing a character to a trapped urn. This memory shows the importance of the emotional connection to character. When all other memories had faded, the loss of a character remained. For another player, who commented on it having been "a million years" since they played *Temple,* still remembered the setting: "I remember delving into an endless maze of rooms divided into four sections that related to the four elements — air, fire, water, earth." For this player, the image of the temple itself seems to have embedded the deepest memories.

The response to the survey indicates that we must not assume that story is the most memorable part of *Temple* or what is most easily transported between media. Elements of story are certainly important, including character and setting. However, a congruent plotline is not necessarily transportable between media. Even players who had engaged with the same version of the text chose to focus on different elements of it in their narration, which lends credence to the idea that different types of players may experience a text differently, possibly even as different genres. I now turn to my own readings of the *Temple* module, computer game, and novel to discuss in more detail the different affordances present in these different media and the way that they work together to form a player's experience with this well-known adventure.

Media Affordances and Versions of The Temple of Elemental Evil

When looking at the TRPG version of *Temple*, we have two different media to consider — the print module and the oral text created by the players. Gygax and Mentzer's (1985) print version of the *Temple* module is more of a technical manual than a narrative. It does have possible narrative interludes, but there is a distinct difference between the text of the module and the story that emerges during the playing of the module. As we have seen from player comments, there is the potential for the embedded story to never completely emerge, as many early gamers seem to have focused on the combat and game-like parts of the module instead. In contrast, even if the computer game focuses primarily on combat, the story will emerge eventually through the cut-scenes and narration that the player unlocks. The relationship between the audience and the narrative, then, is far more variable in the module than in the computer game or the novel. This increased agency can lead to narrative control and exploration, but it can also lead to a rejection of story altogether.

Rather than progress as the novel does from one event in the story to the next, the module is written in four parts (sometimes referred to as T1–4). These sections include "The Village of Hommlet," "Nulb and the Ruins," "the Dungeon of Elemental Evil," and "The Nodes of Elemental Evil". Within these parts of the module, there are further divisions that are numbered according to different locations. Players may encounter these locations in any order, or not at all. At times, these encounters include read aloud text that the DM is instructed to read to the players. Often these passages describe the location, but sometimes they are also used to describe the action of NPCs that are encountered in that space. The read aloud passage on p. 93 begins with detailed description: "Atop the dais to the west is a huge throne of silver, adorned with hundreds of precious gems." However, unlike the majority of passages, this one leads to action. A crone, seen sitting on the throne, "cringes and shrieks when you approach" (Gygax & Mentzer, 1985, p. 93). At times NPCs' actions are narrated thusly, but this information is not always essential to the game.

There is also a great excess of information in the module. There are areas that the players will never explore, characters they will never meet, treasure they will never find. Yet, it is all detailed by Gygax and Mentzer on the possibility that it will be a direction that players choose to explore. The village of Hommlet alone includes 33 locations, some of which are extremely mundane. Other locations serve as points of initiating action where players gain important information that leads them to a quest or meet NPCs. However, no one location or character is key to putting together the story as a whole, nor can it be because there is nothing to make players go to each location. For example, the character of Elmo is detailed in area two, where he lives, but Elmo is just as likely to be met at the inn where he spends a good amount of time. It is up to the DM where the party encounters Elmo. In addition, in the print version of the module, the information about the ruined moat house does not appear until after the detailed descriptions of the various buildings in Hommlet, and the clues are not specific to any one building. Instead, it is simply noted that "the following information may be gleaned, piece by piece, through conversation with the villagers of Hommlet" (Gygax & Mentzer, 1985, p. 21). It is up to the DM exactly where and how this information is obtained, allowing for flexibility in where the players go and who they talk to.

In fact, there would be nothing to stop a DM from actually starting the story at the *Temple* itself and ignoring the towns of Hommlet and Nulb completely. Gygax and Mentzer encourage DMs to adapt the adventure to their campaigns. In part two, "Nulb and the Ruins," a note states that it is "absolutely necessary for the DM to personalize his or her map" (Gygax & Mentzer, 1985, p. 30). The DM is also encouraged to "adjust details to suit your own concept of a fantasy milieu" (Gygax & Mentzer, 1985, p. 28). Interestingly, it is also in this section of "notes for the DM" that the backstory of the temple and Zuggtmoy and Iuz is told. It is not read aloud to players at any given point, but provided to the DM as background to be added in when he or she sees fit. Although it may have gained a reputation for hack and slash combat, it seems clear that Gygax and Mentzer intended DMs to adapt the module to their own campaigns, not follow it to the letter.[2]

One participant in my survey explained that such a variation was indeed how their experience with *Temple* had come about. This respondent explained:

> Ours was ... different. We ran *Temple* in an historical fantasy game, prior to the building of the Cathedral of Mont St. Michel in Normandy. In our version, the "Elemental Evil" was the remains of a Celtic polytheist worship resisting Christianity. Instead of Zuggtmoy we used Cernunnos with "elemental" friends. Apart from that, however, we used the general plot trajectory of a small village, the political subterfuge etc. that is typical of T1–4. It was just less "good versus evil" and more "Christian versus Pagan."

This example shows that the *Temple* module can indeed be used as a manual; as a tool for creating a story rather than as a story itself. In this version, the DM changed the overall setting of the temple, to put it in more of an actual historical context, as well as significant NPCs. Nevertheless, the DM was able to use the module and its story about the rise of a temple and the political maneuverings involved with it to form his or her own adventure. Taking the CRPG or the novel to a new setting like this is an obvious impossibility, as the narrative details are more deeply embedded in the structure of these media. Yet, even this example kept the same basis for setting in the small town and the temple itself. Certain elements remained the same even when major changes were made between the print text of the module and the text of the actual gaming session.

While the flexibility to completely alter the world is only found in the TRPG, the medium of the computer game consists of its own affordances. In particular, the options of visual representation of the narrative are key to the CRPG. In the computer game, cut-scenes serve a similar purpose to the description passages read aloud in the TRPG, but add more visual interest. Cut-scenes are moments in a videogames where the gameplay is interrupted by a visual scene. The player has no control over these scenes, except to skip them, and is presented with visual and often audio narration. These scenes will often reflect events in the story behind the game, and often come at the beginning of a new game and at key intervals. One way that cut-scenes can be used is as narrative rewards. As the player completes key steps in the game, more of the narrative is revealed.

Cut-scenes can also be more purely descriptive as the read aloud text in the module. The opening of the computer game is a fairly elaborate cut-scene that shows the battle at Emridy Meadows where the original forces of the temple were defeated and Zuggtmoy was imprisoned, thus establishing the back-story and history of the temple. However, the scene is purely visual. In contrast, the end cut scene is not as visually appealing but is narrated more orally. It shows a book and candle; and brief, illustrated, narrative scenes as the story of what happens after the game ends. The final cut-scene also varies depending on the actions the player takes in the game. If, for example, the party helps a noble trapped in the temple, the narration will explain that he knights the party in return. If the party allies with Zuggtmoy, the narration will describe her overthrow of Hommlet. If they defeat her, it will describe the way that Hommlet prospers. Unlike the human DM in the TRPG, however, the computer does not recognize which elements of the ending are compatible with other parts. I joined forces with Zuggtmoy and Hommlet was destroyed, nevertheless I still received knighthood from a grateful noble I had rescued, a somewhat illogical pairing of endings. Both the opening and closing cut-scenes capture important stories for *Temple*. Another cut-scene, the entrance into to the temple itself, has no narration at all but serves more to set the mood and visual image of the temple in the player's mind. The medium of the CRPG allows for these important scenes and images to be represented visually while the TRPG players will have to picture them in their imaginations based on the text read orally by the DM.

Another key affordance of the CRPG is the ability to go back to a previous point in the game. When I played *Temple*, a NPC named Otis joined my party for a while; however, once he discovered that my party was evil, he refused to keep adventuring with them. In fact, in one version of my game, he turned on me and attacked. As with other unwanted plot twists, I was glad that I had saved the game before that happened and was able to go back to a prior point, although Otis still left the party. The TRPG might allow for the player to negotiate with Otis rather than fight him, but whatever the outcome, there would be no redoing the scene.

Character is another story element that plays out differently depending on media affordances. NPCs tend to remain the same between versions of *Temple* as well. Zuggtmoy, Iuz, and Cuthbert are part of the pantheon of the gods and demons that run the universe. Hedrack and Lareth are their pawns in the temple. Elmo and some of the characters in Hommlet remain the same also. Again, even in the extremely different version presented by the participant quoted above, the general types of characters remained. However, the player characters are far more variable. Both the TRPG and the CRPG version offer some flexibility in terms of the player characters involved — from heroes to greedy mercenaries. At the beginning of the computer game, the player chooses the alignment of the party, such as whether they are good or evil. The opening narration offers two potential sequences — a good sequence and an evil one. Interestingly, the scene entering Hommlet is the same visually for both the good and evil openings; only the narrated text differs. The player characters have highly different motivations in these two scenarios. However, the entire party, controlled by one player in the CRPG, is given the same motivation. In the module, as with TRPGs in general, the player controls only one character within the game. Thus, each character and each player may have different reasons for embarking on the campaign.

Naturally, in the novel the reader has no control over the point of view that is presented, yet this medium also brings its own affordances. The heroic characters are those that would be player characters in the TRPG or CRPG. We are introduced to, as our primary protagonist, Shanhaevel, a mage and elf; as well as his love interest, the druid Shirral. The novel presents a good deal of depth in terms of character emotions and interactions, as the reader sees the relationship between Shanhaevel and Shirral develop and is also privy to many of Shanhaevel's thoughts. Naturally, in the TRPG, relationships such as this one could also be developed, but all of that material would come from the players rather than the pre-written module. The novel does something else that is a shift from both the TRPG and the CRPG — it shows the point of view of the opposing side. Although it is clear that Shanhaevel is the main protagonist, the story shifts between his point of view and Hedrack, the head of the temple. We become privy to Hedrack's interactions with Iuz and Zuggtmoy in a way that we never see in the TRPG or CRPG, where they are simply villains to be fought in combat or powers to be allied with. In fact, it is completely possible to play either the TRPG or the CRPG with no real understanding or explanations of the forces in the temple. In the TRPG, much of the inner workings of the temple must be discovered by players asking the right questions. For example, if the party captures Senshock (Zuggtmoy's emissary) and uses ESP to interrogate him, they will find out a bit about Iuz and his plans (Gygax & Mentzer, 1985, p. 99). However, if the party kills Senshock or misses this encounter altogether, that information may never be obtained or the DM may need to incorporate this information elsewhere in the game. From some players' comments about the political maneuvering in *Temple*, it is clear that the motivations guiding the NPCs can be a key part of the intrigue. However, from other players' comments, it is probable that not everyone who plays the TRPG learns these details of character development. One of the affordances of the novel, then, is the ability to provide multiple points of view where the reader can shift perspective throughout the novel.

Each medium offers something to the story that the others cannot. Each shapes the story in a different way. In the TRPG the audience has more control over the framework of the story. The DM may choose to reveal information as he or she sees fit or adapt the story to fit within a different campaign world. However, short of incorporating additional media (such as video) into the gaming session, the DM would have a hard time representing the visual scenes in the story the same way that the CRPG does. The computer version also offers the chance to return to an earlier point in the story and begin again with the hope of a new outcome. The novel offers the least flexibility, but it also gives the reader more insight into different characters, allowing for a more complete perspective that is not achievable in the other media.[3]

Transmedia Narrative—The Nexus of Stories

It is apparent from the examples presented here that there are multiple differences among the experience of the TRPG module, the CRPG, and the novel all called *The Temple of Elemental Evil*. What is it then that allows us to recognize all three as the *Temple of Elemental Evil?* How might these texts and others work together to inform our understanding of a particular textual universe?

First and foremost, it appears that structuralist narratologists notion of story as separate from medium does not hold true for the transfer among the TRPG, CRPG, and novel. One very important reason for this is that story in the TRPG exists primarily in the oral discourse created by the gaming group as they play through the module. The module itself has some backstory, but it neither reads like a story nor determines what part of the story the audience will hear. Instead, each gaming group will individually access certain storylines and ignore others. As we've seen, some groups may ignore story altogether and focus more on combat and game mechanics.

What was perhaps not accounted for in the structuralist categories of story and discourse were the ways that elements of story, such as characters and setting, can be removed from the story itself. My study of *Temple* shows that it is not necessarily narrative that transfers between media. Rather, it is narrative elements, particularly the setting and key characters that transfer across media. In all three version of *Temple*, the setting remained constant. They all involved the town of Hommlet, the moathouse, and the temple, in that order. Furthermore, the backstory seems intact. In all three versions, there is the demoness that was trapped in the temple before the current adventure begins. Thus, it seems that main NPCs (clearly Zuggtmoy and Iuz as well as Lareth, Hedrack, and even Elmo) transfer to the most versions of *Temple*. The degree of that each of these characters is important to the narrative, however, may vary in the TRPG, CRPG, and the novel. For example, Elmo is a ranger and agent of the Viscount, but pretends to merely be a drunk. I found his character to be a necessarily ally in the computer game as he is initially a higher level than the player-run characters, and this allowed me to succeed in challenges that were otherwise unplayable. He also figures as a prominent character in the novel, where more of Elmo's story comes out. We find that he only pretends to be a drunk, but instead knows a great deal about the temple and the story behind it. Thus, in some versions of the story, Elmo may only be a drunk encountered in Hommlet, in others he may be a crucial aid to the party.

Another factor that transfers from the module to the CRPG has more to do with gaming than storytelling; the CRPG is based on *D&D* rules.[4] The player characters in both versions have the six ability scores — strength, dexterity, constitution, wisdom, intelligence, and charisma. Characters have a class (such as fighter or wizard) and a race (such as elf, dwarf, or human). They have hit points, gain experience, and go up in level. As discussed in chapter 2, these are the type of game mechanics that made *D&D* so influential to other games, and they are the same core ideas that transfer between the TRPG and CRPG. As the novel is not written as a game, one might suppose that these features do not transfer. However, that does not appear to entirely be the case. A good deal of the book revolves around combat, and the characters clearly belong to a distinct class and race. In the battle scenes, a *D&D* player can recognize familiar spells and skills being used. When Shanhaevel and his companions encounter the illusion of the basilisk, one can almost hear dice being rolled as Ahleage fails his saving throw and is thus deceived by the basilisk and temporarily petrified. Of course the book does not talk about dice or saving throws, but even a casual *D&D* player will recognize this familiar game mechanic.

It seems, then, that the audience for this book is not intended to be significantly different that the audience for the TRPG or CRPG. In fact, the book was released by Wizards of the Coast and is likely meant be read by *D&D* players already familiar with their products or by those with an interest in gaming to begin with. Likewise, the CRPG version held certain advantages for the player who was already familiar with *D&D* and the *Temple* story. A GameSpot review of the videogame by Greg Kasavin (2003) calls it "one of the most authentic PC *Dungeons & Dragons* experiences of the past few years." The problem with this, he notes, is that when advancing a character, a non–*D&D* player may be completely bewildered. The game draws on previous knowledge of the both the antecedent genre and the story and seems designed best for those who want to relive the *Temple* adventure in digital form.

Furthermore, I found that because I was reading the book and playing the CRPG at the same time, I was able to make valuable connections between them. Because I remembered in the book that Shanhaevel and his friends had entered the temple by a secret entrance in a well, I recognized a well I found in the CRPG as an entrance to the temple. In addition, when I encountered Hedrack, I knew right away that he was a major player in the temple, connected to Iuz and Zuggtmoy. I also knew that I needed to find the gems to go in the Orb of Golden Death to defeat Zuggtmoy. Finally, from reading the module, I knew that there was a good chance when Iuz came down to join in the big battle scene, so would his opposing god, Cuthbert. While I experienced each media differently, they worked together for me to form a more complete picture of the *Temple* story, setting, and characters.

This larger picture expands beyond just the iterations of *Temple* in different media. One participant, in addition to relating the story of *Temple*, explained:

> My personal exposure not only included the "Return to Temple of Elemental Evil" PC game but also casual references to it in the 3.5 edition module "Expedition to Castle *Greyhawk*" and minor references to it with the Lareth the Beautiful miniature stat card for *D&D* miniatures.

This participant refers to other texts; those that are not direct retellings of *Temple*, but that draw on the larger textual economy of *Temple*. The TRPG module exists within the larger campaign setting of the world of *Greyhawk*. Thus, other adventures within that setting may reference what occurred at the temple as it became a part of the history of that storyworld. Similarly, the miniature figures that Wizards of the Coast puts out often include specific characters from famous campaigns, such as Lareth from *Temple*. Thus, it is not surprising that many of the participants in my survey had heard of *Temple* without having played it themselves.

While the question of what makes up a particular genre or medium and how texts transfer between mediums is still an important question, it appears that a question of equal or greater importance has to do with the way that textual systems draw on multiple texts within multiple genres and media. *Temple* exists culturally, not as a single text, but as a textual system that draws from a common universe and some common characters with some of the same storylines. Each iteration within the textual system may add to or change the universe; each player will create new characters and the story may change. The media and the genre shape each telling. However, these texts cannot be seen in isolation.

In our current culture, we find more and more that games are made from movies or books and that movies and books are made from games. No longer do we encounter a particular story in only one format. Jenkins (2002) explains that "increasingly, we inhabit a world of transmedia storytelling, one that depends less one each individual work being self-sufficient than on each work contributing to a larger narrative economy." The idea of a narrative economy is one that warrants further discussion in both genre and narrative studies. Rather than assuming that we transfer a story between media, this chapter shows how an audience might take bits and pieces from several related narratives told in multiple media in order to form a full view of a particular story. As audiences, we increasingly decide which versions of stories to accept — do we hold to the view of Harry Potter in our heads from reading the book or do we replace it with an image of Daniel Radcliff from the screen? Perhaps we can do both. *Temple* shows that while each medium gives us certain advantages, certain affordances that shape the telling of a story, texts work together to form a more complete view of a storyworld, characters, and even plotlines.

4

The Reconciliation of
Narrative and Game

So far we have seen that the stories play a key role in role-playing games; both tabletop role-playing games (TRPGs) and computer role-playing games (CRPGs). However the question of whether games should be considered narratives or not and, thus, whether they can be studied using narratological tools, has formed the basis for a heated scholarly debate. Marie-Laure Ryan (2006) gives a thorough explanation of the opposing sides of this debate — the ludologists and the narrativists. Ryan (2006) notes the disagreement often comes down to the different definitions of narrative and the politics ascribed to by scholars following different disciplinary traditions. As she points out, the position of the ludologists[1] to study games (videogames in particular) as unique artifacts is an important one for establishing their work as a new discipline (Ryan, 2006, p. 181). These scholars resist subsuming games under forms of literature and using means of analysis originally designed for the study of literary narrative to look at games.

Yet, the link between narrative theory and the field of literature or literary theory has itself begun to dissolve, allowing for a broader perspective of the study of narrative. Ryan (2006) explains that "the trend today is to detach narrative from language and literature and to regard it instead as a cognitive template with transmedial and transdisciplinary applicability" (p. 184). In addition to seeing narrative as a cognitive template, I would add that seeing it as social and rhetorical force further opens the door for an interdisciplinary approach to the study of all genres and media with narrative elements. I maintain that games and narratives have been seen as incompatible, in part, because of a limited view of what constitutes either. Thus, I revisit the narrative versus game debate with two new perspectives in mind. Ludology, or games studies, has focused almost exclusively on video gaming which, as we have seen, was highly influenced by tabletop role-play but did not replace it. I thus bring to bear on the narrative versus game debate the inclusion of the TRPG as a game genre. Furthermore, the debate hinges on concepts from structuralist narratology; a perspective that warrants challenge from both post-modern and rhetorical theory. I argue here that a rhetorical approach to narrative offers a valuable framework that explains the narrative nature of gaming without discounting its other important features.

Games Versus Narratives

In order to understand the position that games (even those that seemingly have a storytelling element) are not narratives, we must look at the definition of narrative that has been appropriated by many ludologists. This traditional definition comes from early linguistic studies of narrative that rejected anything other than oral storytelling with a clear narrator and narratee. Linguist William Labov (1972) defined narrative as "one method of recapitulating past experience by matching a verbal sequence of clauses to the sequence of events which (it is inferred) actually occurred" (pp. 359–360). Gerald Prince echos this definition in his *Dictionary of Narratology,* originally published in 1987 and revised in 2003. He defines narrative as "the representation of one or more real or fictive events communicated by one, two, or several narrators, to one, two or several narratees" (p. 58). Prince accounts for collaboration here as well as fiction, but still defines narrative in terms of representing (rather than creating) an event and in terms of having narrators and narratees.

To separate them from other types of speech for linguistic analysis, narratives involve longer turns at talk, where an interlocutor recalls the events of the past in an order that shows the cause and effect relationship necessary for the progression of the story. When we hear statements such as "the king drank from the poisoned cup" and "the king is dead," we know that the second statement is a result of the first statement. Cognitively, we have a sense of the linear progression of narrative; thus, we are able to establish a connection between these two events as a story. This sense of causality and linearity from the study of oral narrative persists, even in studies that examine new media. Objections to viewing games as narratives are based often on the non-linear progression of games[2] and the fact that the story is created through play rather than a retelling of the past (Ryan,

2006, p. 186). In addition, Eskelinen (as cited in Ryan, 2006) rejects that games are narratives even if they involve stories because they do not always have a clear narrator (p. 185). By using such a limited definition of narrative — one that was intended for the linguistic study of narrative — scholars have been able to argue that games should not be seen as narratives because they do not fit with this linear or causal model or because they do not have a traditional narrator.

The use of the concepts of story and discourse, and the positioning of the concepts as separate, is another way that ludologists have used narrative theory in order to argue against a narratological approach to games. Espen Aarseth (1997) makes this distinction when he talks about fiction versus narrative. For him, fiction pertains to content while narrative pertains to form. The form of a narrative must be linear. Thus, he insists that a game or a hypertext can be a fiction without being a narrative (Aarseth, 1997, p. 85). For these particular ludologists, a story (or at least a story-world) can exist without an actual narrative. Narrative is seen as the particular way that discourse unfolds, and it is seen as separate from the plot of a story. However, as I have shown in the previous chapter, story is not as separable from discourse as one might imagine. To "separate" a story from the medium is to change the story.

The strongest point from the ludology camp is that games represent something new, something that cannot be explained simply with our old methods for studying narratives. Aarseth (1997) articulates this point clearly saying that "to claim there is no difference between games and narratives is to ignore essential qualities of both categories" (p. 5). He criticizes scholars for ascribing to the "spatiodynamic fallacy where the narrative is not perceived as a presentation of the world but rather as the world itself" (Aarseth, 1997, p. 3). It is easy to see where such criticism comes from when we look at scholars at the other end of the spectrum. The enthusiasm of Janet Murray (1998) for games as narratives extends to games such as Monopoly, which she regards as "an interpretation of capitalism, an enactment of the allures and disappointments of a zero-sum economy in which one gets rich by impoverishing one's neighbors" (p. 143). Even Tetris, she says, has a "clearly dramatic content" (p. 144). While she may have a point that Monopoly or Tetris can be constructed into a story by the gamer or may tap into cultural metanarratives, there is no obvious *narration* within these games. Murray clearly takes things too far and, in light of this, one can see where the instinct to find a new perspective on games emerges. Not only does she blanketly apply the idea of narrative to games, she does very little to separate different types of games from one another.

Unfortunately, in trying to find a unique lens through which to study games, some scholars have ignored the important role that narrative plays in many games altogether. Along with Aarseth (1997), Jesper Juul (2001) and Bernadette Flynn (2004) reject the "spatiodynamic fallacy" and argue that games often involve an exploration of a world without involving a narrative structure. Flynn's (2004) article on "Games as Inhabited Spaces" suggests that games should be seen through an aesthetics of space, which she states is "grounded in immersive aesthetics, maps, tours, modes of navigation and geometric landscapes," rather than in narrative aesthetics (p. 54). However, in Flynn's attempt to avoid conflating game and narrative, she makes her own reductive moves. Her argument avoids placing games into the narrative pigeonhole only by "shoehorning" them into a new slot — one of spatial exploration. To consider every aspect of the game as narrative, is indeed to try to fit something expansive in a restrictive and inappropriate structure. Yet, the same holds true for reducing them only to an aesthetic of space. To recognize that games can fit in both a narrative and a spatial aesthetic is to acknowledge their diverse and complicated nature. Furthermore, the degree to which a spatial versus a narrative aesthetic applies to games depends on the game in question.

Both Jenkins (2002) and Ryan (2005b, 2006) offer possible conciliatory positions in this debate between game and narrative scholars. One of the problems that Jenkins sees with the entire argument is that it deals with games in binary terms, looking only at whether a game is or is not a narrative rather than at what narrative elements might exist in a game. Ryan (2005b) explains that there is a difference between being a narrative and "possessing narrativity" (p 347). A text that possesses narrativity is "produced with the intent to create a response involving the construction of a story" (Ryan, 2005b, p. 347). Many games, including the TRPG, appear to fall into this category.

While Jenkins (2002) is careful not to equate the storyworld with the actual telling of a narrative, he does see the potential for what he calls "spatial storytelling." What he means by this is that storyworlds are created in games that either provoke previously known stories or provide the potential for creating new stories. For Jenkins (2002), games are "spaces ripe with narrative possibility." Similarly, Ryan (2006) talks of games as "machines for generating stories" (p. 189). In these more recent studies, we see that the earlier debate suggesting that games must be viewed either through a narratological or a spatial aesthetic falls to the wayside when we think of the way that spaces create the potential for narrative experience rather than sticking to a strict structural analysis of narrative forms.

What we have seen throughout this debate on whether or not games should be studied as narratives is a disciplinary and methodological struggle. As new texts emerge, we have been forced to test whether or not our old methods for studying texts are still applicable. Thus, a discussion of traditional narratological definitions, such as that found in Labov's 1972 study, has been warranted. When videogames first came on the scholarly scene, this debate caused a separation between those who wished to create new methods to study them and those who wished to apply and adapt already existing methodology. This split is only now beginning to be reconciled as scholars work to expand both the definitions of narrative and games. Yet, the majority of the discussion of games still revolves around videogames. If we keep the discussion focused only on new games and emerging technologies, it seems we will never get past this continual re-evaluation of older methods in the face of new texts. Videogame technology is evolving at a pace that moves much faster than our scholarly debates about it. It seems to me, however, that there is value in looking at the debate not in terms of new technology, but in terms of longer existing genres that may also challenge our methodological views. I thus present the TRPG, rather than videogames, as a test case for the argument surrounding defining games and narrative. Showing that a game nearly as old as Labov's definition can present a challenge to these definitions may very well prove to shake the foundation of narrative and games studies in a way that a more modern critique cannot. It is one thing to say that our definitions of narrative and games must change to account for new technologies; it is another to say that they have never completely accounted for existing ones. The social and rhetorical elements of narratives did not enter the scene with digital technology, but have always been a neglected part of our narrative worlds.

Campaign Settings in D&D

One clear objection to seeing games as narratives is that games draw on vast spaces, storyworlds that players explore with or without an actual story present. With seemingly endless maps of dungeons, to what degree is *Dungeons and Dragons (D&D)* about an exploration of space? To what degree is it about creating spaces that serve as storyworlds for *potential* narratives, but not about the narratives themselves? The next section looks in-depth at how worlds are created in *D&D* during gameplay and by Dungeon Masters (DMs) and game designers. First, I look at spatial exploration during gameplay. I argue that while TRPGs involve a degree of spatial exploration, this aspect is far less important than it is in most CRPGs. The *D&D* storyworld is filled with unrealized narrative possibilities. Nevertheless, the argument that games should be considered in terms of spatial rather than narrative aesthetics does not hold up when we look at the TRPG.

Jenkins (2002) mentions that before collaborative story development can take place, the DM must create the space for it. In order to know more about how world building works in *D&D*, I talked to both the DM of the Sorpraedor campaign and well known game developer, Monte Cook. In particular, I discussed with Cook the way that he developed the *Ptolus* campaign setting. Rather than a module that is meant to be played in one setting, *Ptolus* is a published campaign world. It involves the details about the city of *Ptolus* and the world surrounding it. Furthermore, it involves a set of adventures for players to engage in and non-player characters (NPCs) for players to interact with. Both Sorpraedor and *Ptolus* are considered campaign settings. In other words, they are settings for the adventures in a *D&D* campaign to take place in. The major difference between these two worlds is that Sorpraedor was created for a home campaign by one gaming group and DM, while *Ptolus* has gone on to be published for multiple gaming groups to use.

Sorpraedor, like *Ptolus*, is based on the rules from the *D&D* rule books, yet, as a creation, it stands as a text on its own. Scott created multiple maps that visually laid out the world. Much like Earth, Sorpraedor has continents, bodies of water, countries, cities, mountain ranges, etc. The DM must create more detail about the world than he or she conveys in the narrative. However, while the world exists independently from the way the characters and players progress through it, the participants of TRPGs do influence the development of the world. For example, Scott created a town named Lugyere that had twin brothers as rulers. He knew that that one brother was good and the other was evil. However, it was not until the party decided to visit Lugyere that he fleshed out the motives of the two brothers and their city. Any part of the Sorpraedor world can be fully created as the participants express an interest in it.

In addition, players may influence parts of the world as they determine the background for their characters. The way that *Ptolus* evolved as a storyworld is very similar to the way Sorpraedor evolved. Monte Cook explained to me that he created *Ptolus* as the world for his own home run *D&D* campaign. Like Scott, Cook added certain elements of the world based on player interest. He explained that one of his players really wanted to create a character with an Arabian sort of background, so Cook incorporated a setting where this was possible in the world of *Ptolus* (personal communication, June 30, 2009).

The interests of the players and the questions they ask also affect the world in more detailed ways that more directly influence the narrative. For example, the following section of the Blaze Arrow story shows the way the players both explored the spatial environment, but also added details to that environment.

> I slide the message down the tube and a whooshing sound carried it away. I then composed a message to Gateway, "Orcs took Blaze Arrow, 12 dead. Orcs after Skullbash group in the mountains near Barrenstone. We told them to leave humans alone. So far they have complied." As I dropped this message in the tube, it made a sputtering sound like it had gotten stuck. I looked at David. We decided to send a "test" message to the Black Tower tube asking them to confirm receipt. About three minutes later a note arrived back saying the message was received. I replied that the tube to Gateway seemed not to be working and asked them to forward my message and ask the magistrate to reply directly to me.
>
> While we were waiting for a response, David began examining the machine. He discovered that the label for Gateway was loose. "Perhaps it has been switched," he suggested. We decided to try a test message through the third unmarked tube. Almost immediately we received a letter back, "Message received. What status?" I repeated the story once again and told them the tube had been mislabeled. The operator on the other end replied that they had been attempting to connect the tubes to Barrenstone but so far had been unsuccessful. We were of course suspicious as to why the labels had been changed — that someone was purposely trying to screw up communication.

In this sample story, the detail that the labels on the message tubes were switched was not included until Alex (playing David) asked about the labels. This fact was added in by the DM on the spot as a response to the player's question, and it changed the way the characters interacted with that encounter. My party was entirely convinced that the labels being switched meant that someone had purposely tried to disrupt communication at the Blaze Arrow outpost, when in fact this was simply a detail added at the whim of the DM to answer Alex's (playing David) question. From reading the final narrative, it is impossible to tell which details were created beforehand and which were added during the gaming session (although my interview with the DM revealed this). Some stories, then, come not from the space created before the beginning of the game, but from questions asked and directions suggested by the players during the game.

Many details of the world get fleshed out only as the players (characters) progress through them; however, certain events in the world progress regardless of the characters' involvement with them. For example, my interview with Scott revealed that once the party had moved on from their encounter with the orcs, the Blood Fist tribe continued on to fight the Skullbash tribe and win. This storyline is one of many in the world that was not narrated (at least not until my interview), but it clearly shows that an expansive world exists outside the narrative. In this way, we see that the storyworld itself does not mean that any given story will become a part of the game.

Campaign settings are designed not to tell stories, but to create spaces for stories. Monte Cook explained that he consulted travel guides in order to get a feel for the layout and format he wanted for the published version of *Ptolus* (personal communication, June 30, 2009). He wanted his manual to read like a travel guide to a fictional world. While he did include a set of adventures that DMs could run within the *Ptolus* world, Cook also created a space with the potential for many stories, not just those he engineered.

Manuals for Stories

In addition to ready-made campaign settings, gaming companies also publish ready-made adventures, or *modules*. These modules give the DM a setting, NPC characters (complete with motivations and suggested actions), and a plot outline. As we have seen in the case of *The Temple of Elemental Evil (Temple)*, which is part of the *Greyhawk* campaign setting, the form of these modules often reads more like an instruction manual or report than a narrative. For example, there may be an overview of the entire adventure at the beginning, like an abstract. Then, there might be a list of characters, or a list of locations. These characters may be given certain motivations, and certain events may be triggered at certain locations. However, the players may never visit certain locations or may visit them in a different order than the DM anticipates. It isn't until the DM arranges the features in the process of the game that the text begins to resemble a narrative format.

Often these modules are intended to be one-time adventures, although a DM may string together a series of them to create a more coherent campaign. In doing so, the DM often adapts these modules to fit his or her needs and, thus, takes a degree of authorship over these texts — a point I engage more fully with in chapter 7. For example, although the world of Sorpraedor was created by Scott for his campaign, he continually took aspects of this world from already existing modules. These modules might provide a map of a city, or an interesting NPC, or a plotline that Scott found appealing. However, he would only take that one piece of the preexisting text rather than the module as a whole. These practices are common among gamers and accepted by the gaming industry. Modules are not published with the expectation that they will be read exactly as written, rather, that they will act as a guide for a DM.

However, modules can also be played in their entirety, and they offer some narrative passages within the preprinted text. Most modules have sections of text that are meant to be read aloud to players, and it seems that this might be a good place to look for a more narrative structure. Returning to the idea that in linguistic narratives the narrator takes a longer turn of talk, we might be tempted to say that these sections set aside for DMs to read aloud are narrative passages. An analysis of these passages finds that they are often almost exclusively description. The following excerpt from one of these passages in the module shows the detail often used in the description of space:

> As you approach the Temple area, the vegetation is disconcerting — dead trees with a skeletal appearance, scrub growth twisted and unnaturally colored, all unhealthy and sickly looking or exceptionally robust and disgusting. The ruins of the Temple's outer works appear as dark and overgrown mounds of gray rubble and blackish weeds. Skulls and bones of humans and humanoids gleam white here and there amidst the weeds. [...] Everything surrounding the place is disgusting. The myriad leering faces and twisting, contorted forms writhing and posturing on every face of the Temple seem to jape at the obscenities they depict. The growth in the compound is rank and noisome. Thorns clutch, burrs stick, and crushed stems either emit foul stench or raise angry weals on exposed flesh. Worst of all, however, is the pervading fear which seems to hang over the whole area — a smothering, clinging, almost tangible cloud of vileness and horror [Gygax & Mentzer, 1985, p. 35–36].

The deliberate break from gameplay for oral description calls attention to setting in the TRPG, but does it create a narrative?

Just as these descriptive interludes may be considered a break from normal gameplay in the TRPG, descriptive utterances have often been considered separate from narrative. This claim exists on the premise that description does not seem to need to follow a particular order, whereas in narrative there are causal connections between events. However, as Meir

Sternberg (1981) points out, the relationship between description and narrative is extremely complex. According to Sternberg (1981), "description is no more doomed to disorder than a narrative of events" (p. 65).

Often, the descriptions given by the DM in *D&D* are chronologically organized. If we return to the story of the orcs from the Sorpraedor campaign, we find that the order of the description does establish a narrative order.

> You approach the Blaze Arrow outpost. The bastion that guards the frontier of the city of Gateway is silent except for the distant cry of gathering carrion birds. You notice that the ground around the outpost has been scarred by the hobnailed feet of dozens of invaders. The three story tower is surrounded by a now broken gate. The smell of burning orcish flesh, the smell of death, profanes the air. As you enter the gate, you find the remains of a ballista that once defended the outpost. Another rests farther in, still fully loaded, its human operator dead beside it. All in all, twelve human bodies lie around, evidence of the attack that took place only hours ago. It appears the victors have suffered losses as well, but their dead have undergone the cremation rituals known to exist in orcish societies. There are also orc bodies piled up and smoldering. Yet the process seems to have been done quickly and was perhaps not completed. Some remains of orcish clothing and some shields have been left behind. They are marked with the symbol of a bloody hand, which you recognize as the sign of the "Blood Fist" tribe of orcs.

First, there is the order of progression followed by the reader. At the time of the gaming session, this description was presented in the general order that the party came upon Blaze Arrow. First they would see the footprints leading to the tower, then the broken gate, then the bodies inside the gate. Had the party approached Blaze Arrow from a different direction, the description might have been different. Furthermore, the way in which the DM constructs these descriptive passages also clues the party in to the events that happened previously. Orcs advanced on the tower (the footprints), they broke down the gate, breached the tower, and killed the soldiers. Stories like this are rarely narrated directly by the DM; rather, he or she will present the evidence in a descriptive form that allows the group to formulate an event sequence in their minds. The cognitive power of narrative is still present here, and it allows the audience to establish connections between the descriptive details that form a sequence of events. Sternberg (1981) claims "that spatial features are subject to chronological or even causal sequencing, which explains their order of presentation in terms of some order of occurrence, is no paradox" (p. 72). Description and narrative are not necessarily at odds, even when we limit the definition of narrative to the progression of causal events. The descriptive accounts in *D&D*, while immersing the player spatially, do not necessarily negate the progression of plot.

Descriptive passages offer the ability for players to reconstruct past events in narrative form. As we have seen with the *Temple* module, though, players may never completely uncover the story embedded within the modules. In terms of looking at the TRPG as a narrative, the print sources — both campaign settings and modules — are used as reference materials and can not be seen as narratives any more than an author's notes for his novel can be. On the point of spatial exploration, looking at the TRPG seems to support ludologists claims that a narrative perspective does not account for all aspects of gaming. Both campaign settings and modules are written more as manuals, devoid of narrative form; nevertheless, they create a storyworld.

However, the TRPG is not simply an exploration of this storyworld. Unlike a computer game that may be focused on graphic and visual elements of game design, TRPG space seems to revolve more around its narrative potential. While a skeletal outline for the world of Sorpraedor exists, only parts of interest to the narrative become fully developed spaces as they are enacted in the gaming session. Similarly, areas of a module may not all be explored and, thus, may never be developed or narrated. Spatial exploration does not seem to drive the TRPG narrative as much as the narrative drives the spatial exploration.

Any game (whether it uses a module or not) allows for some flexibility, but games played as one time events or in the context of conventions may be more limiting. Where players in a home game may have greater freedom to explore whatever parts of the world they choose, gamers at a convention have to stick more closely to the chosen module. However, I would argue that the exploration of space in more restricted games is even more driven by narrative progression. The Role-Players Gaming Association (RPGA) is an official gaming organization run by *Wizards of the Coast*. They hold tournaments and events both on a local and national level for gamers to get together and play adventure modules in worlds such as *Living Greyhawk* and *Living Forgotten Realms*. Because members of the RPGA move from one adventure to another, often with different DMs or players, there must be some attempts to maintain consistency in the world and the plotlines experienced. Thus, the DM of an RPGA game does not have the same flexibility that other DMs enjoy. In addition, time is often a constraint. In the game I observed, sessions were scheduled for six hour blocks and DMs were expected to wrap up the module in that time period. As the group I watched got sidetracked, partook in a dinner break, and generally took their time working through the adventure; the DM was forced to speed through both the exploration of space and the storyline. Because he was expected to get to a certain point in the story by the end of the session, it was very important for players to only explore locations that were key to the story. As time was called for the gaming session, he quickly gave an overview of what the group did not get to. The group quickly switched from an interactive narrative experience to direct narration by the DM. In a home campaign, the session would have gone longer or been resumed at another time. However, the constraints of the RPGA convention meant that the DM needed to convey certain information about the world and the story for these players to move on to other games during the course of that weekend that would build on this adventure. Therefore, rather than exploring whatever areas of space and elements of plot interested this particular gaming group, there was a pressure to cover certain storylines.

We see that space is important to the TRPG, so much so that entire books are written only to describe storyworlds. Nevertheless, the actual exploration of that space within the game is almost always connected to narrative. Just as a narrative aesthetic may be grounded in a history of linguistic and print texts, the idea of spatial aesthetics seems more appropriate for digital environments with strong visual elements. While it may take hours of gameplay in a CRPG of exploring space to find the right location and that gameplay may be satisfying because of the visual display involved, often in the TRPG the players can skip ahead to important locations. For example, when playing the *Temple* CRPG, I had to go into every building in town in order to ascertain its purpose. As a player, I needed to keep notes on which building was which so that I would know where to return. While a TRPG could certainly be run like that, more often players make statements such as "I go to the tavern," and the DM then assumes that the players are able to locate the tavern and begins describing the scene there.

Explicating these differences in the use of space between CRGPs and TRPGs shows the difficulty with turning to a spatial aesthetics to study the TRPG. As previously noted, the majority of current studies have focused on videogames and thus do not account for the way these concepts might or might not apply to other games. Because space is virtually unlimited in the TRPG, spaces are only revealed as they have relevance to the story. This is very different from playing a CRPG where a storyline may be complete, but the player continues to explore space because there is still a black unexplored area on the map. However, this player also knows that there will be boundaries to his or her exploration and that a point will be reached where their exploration is complete and can go no further. No such point exists in the TRPG, even a module can be added to by a knowledgeable DM. Thus, on the point of games as spatial exploration, we find that an analysis of the TRPG neither falls on the side of the narrativists or the ludologists. They are neither narratives in their entirety, nor are they journeys of social exploration. Rather TRPGs represent a combination of space and narrative in a way that may be specific to their medium.

Narrators and Narratees

The other main objection that ludologists have to viewing games as narratives is the lack of a clear narrator and narratee. Again, this perspective does not account for various types of games. Even within videogames there are often scenes with more direct narration or logbook features, where character actions are listed in narrative fashion for review. In the TPRG, the DM most often acts as a narrator. In addition to the descriptive passages like those seen in this chapter, the DM may recap what players suggest for their characters to do. The player may articulate the desire for their character to complete an action — *I take out a dagger and cut through the rope to escape from the orcs.* The DM may then narrate the success or failure of that action — *You feel the ropes loosening as your dagger slips between the knots.* The story goes back and forth between the player and the DM, both of whom narrate key parts. The other players serve as narratees listening to the story as it is being told.

At other times, the DM may take full control over the story. The following passage is from Maureen's story. It was narrated exclusively for Mary through a private message. Although this particular passage transpired via email in order to keep Maureen's experience secret, similar narrations frequently take place orally in the face-to-face game setting. In this story, Maureen had decided to take the blood suckle drug, a drug that caused a metamorphosis over which Maureen (played by Mary) had no control. Scott, as DM, completely narrates the scene:

> You lie down, though you feel energy coursing through your veins, and close your eyes for a second. Then the visions hit you, and it is a strange dream where you feel like you are running through fog and everything seems blurry around the edge of your vision.

You are sleek. Muscular. Darkly beautiful. You see a few people — some thieves, some guards, a few stragglers coming home — and you see them playing a game of cat and mouse as they try to catch their prey and escape from their predator. They are so fragile, these people — you see this now. So puny, and so weak. But almost none see you; you seem to be able to melt into the shadows, and fast. Oh yes.

On a whim, you leap to a roof of a building and move closer, just to see what someone will say when they do see you. You drop into the alley behind someone dressed in soiled black clothes. You can smell the fear on him even before you see him turn in slow motion and his eyes widen. He holds a rusty blade in one hand as you advance and makes a feeble attempt to stab you.

You smack the weapon from his hand and knock him across the alley with hardly a thought. You hear his heart stop beating and you realize that he dies before the scream on his lips even had a chance to come out.

You start getting confused and then everything goes black. When you open your eyes from the dream with a start, you still feel powerful but very tired. You also notice that your sheets are completely ripped to shreds and your fingernails have a little blood on them. Probably yours, seeing the condition of the bed, and you must have cut yourself in tearing the sheets as you acted out your dream.

Unlike the descriptive passages from the module, there is clearly action here. One event leads to another. Maureen takes the blood suckle drug, she transforms, she jumps from the rooftops in her panther form, is confronted by an assailant, kills him, and returns to her room, unaware of what has transpired. Or we could interpret the entire story as a dream sequence that Maureen hallucinated after taking the blood suckle drug. Despite a clear chain of events, this narration is still somewhat unusual because it is in present tense and addresses the narrattee in second person. Monik Fludernik (1994) explains that "second person texts frequently undermine this story-discourse dichotomy by the very nonnaturalness of their design, telling the narratee's or addressee's story." As such, she sees second person narratives as post-modern — they reformulate the relationship between narrator and narratee from traditional structuralist terms. In the sense that a story is told to one person (a narratee) by another person (a narrator), this passage clearly fits the definition of a narrative. However, even in these passages that consist clearly of storytelling, the story is far from traditional.

Furthermore, while the DM may act as narrator, this is not the only role that the DM fulfills within the gaming session. He or she also rolls dice to determine actions, voices the parts of NPCs, and maintains social order to the group. Again, no single perspective can account for the multiple layers of the game. A narratological stance would analyze the DM as narrator, but might not provide a framework for the DM as world builder or as rule enforcer. Although the TRPG cannot be excluded from narrative status on the grounds that it does not have a narrator, it also must not be limited to only studying this one aspect.

A Social and Rhetorical Approach to Narrative

When I say that the TRPG "possesses narrativity," I mean that it contains narrative, but is not *exclusively* a narrative. The game does appear to favor story over exploration of space, and does consist of narrative interludes with a clear narrator and narratee. More importantly, whether or not ludologists or narrative theorists would consider games such as *D&D* narratives in terms of their formal structure, many gamers feel that their experience with the TRPG is a narrative experience. Rather than dismiss the views of gamers for not using the careful terminology as defined by scholars, it is our obligation to reconcile the actual gaming experience with our scholarly accounts, even those produced by scholars who are themselves gamers.

If we take a social rather than a formalist approach, we quickly see that narrative is an important element of gameplay for many role-players. Ed Stark from Wizards of the Coast, the company that now owns *D&D,* comments that "people often say playing *D&D* is like writing your own movie" (as cited in Waters, 2004). When asked by BBC News Online to comment on their memories of *D&D* for its 30th anniversary, participants noted the feeling of controlling a storyworld. James Dodd of the UK states that *D&D* provides "a chance to star in your own subjective version of any film or novel." Paul Grogan also says that *D&D* gives you a chance to "recreate cinematic moments, kinda [sic] like being in a film where there is no defined script." Diana Thirring agrees, noting that "it is like writing a story without knowing the outcome" (as cited in Waters, 2004). Whether or not a formal analysis reveals a story in narratological terms, it seems clear that those participating in the TRPG are aware of a story behind the game.

Furthermore, narrative can be seen not as a form, but as a response. When talking more broadly about rhetoric and the rhetorical situation, Lloyd Bitzer (1968) argues that "we need to understand that a particular discourse comes into existence because of some specific condition or situation which invites utterance" (p. 6). Bitzer talks of discourse here in terms of speech, but his basic idea has more widely applied. The argument that a situation is rhetorical and that such a situation calls forth a particular response is also the basis for the rhetorical definition of genre applied in chapter 2. Something about the TRPG invites a narrative response, and it seems that narrative theory, whether or not it can elucidate all aspects of the gaming genre, can help us explain why we respond to this form as a narrative.

This notion of experience rarely factors into definitions by ludologists or narrativists, although Ryan (2006) opens the door for such an approach. While she doesn't argue that retelling what happened during a game makes the game a narrative (in a structural sense) as it is being played, she does say that "the greater our urge to tell stories about games, the stronger the suggestion that we *experienced the game narratively*" (Ryan, 2006, p. 193). We see an important move here away from Aarseth's (1997) view of narrative as a form to see narrative as an experience (whether that be a cognitive experience, a social one, or both). That we can experience something as narrative, regardless of its form, is an important shift in perspective when looking to explain the comments of gamers that they see themselves as a playing a role in an ongoing movie or novel. Aarseth's (1997) notion that in hypertext (as well as in games) the "reader must produce a narrative version" and that the text "does not contain a narrative of its own" (p. 95) is ultimately not at odds with studying games as a narrative experience, only as a narrative form.[3] The insistence of ludologists that narrative does not exist as a form in games needlessly restricts us to a formalist view that limits the study of games, rather than establishing a new lens for their study. In contrast, a rhetorical perspective allows us to bring the study of narrative into the study of game by focusing on the experience of the players, thus reconciling the either/or debate between ludologist and narrative perspectives on game studies. This perspective is especially important to the TRPG because of the social nature of the game.

5

Frames of Narrativity in the TRPG

The tabletop role-playing game (TRPG) does and does not fit traditional definitions of narrative. A narrative is a frame through which the audience sees that world. It is that act of re-framing that constitutes a narrative act. Linguist William Labov (1972) explains that the abstract, which begins an oral narrative, is a way of re-centering to a narrative world; and the coda, which ends the narrative, is a way of returning to the actual world (pp. 363–365). Traditionally, linguistic narratives have been described as longer turns of talk by one individual. The re-centering to the storyworld occurs, the story is presented, and the conversation returns to the actual world. However, gaming groups frequently shift between conversation about the storyworld, the game, and the actual world. Thus, the linguistic structure of the TRPG is necessarily different from that of oral narratives. It is clear that re-centering to multiple worlds takes place during the gaming session, but these worlds may or may not be *story-worlds*. I analyze the different frames of the TRPG, the types of speech in the TRPG, and the degree that narrative is present in each.

To date, there have been very few studies of the TRPG that focus on narrative, yet nearly every analysis features a look at the multiple layers or frames in the genre. Gary Fine (1983) uses frame analysis to talk about gamers as people in a social world, players in a game world, and characters in a fantasy world (p. 186). Sean Hendricks (2006) accepts Fine's three frames, but focuses his own analysis mainly on the fantasy frame (p. 43). Daniel Mackay (2001) splits Fine's game frame category into three frames for a total of five frames:

> [T]he social frame inhabited by the *person*, the game frame inhabited by the *player*, the narrative frame inhabited by the *raconteur*, the constative

frame inhabited by the *addresser*, and the performative frame inhabited by the *character* [p. 56].

A key move that Mackay makes in his redefinition of Fine's frames is use of the term *narrative*. Fine, instead, seems to conflate the narrative world with the fantasy world, a separation that both Mackay and I find important. As shown in the previous chapter, a fantasy world is not always a narrative world. Mackay (2001) also focuses on the dramatic aspects of the TRPG and thus it is important for him to separate out constative utterances; which include description that becomes the narrative, and performative speech that involves participants speaking in-character (p. 55). I, too, find this distinction useful. However, I argue that both constative and performative speech work to form the narrative and are thus both part of a narrative frame. As *constative* and *performative* are terms that are fairly specific to drama and speech theory, I will instead refer to *narrative speech* (which is constative) and *in-character speech* (which is performative). I use the term *narrative frame* to distinguish between the fantasy world and the narrative as told during the gaming session. Like Fine (1983), however, my model separates the TRPG into three frames. In addition to the narrative frame, there is the *social frame* of the actual world and the *gaming frame*.

The Creation of Possible Worlds in Fiction

Because of the many different worlds referenced during the course of playing a TRPG, there is an obvious connection between TRPGs and possible-world theory. Possible-worlds theory originally comes from the study of philosophy and logic. It helps explain how someone can say, "If it rains tomorrow, I will wear my jacket" when the current situation does not involve rain. Logically, the speaker can think of a world where it will rain. That world is not the present state of reality, but based on previous reality, the speaker is able to logically think of a possible world where there is rainy weather.[1] This theory has been appropriated by fiction scholars in order to show how we can logically explain the truth within fictional worlds. The actual world is current reality. Possible worlds are everything else.[2] We are able to understand the storyworld because of our comparison with our own actual world. We recognize that things are true in this possible world that may not be true in the actual world because we recognize the logic of that storyworld. Thus, possible-world theory accounts for the idea of truth in fictional stories.

Daniel Punday (2005) also makes the connection between possible worlds and tabletop role-playing, however, he ultimately uses TRPGs to help define concepts within possible-world theory rather than to create a model for future study of the TRPG. It is important to note, as Punday (2005) does, that possible-world theory does not consider the way that an author creates a world but the logic that governs these worlds apart from an author's intentions (p. 129). Regardless of what an author conceives, a reader will be able to understand certain things about a world because of the logic inherent in narrative and in narrative worlds.[3]

I find that possible-world theory is especially useful in the case of the TRPG because it does not just involve a storyworld created by an author but multiple worlds with their own logic rules that are referenced and understood by players in a TRPG session. The multiple frames that Fine (1984), Mackay (2001) and Hendricks (2006) use for the TRPG can be seen as different possible worlds. They all contain their own systems of logic, and players are able to shift between the worlds without confusion because of these separately functioning logic systems.

For understanding this particular use of possible-world theory, I draw on terms used by Ryan (1991) in her book *Possible Worlds, Artificial Intelligence, and Narrative Theory*. These terms prove useful for explaining the different worlds referenced in the TRPG and thus I give an outline of them here (see figure 2). There can be only one actual world (AW), which is the current physical reality. However, multiple alternate possible worlds (APWs) can exist and are treated as AWs in fictional stories. These APWs, however, are not narratives in and of themselves. Instead they hold the potential for many stories, as does the AW. The text reference world (TRW) is the APW that the text refers to, while the textual actual world (TAW) presents the view of the TRW that the author projects (Ryan, 1991, p. vii). Thus, the TRW is one of many APWs. Finally, Ryan (1991) also includes a category for the narratorial actual world (NAW), which is the view of the TRW provided by the narrator (p. vii).

This separation between author and narrator can be useful when looking at fiction. At times, the view of a narrator does indeed work against the view of an author. This distinction is more important if we look at TRPGs that build on published campaign modules and settings. In this case, the TRW might also refer to worlds such as *Ptolus* or *Forgotten Realms* that are created as references for the Dungeon Master (DM) to use. When the DM then reads a passage directly from a module, one might say that the TAW becomes the NAW because the text in then narrated. A clearer distinction exists between the TAW and the NAW in games that utilize a

---

Figure 2: Terms from Possible-World Theory

AW: The actual world is our reality.

APW: An alternative possible world in a different system of reality, a fiction that is accepted as true when the reader shifts to this world.

TRW: The textual reference world is the world that the text claims as factual. It is the alternative possible world that the text refers to.

TAW: The textual actual world is the view of the text reference world that is presented by the author.

NAW: The narratorial actual world is the view of the world that the narrator presents to the narratee.

(adapted from Ryan, 1991, p. vii)

---

pre-generated module than in those where the DM is also the creator of the world because textual worlds exist in print outside of the gaming session, making them separate from narrative worlds. For a home campaign such as Sorpraedor when the world becomes a *textual* world defining the type of world becomes more problematic. Scott may bring thorough notes to the gaming session; in which case we might say that they represent the textual world of Sorpraedor. Players may ask questions or pursue lines of the story that Scott didn't think of in advance, however, and, thus, there is no textual representation of these parts of the story or world until they are articulated in the actual gaming session. As we have seen, the same kind of off the cuff narration can also take place when a published module is used. Thus, instead of making a distinction that is ultimately problematic, I chose to use the terms TAW and TRW to refer to those worlds that are embodied textually. The text, in this view, is the discourse provided by the actual gaming group. It is created and narrated by the gamers themselves, particularly the DM. Because I take the text to be the discourse created during the gaming session, I, thus, collapse this distinction and refer only to the TAW.

When we step into a fictional world, we behave as if it is the AW; we ascribe to the truth of the particular APW we are presented with. Both the AW, and the APW exist outside of any narrative structure, much the way both this world and the world of Sorpraedor exist. The TRW and TAW come into being with the creation of the text. The author refers to the TRW but controls our view of that world by presenting only pieces of it in the TAW. Thus, a narrative structure involves only a selection of a possible world rather than the entire thing—a view into a world that an author allows us to see. In the case of the TRPG, we might say that the DM controls the world in this way, allowing players to only see parts of the world that he or she presents. However, Mackay (2001) notes that "the entire role-playing game narrative [is] unavailable to the gamemaster" (p. 87). Because the DM cannot predict players' actions, he or she can not know what direction the story might take or what parts of the world might be explored. While the DM may control the world to an extent, this control is far more ephemeral than that of an author.[4]

TRPGs involve continual frame shifting between different possible and AWs. In our example, the world of Sorpraedor can be seen as an APW. Sorpraedor is a large world and at the time of the orc tale, our group had not yet heard of parts of the world such as the Iron Mountains or the city of Lugyere. However, Scott had created these worlds in his head. Despite all of Scott's planning, it was not until the Sorpraedor campaign began that Sorpraedor became a TRW because prior to that time, no text existed to reference that APW. For the world to take on its life as a text, then, it must be embodied in discourse rather than merely thought. It must also have an audience.[5] Nevertheless, there are things in the TRW that are not always apparent to that audience. Textual worlds are populated with complete human beings who can be assumed to have existed and experienced certain events even if these events are not told as a part of the story (Ryan, 1991, p. 23). In our sample story of Blaze Arrow, Grumbach and the Blood Fist tribe have already attacked the tower before the party arrives. They also have a history and a reason for being there that stems from events that occurred before the story began. When the DM refers to these events, the world of Grumbach and his orcs also becomes a part of the TAW. The way in which the DM describes Grumach and the orcs is the view of them that exists in the TAW, which may or may not be the same as the "truth" of the TRW (the DM could be trying to intentionally mislead characters). However, whether or not the players discovered the motives of the Blood Fist tribe, these motives do not cease to be true in the TRW. Similarly, although it has not been narrated, the Blood Fists' victory is a matter of truth in the world of Sorpraedor.

Likewise, when players propose actions for their characters, their discussion exists in the AW but refers to the actions that may happen in an APW. Nick may refer to the possibility of Fletch finding treasure in the APW, but unless it happens, that event never becomes a part of the TAW, just as his own thoughts of winning the lottery do not make it so in the AW. Dice rolls may affect the TAW, but they are made in the AW. Nick, the player, may roll a die in the AW to determine whether or not Fletch notices the gold in the APW, but if that gold never existed in the TRW he will inherently fail. Unlike a traditional narrative, though, Nick might be able to convince Scott that something should exist in the world of Sorpraedor and thus it may come into being in the TRW.

Thus, in contrast with most texts, in TRPGs, decisions made in the AW directly affect the TAW. For example, in the interview I conducted, Scott noted that if the party had not chosen to talk to the orcs and had not asked the right questions, he would not have explained the motivation for the orcs' attack on the towers. The motivation would not have disappeared from the APW or the TRW, but the view of the orcs presented in the TAW would have been quite different. Furthermore, the way in which the DM presents the TAW affects the decisions the players make in the AW. These decisions, in turn, have an effect on the APW. If the players had not asked the right questions and had not made successful rolls to convince the orcs to respond to those questions, they would not have discovered the motivation for the attack and might have responded differently. Scott explains that he planned for several different possible outcomes before the session, though he was also open to other outcomes based on the players' actions. If the party had defeated the orcs and prevented them from making their journey into the mountains to defeat the Skullbash tribe, Scott had planned that the orcs would have vowed vengeance and in several months time they would have accumulated a greater army and come to attack the city of Gateway. This outcome was certainly affected by both the TAW and the AW, for had the players not been presented with the motivations of the orcs, they would likely have reacted differently to the both the narrative and the gaming situations.

How does one keep all of these actual and possible worlds straight? Especially when Ryan (1991) states that stepping into the APW means "erasing the linguistic signs" that this world is a fiction (p. 23)? Participants in *Dungeons and Dragons (D&D)* continually switch between the APW and the AW; but once they have entered the APW, they do not need to continually signal that it is not the AW. The actions that the players take don't need to begin with the phrase, "Let's pretend that." Even though participants continually go back and forth between the AW and the APW, they rarely clarify whether they are referring to the AW or the APW. Ken Lacy (2006) points out that even when going from out-of-character to in-character roles involves a gender change, participants rarely use traditional linguistic markers to call attention to these changes (p. 106). While this occasionally causes some confusion, the majority of the time there is no question about which world is being referred to. In reference to gaming in general, Goffman (1961) explains that the notion of frames allows gamers to sustain both a side encounter and the main encounter with relatively little confusion (p. 20). This holds true for *D&D*, even though the frames are extremely complex.

Levels of Narrativity in D&D

Separating the TRPG session into frames that refer to different possible worlds and that use different types of speech lends insight into the question of how to separate the narrative from other modes of immersion in the gaming session. The types of speech used in the TRPG have vary-

High Narrativity	
The NARRATIVE frame: Players create the textual world of the narrative.	**narrative speech** DM narrates and thereby creates the TAW (use of past or present tense, use of 2nd and 3rd person) players narrate actions that do not need confirmed by the DM, creating the TAW (use of present tense, 1st person)
	in-characters speech players and DMs interaction contribute to the TAW (use of quotative markings)
The GAME frame: Players engage in game play and are immersed in the game world, which exists as a part of the AW.	**dice rolls** DM and players' dice rolls in the AW determine whether their suggestion actions succeed in the APW (numbers announced for players, not for DM)
	narrative suggestions players suggest actions in the AW for their characters in the APW (use of present or future tense, use of 1st person)
The SOCIAL frame: Players interact in a social setting.	**narrative planning speech** players negotiate rules and how the game will be played out in the AW
	off-record speech players comment on the story world, or engage in everyday conversation in the AW
Low Narrativity	

Figure 3: Levels of narrativity in tabletop role-playing game discourse.

ing relationships to the actual world and the APW and indicate that both narrative and non-narrative can exist within the same text. Rather than concluding that the entire *D&D* session is or is not a narrative, I propose a model for TRPGs (figure 3) that involves levels of narrativity that reflect the relationships among the multiple worlds accessed during the game. Thus, my model shows how the TRPG "possesses narrativity" to varying degrees depending on the level of discourse. This model incorporates the terminology of both Ryan (1991) and Cook-Gumperz (1992) to explain the multiple frames that exist in *D&D*.

In her article "Gendered Contexts," Jenny Cook-Gumperz (1992) studies discourse samples from the make-believe games of two three-year-old girls. Although her main goal is to observe the formation of gender identities rather than the structure of narratives, Cook-Gumperz gives an in-depth model for this format of storytelling and the frames that it involves. She explains that because the children work together to develop a plot, make-believe sessions may be understood as *narrative games* (Cook-Gumperz, 1992, p. 182); a term that corresponds directly with the way Rilstone (1994) referred to TRPGs as producing narratives and Mackay (2001) defined the RPG as a *story-creation system* (p. 4). Although adult TRPGs operate on a much more sophisticated level, they do have many similarities with childhood fantasy. The ability to shift frames is one of these similarities. Like *D&D*, children's make-believe games rarely involve one act of re-centering to the storyworld but, instead, continually shift between the AW and the APW. Another useful way to look at TRPGs, then, is to compare the frames used in them to those used in make-believe games.

In these make-believe games, Cook-Gumperz (1992) recognizes three distinct voices used by the children: narrative speech, in-character speech, and off-record speech. Narrative speech is used to describe objects and events in the storyworld. In-character speech involves speaking as a character in the make-believe game. Off-record speech is grounded in the actual world and involves organizational planning of the narrative game as well as statements not directly related to the story being told through the game (Cook-Gumperz, 1992, p. 184). Off-record speech includes narrative planning speech, which is used to counter what someone has done or alter the course of events in the story that the children are developing (Cook-Gumperz, 1992, p. 188). These types of speech possess different levels of narrativity, from direct narration in narrative speech to little or no narrativity in off-record speech. I now turn to a linguistic analysis that shows how these forms of talk are nearly analogous to those found in the *D&D* game.

The Social Frame

The social frame takes place in the here and now of the actual world, rather than the fantasy world. Nevertheless, it can be highly influential on decisions made in the APW. This level consists of two types of speech, off-record speech and narrative planning speech. Both of these types of speech involve players interacting as players within the social setting of the TRPG.

The bottom level of the model is *off-record speech*, which contributes the least to the narrative and is often everyday talk rather than part of the narrative. Off-record speech shows the players reacting to the story as an audience by relating events to other cultural texts or making jokes about the actions and characters in the story. It exists in the AW, although it may comment on the textual world and even add to the audience's understanding of that world. Hendricks (2006) explains that references to popular culture "strengthen the fantasy frame by creating an avenue by which a gamer can access the fantasy frame," and also allows for "other players to elaborate on the fantasy frame so as to continue to narrow its possible variations" (p. 50). Such references help the players form a common view of the world they are creating, thus adding to their immersion in and enjoyment of the game.

Off-record speech may or may not be related to the game and narrative frames, but is clearly a part of the social frame. Mackay (2001) finds that gamers often refer to other popular texts such as sci-fi or fantasy books, or films, and that if the "setting, story, and characters are not sufficiently engrossing, there is the danger of digressing into out-of-character anecdotes and free association of popular culture references from which the players never return" (p. 75). While these pop culture references may actually add to the immersion in the storyworld by allowing players a common reference point, they can also branch into tangents that have little to do with anything other than maintaining the social atmosphere. Often, Sorpraedor sessions are a bit slow at the beginning because players engage in this sort of off-record speech while waiting for others to arrive. Likewise, during breaks for food, the pleasure of socializing can make it hard to re-start the game.

Off-record speech can also show how something in the real world is connected to something in the game world. In the beginning of the orc adventure, two heads that Whisper recognizes as the twins Mirador and Mardowin land in the middle of the camp along with the cursed scroll tube. While Maureen and Whisper did not initially tell the group who Mirador and Mardowin were, Mary and I explained to the new members of the gaming group that they had been the characters played by our last gaming companions. This led to an out-of-game discussion on different types of gamers and why these particular players did not fit in with the gaming style of the Sorpraedor campaign. This discussion was off-record in the sense that it did not forward the narrative or the game; however, it both explained the bodiless heads in the storyworld and gave the players an opportunity to discuss the way in which they preferred the game to progress.

Sometimes, though, off-record speech will more clearly relate to the narrative being formed by the game. The following transcript from a Sorpraedor gaming session clearly shows the way off-record speech can work. In this scene, the characters are at a tavern enjoying themselves. They have been drinking the ale provided by the establishment and are discussing whether or not this would affect Mary's character Gareth's ability to perform his musical act at the tavern.

1. DM: All of you that rolled a ten or less
2.   You get a plus two to your constitution
3.   but you do have a minus four to your wisdom and dexterity
4. (laughter)
5. MARY: Ah, but as it turns out my charisma's still doin' its thing
6. DM: Oh, yeah, drinking doesn't hurt your charisma.
       [
7. MARY: So I can...
8. (laughter)
9. MARY: Although technically speaking, like, maybe we should make a rule for this because that
10.   would mean that I could play my---my performance roll would be as high as it has been
11.   when I'm drunk.
12. ALEX: But it's arguable that it should be.
       [
13. MARY: But if my dexterity is like
       [
14. MARK: Well, if everyone else in the tavern is drinking the same thing and rolling the same
15.   tonight then that means the bard's--- the HALF ORC is looking good right now.
16. ALEX: Well, that's what I was thinking--- it's based on the interpretation
       [
17. MARK: If everyone's plastered then
18. ALEX: You could also argue that this is a skill that is so innate, it's one of the last things to go.
19. DM: I--- for your evidence in exhibit A: Joe Cocker.

The reference here to popular culture icon Joe Cocker, known for performing his music while intoxicated, helps to determine whether or not Gareth might also be able to entertain in such a state. While the reference is off-record in that it no longer refers to the TRW, but to the AW, the example helps to clarify circumstances in the APW. In cases like this one, off-record speech begins to morph into the next category, narrative planning speech.

The next category of speech that Cook-Gumperz (1992) refers to as *narrative planning speech* (p. 188) is essential both to the children's make-believe games and *D&D*. While planning for the three-year-old girls consisted of deciding who would use what doll and the like, adult games involve much more complex planning. Often this form of talk involves complex negotiation of the game rules. This type of talk can also be seen in the above transcript. The dice rolls that determine Gareth's success as a musician are based on the charisma ability score. According to the official game rules, charisma is not affected by drinking (Cook, 2002). Mary sees that logically playing a musical instrument would also involve dexterity, an ability that is affected by intoxication. Thus, she challenges this rule, and the group negotiates it.

Although Cook-Gumperz (1992) includes narrative planning speech as a subdivision of off-record speech, my model places it above off-record speech on the narrativity scale because in this type of discourse the players are no longer a passive audience, but actively involved in planning how the game will progress. This level still exists outside the narrative in the AW but creates a bridge between the actual world and the game world through its discussion of gaming tactics. However, just as everything discussed in this frame does not become a part of the narrative, every idea posed in this frame does not become a move in the game.

Although the social frame affects the narrative, the final story that is created from the role-playing gaming session does not usually reflect this stage of thought. A several-hour debate over what action to take next and the rules surrounding the action is reduced to one line in the write-up of the orc adventure: "We discussed amongst ourselves the political repercussions of the situation and decided that if at all possible it would be best for humans to stay out of this orcish war." The players were involved in a complex discussion of the storyworld here, yet the discussion did not take place in the storyworld. Likewise, narrative planning speech is not the actual oral narrative, but instead stalls this narrative while details are negotiated between the players.

The Game Frame

Like the social frame, the game frame operates in the actual world in that the players are sitting in this reality face-to-face playing the game. However, a new sort of logic comes into play in the game frame — the logic that governs the rules of the game itself. Because the make-believe games Cook-Gumperz (1992) studied did not involve the type of complex game mechanics seen in *D&D*, she does not include a type of speech for actions such as statements of intention or dice rolls, both of which are crucial to the game frame of TRPGs. The game frame is governed by the rules of the game and is composed of moves in the game. It thus accesses another possible world — that of the game — which is governed by its own logic separate from both the logic of the AW and the narrative world.

The transcript in the previous section shows how game logic may be different from logic in either the AW or the narrative world. Mary asserts that it is not logical to be able to perform a musical instrument at full capacity while intoxicated in either the AW or the narrative world. However, the game logic, governed by the game rules, maintains that this is fully possible. The participants go on to negotiate how this logic of the game syncs up with logic in the AW and the APW; yet the game logic exists as a system of its own. In fact, gamers often joke about the way that game logic can conflict with logic in the AW and APW. When a character goes up a level, he or she gains additional abilities. Yet, these abilities are usually not a direct consequence of anything in the narrative world. A rogue may suddenly be able to pick locks better even when he or she has been adventuring in the forest far from any chance to practice lock picking technique. This increase in skill makes logical sense within the logic of the game world rather than the narrative world and thus is accepted by most players.

I identify two types of talk in the game frame: *narrative suggestions* and *dice rolls*. Narrative suggestions involve statements of intention in which the player describes the actions his or her character attempts, which may or may not involve dice rolling. Like narrative planning speech, narrative suggestions have a greater effect on the TAW than off-record speech because actions taken within the game cause what happens next in the story. The main difference between narrative planning speech and narrative suggestion is that narrative planning speech often involves a good deal of negotiation and discussion of ideas that may or may not end up being followed by the players. The group may discuss whether or not to attack the orcs, for example, and if they attack how to orchestrate that attack.

This discussion of tactics is not taken seriously as a narrative suggestion until it is articulated in the game frame. A player may suggest that Alex's character, David, attempt to entangle the orcs before attacking, but until he states, "Ok. I try to entangle the orcs" or "I cast the spell entangle on the orcs," this speech does not constitute an action in the game world.

In my observations, players use either future tense or present tense when stating the actions of their characters. Lacy (2006) determines the present tense is used most frequently in TRPGs. He states that the use of present tense serves to mark "re-orientating to the RPG frame" (Lacy, 2006, p. 64). Although further linguistic study is necessary, the use of tense initially seems like a way to distinguish between narrative planning speech and a narrative suggestion. The use of present tense may also serve to show how certain a player is of the success of their suggestion, in terms of it being incorporated into the narrative frame. Observe the tense usage in the following transcript from the Sorpraedor campaign. In this scene, Mary's bard (Gareth) tells us about her upcoming gig at the Foppish Wererat tavern.

1. MARY: Well, I've got to go, um, meet up with Ka'Goth (laughter)
2.   the, uh, Orcish bard (laugh)
3.   later this evening, uh...
4. MARK: Yeah, uh, I'm going with you.
5. JENNY: Yeah. Yeah---
       [
6. MARY: At the Foppish Wererat, so...
                                [
7. JENNY: I'll go with you too.
8. MARY: ... I don't know if you guys want to come or go or
9. ALEX: (snicker) Oh, I wouldn't miss an Orcish bard for an instant.
10. MARY: (LAUGH)
11. DM: Ok, then.
12. MARK: We go clubbing.
       (pause)
13. DM: All right.
14.   It's a very short journey across the
15.   couple open, uh, courtyard areas and to get to the court---
       the Foppish Wererat
16.   (to Mary)You've been there before.
17. MARY: Right, right, right, I have.
18. DM: And, uh, actually, uh
19.   a couple of people up front wave at you
20.   (3) You remember them from last night.

At the beginning of this transcript, we see the group going back and forth both planning what is next and stating their actions. Mark states, in present tense, that he is going with Mary. However, I state in future tense that I will go with Mary. Mary seems to be in the frame of planning as well as she expresses uncertainty over whether or not this part of the story is one that the group as a whole would like to pursue or whether it is something for her character to do alone. When we reach line 12, however, there is a clear move to narrative suggestion. Mark no longer states his individual intent, but speaks for the party and their decided action: "We go clubbing." The DM then proceeds with narrative speech describing the journey to the Foppish Wererat. Because going "clubbing" is not the sort of thing that requires a dice role to confirm, this narrative suggestion skips over this stage and becomes a part of the narrative.

If dice rolling is necessary, the player moves to that level on the chart. Dice rolling acts are higher in their degree of narrativity because once the dice are rolled, there is usually no going back to the point of suggestion. A player will call out the dice rolled, such as "I got a 23," and the DM will respond by narrating the action within the narrative itself, "You hit the orc." A narrative suggestion may lead to a dice roll or may be overturned by the DM. Alex may say, "I cast the spell entangle on the orcs" as a narrative suggestion, but the DM may state, "Your character doesn't know that spell," thus preventing this narrative suggestion from taking root in the narrative frame. More likely, however, the DM would state, "Roll the dice to see if you hit." At this point the success or failure of the dice roll will then determine what happens in the narrative.

The Narrative Frame

Once the players begin to discuss things in-game as characters, they begin to compose the textual world. The narrative frame differs from the game frame because it involves the actual construction of the textual world. It thus possesses the greatest level of narrativity. This frame is made up of in-character speech and narrative speech. Cook-Gumperz (1992) refers to moments when the player takes on the voice of the character as "in-character speech" (p. 184). In addition to in-character speech, the TAW consists of narrative and descriptive utterances spoken by the DM. Cook-Gumperz (1992) observed similar types of speech in the children's games. Instances when the children actually narrated the story they were creating are examples of "narrative speech." Cook-Gumperz (1992) found that when the children explained events as if they were telling a story, they maintained a "reading tone"; an even tone with careful word enunciation

(p. 184). I also observed this type of tone when the DM narrated the action of the *D&D* adventure. At these times, the DM is often granted a longer turn of talk, which is characteristic of narrative speech. In the case of a pre-written module, the DM may literally be reading as certain passages in these adventures are often set aside for the DM to read directly to the players. As mentioned in the previous chapter, these accounts can also contain description, such as when the DM described the scene at Blaze Arrow. However, even these descriptive scenes can be seen as temporally motivated. The description of Blaze Arrow tells the story of the battle that happened before the party arrived. Passages like this both describe the scene and advance the "plot" of the story.

In-character speech and narrative speech possess the highest levels of narrativity because they are the TAW formed by the oral discourse of the gaming session. However, in-character speech is one level below narrative speech because it involves both the DM and the players and is thus always subject to the authoritative power of the DM (who may retract it). For example, when Whisper went to open the cursed scroll tube, Nick made a statement in-character as Fletch, saying, "No, don't do that!" However, the DM ruled that Whisper's action took place so quickly and by such surprise that the characters did not have time to react and thus Fletch's speech never reached the TAW of the narrative. However, unless directly countermanded by the DM in this way, in-character speech becomes a part of the TAW and does not need to be re-stated when the DM narrates the action.

While it may seem that narrative speech is only available to the DM, there are instances where players may also engage in it. When a player is fairly certain that an action will not require a dice role, he or she will go ahead and narrate it more directly. Similarly, narrative suggestions that go unchallenged by the DM or do not need dice rolls to determine their success or failure may rise to the level of narrative speech. However, these are below narrative speech by the DM on my model because it is the DM that ultimately controls whether players' narration becomes a part of the TAW. A player may declare, "I order some ale at the tavern." This sort of suggestion does not usually require a dice roll and would become narrative speech. Thus, this type of speech may function as both a narrative suggestion and narrative speech. However, there might be special circumstances in which the DM would determine that a dice roll is needed. If the bartender had a grudge against this particular character and was ignoring him, the DM might ask that player to roll for diplomacy to see if he or she is able to get the attention of his unwilling host. Thus, it is ultimately the DM that determines whether a narrative suggestion stands as narrative speech or whether the action must be further negotiated before entering the TAW.[6]

In TRPGs, the amount of in-character speech varies depending on the style of play that the group of gamers prefers to engage in. In general, the Sorpraedor campaign does not involve a lot of in-character speech; however, there were several notable instances of it during the orc adventure. When Cuthalion negotiated with Grumbach, Mark delivered an in-character speech as Cuthalion[7] that was so eloquent, the DM granted him extra experience points[8] for it. The DM also uses in-character speech when representing another character in the story. For example, after Cuthalion's speech, the DM responded in-character as Grumbach. In his linguist analysis of TRPGs, Ken Lacy (2006) finds that players often mark speech as in-character by prefacing it "quotative markings," or statement such as "I say" (p. 67). I also found this to be true of in-character speech. Even when direct quotative markings were not present, a change in intonation marked in-character speech. However, because the game world includes its own logic system, these devices are not always necessary to show when a character versus a player is being referred to.

Because narrative speech creates the TAW, it represents the top level of my model with the highest degree of narrativity. Narrative speech is most often spoken by the DM. If the DM is describing a scene, such as the scene upon entering Blaze Arrow or the *Temple of Elemental Evil*, the present tense may be employed to give the players a sense of temporal immersion, or if the DM is responding directly to the narrative suggestions, he or she may declare that the action in question was a success in past tense. The use of past tense here is different from the prevalence of present tense during the majority of the game. Also, as Lacy (2006) notes, the DM's speech is more often in third person rather than first person (p. 66).

The following transcript takes place just after the previous transcript as the players meet up with Ka'Goth at the Foppish Wererat. It illustrates some of the linguistic differences between players and DMs.

21. MARY: Ok, well,
22.   so does Ka'Goth say anything to me?
23. DM: Yeah, he---he
24.   culminates in a---like a little crescendo of drumbeats and
25.   comes over and gives you a big shake of the hand (3)
26. MARY: Ok, uh...
27.   / "Well, should we play a tune?"

28. DM: "YAH!"
29. (laughter)
30. MARY: All right. Well, I'm gonna whip out the old vi:ola (laughs)
31. DM: Ok then.
32. MARY: (dice roll) Uh, 25.
33. DM: Ok...
34. MARY: But I'm assuming that, you know, I've been playing some
        melodic, pleasant songs,
35.   like, for everyone thus far but that I might be able to adapt
        my style to be more
36.   tailored to these---
              [
37. DM: Well, he's
              [
38. MARY: ---the drumbeats
39. DM: And he's actually already doing the same

Note here that the DM refers to the non-player character in third person, stating "he's doing the same." Because the DM runs multiple characters, he remains far more removed from those characters than do the players.[9] In contrast, Mary refers to her character Gareth in first person, even when the separation between character and player could be potentially confusing. In fact, in line 34, the "I" that "assumes" is Mary reacting in the actual world to the narrative world. She assumes, but needs the DM's confirmation, that certain events took place in the narrative. The "I" that has been playing songs is Gareth, the character in the narrative world. Ultimately there is not room for confusion here because it does not make sense in the logic of the narrative world that Gareth would be wondering whether or not he had performed certain actions, and it does not make sense in the actual world that Mary has been playing songs. Possible-world theory, then, helps to explain the lack of traditional linguistic markers when moving in and out of character.

In this example, also note the use of in-character speech in lines 27–28. This speech is preceded by a change in intonation. Aside from the dice roll in line 32, which Mary makes to determine how successful Gareth is at joining in the music, this transcript takes place mainly in the narrative frame. Together, Mary and the DM narrate the scene in the Foppish Wererat that the rest of the party observes. However, at many times narrative speech may be a long narration by the DM alone.

In TRPGs, multiple worlds exist, but the world presented in the DM's narrative speech directly creates the storyworld. It is this level that possesses full narrativity. Because of this level, players feel as though they are immersed in a story, even as they continually shift between frames and worlds. This sense of being immersed in a narrative world is one of the main reasons for playing TRPGs. The narrative speech frame may be the least interactive of the levels in my model, particularly when it involves only the speech of the DM. However, the significance of the narrative speech frame is directly impacted by the other levels of the model. Thus, interactivity and immersion go hand-in-hand in the TRPG.

Because players' actions in the game frame influence the narrative frame, their level of immersion in the narrative frame is directly related to their level of immersion in other frames. The sense a narrative experience of the TRPG comes not from one frame, but from all three frames; and all three frames affect the narrative to varying degrees. Off-record speech is least likely to affect the narrative; this is particularly true of off-record speech that serves only as a bond within the social sphere. Yet, if this social sphere collapses, so does the narrative sphere. If players do not return to the game because they do not fit in the social setting, their characters may end up with their heads thrown into a camp as a warning, as with the twins Mirador and Mardowin. All the frames are necessary for an enjoyable narrative experience. We need not see all levels of the TRPG as narratives in order to see that this is, as Cook-Gumprez (1992) calls make-believe, a "narrative game."

6

Immersion in the TRPG

I saw David take the amulet down the passageway toward the drow, convinced that he meant to betray us. I had given it to him in good faith, to show that I could be trusted, and he had outright stolen it. The party was divided; they scattered. I came across Cuthalion's paralyzed body, and while searching for a healing potion, I saw it. Somehow he had the amulet. After all that! I took the powerful magic item back, forced some magic healing liquid down the elf's throat, and quickly ran off. I had always thought Cuthalion understood, but to find him with the amulet—I wiped away a tear—it seemed I had no friends left. After wandering alone in the woods, I stumbled across an abandoned cottage and stopped to sleep, to rest, to think...

When we turn to look at narrative in terms of an experience — when we look at it as social and rhetorical — our questions about narrative and the relationship between narrative and game shift. For one, we must ask, what constitutes a narrative experience? Furthermore, what does a narrative experience offer us? What is the rhetorical exigency that elicits a narrative response? What needs does it meet? Tabletop role-playing games (TRPGs) can be extremely immersive for the players involved, and this immersion can bring together a group of people through their common reaction to the role-playing game text being created.

While Whisper was waiting in the cottage attempting to sleep, as a player, I was temporarily removed from the rest of the Sorpraedor group. As I awaited my turn, I wrote the following in my personal blog: "For those that don't play, I can't really explain it to you. But I've had a total adrenaline rush going since about 4:00. The tension, the excitement ... all maxed out. It's amazing. And the story. Oh, my god ... the story is *so good*" (Jan. 11th, 2004, at 7:40 P.M.). The game that continued that evening was one of the ones I remember most from my time during the Sorpraedor campaign. It continued as follows:

I had barely drifted off when I heard voices, familiar voices. The party had found me. I prepared for the inevitable confrontation, perhaps even death. David entered the cottage and immediately called me out. I tried to leave, but he pulled out his sword as if to attack me. Gareth was next, and seeing the situation, immediate attempted to come between us. Fletch also stepped between us, his sword drawn. Suddenly, Gareth's magical viola was casting a spell, though I couldn't tell what spell it was. Fletch seemed to recognize it though, and attacked the viola, at which point, Gareth grabbed his musical instrument and informed the party he would be back in town.

But it only served as a momentary distraction from the larger conflict between David and me. Cuthalion was in the doorway, pointing his bow and arrow, and instructing us all to lower our weapons.

"I don't know what she's done to you," said David, clearly indicating me, "But you know as well as I, this can't go on." With that the halfling lunged at me with his sword, while I attempted only to disarm him.

In the back of my mind I thought, "I have my claws. No one knows about my dragon claws. Even with no spells, I can defend myself. But I mustn't fight my fellow party member. For the sake of the rest of the group, he cannot die by my hand." And indeed he did not. I continued to dodge his blows, while Fletch and Cuthalion sided with me. An arrow landed in the halfling's back and he slumped over. The conflict was over.

This personal example was an extremely immersive gaming experience for reasons that I outline in this chapter. However, my own experiences are well supported by the comments of other players, and this chapter will draw on both my experiences and the comments made by other roleplayers in online forums and on the online survey I distributed. These combined experiences show that the TRPG is valuable to players because of the way it immerses them in a narrative experience.

One of the key features of the TRPG is its ability to immerse the players in the world and story that the game creates. As we have seen, examples of narration from *Dungeons and Dragons (D&D)* adventures often address the readers in the second-person, pulling them directly into the storyworld, situating them in a place, and immersing them. Yet, not all of the TRPG is spent being immersed in the story. In fact, a character is sometimes the strongest immersive feature of role-playing because of the players' direct connection with their avatars. Spatial, temporal, and emotional immersion work together in the TRPG to give the player a narrative experience.

In order to understand the overall significance of immersion as part of the TRPG form and the way in which it contributes to the ability of TRPGs to respond to the needs of their players, we must first define what it means for a text to be immersive. Some modules may be played in just one evening, but in order for a TRPG campaign to continue for several years, player interest must be maintained. To do this, TRPG campaigns must immerse their participants in more extensive worlds, such as Sorpraedor. They must have interesting and exciting stories, and they must have engaging characters. Furthermore, the gameplay itself must maintain suspense and interest. Fine (1983) states that players "must lose themselves to the game. The engrossment is not total or continuous, but it is what provides for 'the fun' within the game" (p. 4). This ability to sustain interest is often much less of a concern in games that are only intended to last for one session; however, even these adventures hold a great potential for immersion. To be immersed is to be interested.

In her book on virtual reality, Ryan (2003) outlines three modes of immersion — spatial, temporal, and emotional. Ryan (2003) contends that spatial immersion is a "response to setting," temporal immersion relates to plot, and emotional immersion relates to characters (p. 121). Yet these definitions only pertain to immersion within a narrative. I take a more literal approach to these three type of immersion to explore the ways that players are immersed in terms of space, time, and emotions in the TRPG. The degree to which players are immersed in the story is directly related to the social environment in which the game takes place.

Spatial, Temporal, and Emotional Immersion in the TRPG Storyworld

Ryan (2003) states that for a text to be immersive it must create a space to which the reader can relate. This spatial setting is a place for "potential narrative action" but is not narrative because it "may lack the temporal extension [required] to develop this action into a plot" (Ryan, 2003, p. 15). As discussed in chapter 4, a storyworld does not presuppose a narrative structure. Spatial immersion is found in narratives, but also in games — even those without narrative elements.

TRPGs do involve an exploration of a world, yet the way in which this space is created and the extent to which it can be immersive, differs in face-to-face TRPGs from computer games. For example, Murray (1998) notes that "the slamming of a dungeon door behind you" is more concrete in an online visual environment than in a face-to-face *D&D* game (p. 82). The lack of a visual element may make spatial immersion more difficult to achieve in *D&D* than in more visually oriented games; however, this type of immersion is still important to the game. Without the visual component to TRPGs, players may have difficulty picturing the exact setting that the DM lays out. Wizards of the Coast's market survey shows that in 2000, 56 percent of gaming groups used miniatures to solve this dilemma (Dancey 2000). This number has no doubt increased since Wizards of the Coast came out with their new line of *D&D* collectable miniatures (minis).[1] Each player selects a small figure to represent his or her character.[2] The DM will select additional figures to represent monsters or non-player characters (NPCs). When the game calls for exploration of space, players often use graph paper to map out the journey for future reference. Similarly, the minis are often used to show the relative position of characters to one another on their journey. These minis can also be placed on a battle map, a plastic surface with graph paper-like hexes, each representing five feet. Because *D&D* combat rules often offer suggestions as to what you can or cannot do at certain distances, these battle maps help players visualize the scene and decide on their actions. The Sorpraedor campaign often uses battle maps and minis during battle sequences; however, some gaming sessions that focused more on information gathering or puzzle-solving would progress completely without them. Players may change minis frequently depending on what is readily available at the time of play. An unused die or token has been known to stand in for a monster or NPC when needed. Battle maps are marked on with erasable markers to roughly mark out terrain, only to be erased and remarked time and time again. Even though some gamers may get more interested in the visual representation of space by painting and designing scenery such as miniature castles, these tools exist more for showing spatial relationships than for immersing players visually.

Despite the lack of a visual element, the setting of a TRPG still appears to immerse players. As we saw in chapter 4, TRPGs often include elaborate oral descriptions of locations that players can then imagine. Role-players who explained the draw of TRPGs in my survey often mentioned setting, although it was rarely mentioned as the sole reason for playing TRPGs. For some participants, the genre of role-play does not make a difference, so long as there is an interesting fantasy world. One participant explains, "I enjoy exploring fantasy worlds in any type of game." Another feels that there is less pressure surrounding the exploration of a TRPG world than might exist in other genres. "I like tabletop because it enables me to spend some time with my friends and explore these different worlds without too much worry," this participant says. Another explains, "I enjoy tabletop games because of the interaction with good friends to share a tale or imagined universe together," while a forth lists "to explore new places" as one of several reasons to play the TRPG. While spatial immersion seems to be a key reason for some players to engage with the TRPG, it alone does not seem to create the narrative experience that players desire.

Temporal immersion relates to plot (Ryan, 2003, p. 121). It is therefore the type of immersion most characteristically associated with narrative structure; however, there are types of temporal immersion in games that also seem unconnected to narrativity. When the reader or player is engrossed temporally, there is the suspense of what will happen next. Ryan (2003) explains that temporal immersion is most suspenseful when situations have "diverging, but reasonably computable outcomes" (p. 141). She goes on to elaborate by explaining that situations become more suspenseful, and therefore more immersive, as the range of possibilities decreases (Ryan, 2003, p. 142).

This sort of suspense figures significantly in gaming but, again, may not be the most powerful draw of the TRPG. In many situations in the TRPG, multiple possibilities exist, and therefore the amount of suspense is limited. In the single session game I attended at the NC State Game Day, a member of our party used an extra powerful spell to blast to the bottom layer of the dungeon to where the treasure lay, completely bypassing the obstacles or clues the DM had intended for the party to run into, had they taken the standard method of following the stairs. Similarly, if the Sorpraedor party in the orc adventure had decided to go straight to Barrenstone and bypass Black Tower, the story would have had a very different ending because they would not have received the clues at Black Tower. In either case, there was no real anxiety or excitement about which option would happen next because many multiple options were possible. In contrast, the scene involving the conflict between Whisper and David was extremely suspenseful because the number of paths seemed significantly reduced. The relationship between these characters had degenerated to the point where it seemed clear that one of them must go, but not knowing which one or how the confrontation would go down was incredibly suspenseful for those involved.

However, in some ways the greatest temporal immersion and the greatest suspense does not come from the story surrounding the TRPG, but from the gameplay itself. Thus, temporal immersion may not always be linked directly to narrative elements. In Ryan's (2003) terms, complete temporal immersion exists when an action has only two possible outcomes (p. 142). The most suspenseful situations in *D&D* involve dice rolls, which are either/or situations. Players have a great deal of control over their characters' actions; however, they often have to roll dice in order to determine whether or not those actions succeed. In these situations, there are only two options — success or failure. When I rolled the dice to see if Whisper would succeed in disarming David, I knew that she would either make the roll and disarm him, or she would not (meaning his deadly attacks would continue).

For Murray (1998), temporal immersion is linked to causality. A plot involves events, and each event in the plot causes the next. Murray's (2008) view is that if players feel as though they cause the events, their immersion level increases (p. 207). Rolling dice may seem to violate this condition of causality, but as Fine (1983) observes, TRPG players have a rather illogical view of their ability to control the dice. He calls this "dice beliefs" and explains that when a computer system which randomly generated numbers between 1 and 100 for players was used in place of dice, players objected because they felt a certain amount of control had been taken away from them (Fine, 1983, p. 98). Fine (1983) observes that "the belief in the efficacy of dice is so ingrained that players deliberately change dice when dice are not performing well, in the belief that there are luckier dice" (p. 94). Gamers, of course, will not always confess such beliefs, but my own observations coincide with the behavior that Fine observed. Although these behaviors may seem illogical, Fine (1983) states that these beliefs are "engrossment beliefs" because they are legitimate inside the context of the game but not outside that context (p. 92). Not only do these beliefs arise from being immersed in the game, but they also add to immersion. A reasonable explanation for such illogical behavior is that believing one can control the dice adds to the temporal immersion and thus adds to the enjoyment of the game.

Dice rolls become increasingly suspenseful if the outcome in question is particularly important to the game. For example, if in a battle a character is low on hit points (life points) and may not be able to sustain another blow from a monster, the stakes of a given roll are particularly high. Rolling the dice also comes into play more during battle sequences than other parts or the game. However, it's not just a matter of combat; the player has multiple choices for how to get out of a situation such as this one. They might attempt to kill the monster, but they might also attempt to tumble out of the monster's way, or take a healing potion. Whatever they decide, a roll at a time when the stakes are high like this will obviously cause suspense, even when there are multiple options for success. Because of the turn-taking sequence present in *D&D*, the player may only get to attempt one of those options before the monster lands its final crushing blow.

In fact, when players somehow fail to make the dice roll the way they want them to, they are known to cheat. As Fine (1983) points out, cheating is "particularly likely to occur in 'must situations'— occasions that will influence the character for the rest of the game" (p. 101). It is also more socially acceptable to cheat in TRPGs than other games. Fine (1983) observed that Dungeon Masters (DMs) will often tolerate cheating or even let a player re-roll if the dice affect the story in a way that appears detrimental (p. 101). In my experience, outright cheating on the part of the players is discouraged, and it is usually the DM that is called upon to adjust the rolls if necessary. In fact, I had no idea how necessary this behavior was until I attempted to DM a game myself. Upon realizing how easily characters could subvert my intentions, I found myself frequently modifying dice rolls in order to present more of a challenge for the players. While players make their rolls in the open, the DM often makes his or hers behind a screen, allowing him or her a greater opportunity to cheat or adjust the roll without affecting the immersion of the players.

Besides cheating, there are other ways to get around dice rolls. When I observed the RPGA game, the players had special cards that would allow them to add to a dice roll or reverse the outcome. While leaving the outcome completely to chance does add suspense, the ability to be more involved in the outcome of the story can also cause greater immersion in the storyworld. In other words, a decrease in temporal immersion may actually lead to an increase in either spatial or emotional immersion. There may be less chance and suspense, but the increased control will allow players to feel more a part of the story setting and their characters' lives. In fact, some TRPGs have done away with dice rolls altogether in favor of more player-determined actions.

In addition, before the dice are even rolled, the player may need to convince the DM that an action should be attempted. For example, in a later Sorpraedor adventure, a gnome decided that she would add to her ability to kill the enemy by lighting her socks on fire and attaching them to her arrow to create a flaming arrow. Before making her dice roll to see if her arrow did damage, the player needed to convince the DM to allow her character to attempt the action. These situations then exist both in the storyworld and in the game world. Players are temporally immersed in the game actions, such as rolling the dice, that have an either/or consequence, but also in the story actions; and it is impossible to completely separate the two.

Emotional immersion may very well be the most intense type of immersion in the TRPG. As one of my survey participants noted, "I enjoy role-playing a character. Yeah, we'll do some dice stuff to help resolve conflict, but that's just there to make sure everyone is treated fairly. The point is the character and the story, not the dice." Ryan (2003) defines emotional immersion as a "response to character" (p. 121). This type of immersion is, perhaps, the one that has led to the societal fears about the power of TRPGs that began in 1979 after a Michigan State student who enjoyed *D&D* committed suicide. The public voiced fear that players could become so engrossed in their alter egos that they would have trouble re-emerging. Aarseth (1997) states that this sort of role merging can take place in any game that involves an avatar, and that players, in general, see avatars as extensions of themselves (p. 113). However, Fine (1983) explains that there is a difference between "role embracement" and "role merger" (p. 207). Whether or not a player creates an avatar that resembles him or herself, the constant movement in and out of character prevents a complete role merger.

New players may be more likely than experienced players to see avatars as extensions of themselves, according to Nephew (2006). She explains that a great deal of insider knowledge comes into play when developing a character. Therefore, a less experienced player may have to rely more on their external experience for character creation, resulting in a character that more nearly mimics the self (Nephew, 2006, p. 123). A character that is closely related to the self may indeed increase emotional immersion. However, a new player overwhelmed by the rules of creating characters may also go the other direction and allow someone else, usually the DM, to create a character for them. In addition, games that are pre-made modules may come with pre-generated characters. This was the case when I participated in NC State Game Day and Worldwide *Dungeons and Dragons* Game Day. Both of these gaming experiences involved pre-generated characters and modules, and the emotional immersion in these games was far less than in an ongoing campaign where players create and continually improve their characters. In fact, during these sessions, I noticed that the DM and other players did not try particularly hard to memorize the names of the characters, but would instead refer to them by their class or race. Rather than asking "What does Whisper do?," the DM might look at me and ask, "What does the sorceress do?" However, in an ongoing campaign not only was individual investment in the character more clear, the group also knew each other by character name and was emotionally immersed in the characters as a party.

Just as in Murray's (1998) notion of temporal immersion, the degree that the player has control over his or her character also increases the emotional immersion. Author and *D&D* player Shelly Mazzanoble (2007) clearly demonstrates this connection in her book *Confessions of a Part-Time Sorceress*. The title alone makes the connection between Shelly and her sorceress character, Astrid. When Mazzanoble (2007) describes creating her character, she immediately identifies with her in a motherly sort of way: "Cradling my mini me in the palm of my hand, I realized that *D&D* isn't just a game — it's a lesson in DNA" (p. 39). She talks of her creation as "a new life" that she has created and sometimes refers to herself as her character's mother.

Creating a character is one of the times when the player has the most control over the game. In the Sorpraedor campaign, both Cuthalion and Maureen had elaborate backstories. Mark created multi-paged files detailing the lineage of Cuthalion and his elven heritage. Mary also decided that she wanted her character to have an interesting backstory; however, she collaborated more with Scott in order to make her character's story fit in with the campaign.[3] Even though players have a lot of control, that's not to say that nothing is left to chance. Dice rolling can come into play when creating a character as well. In *D&D*, each character has ability scores such as strength, wisdom, and dexterity. These scores are often determined by rolling dice, although the player can determine which roll serves for which score. Another method for determining ability scores is to give players a certain number of points that can be distributed among the ability scores as the player sees fit (Tweet et al., 2003). Sometimes these points may help a player determine the backstory of a character. For example, if one roll is particularly low, the player may assign that to a certain ability score and then come up with a backstory to explain why that character is particularly deficient in that area. Perhaps the character has an extremely low charisma because he or she grew up in a very isolated part of the forest with little human interaction. In the game reality, the score may be low because of a poor roll on the dice, but adding backstory to explain it allows for greater emotional immersion on the part of the player.

In addition to initially creating a character, players continually get to outfit their characters. As characters progress in the game, they gain levels and additional abilities. For example, every few levels, the character gets an extra point to add to one of the ability scores. A DM may ask players to explain these additional skills in terms of the story in the game. For example, a wizard may need to explain and possibly role-play how he encountered a higher level mage that taught him a new spell. More often than not, however, these upgrades are more a matter of game mechanics than story. In addition, players may find or buy items to outfit their characters as they go. At times this may become a part of the role-playing, such as when Mary's character Gareth decided to have her musical instrument imbued with magical abilities. The viola, as seen in the story at the beginning of this chapter, developed its own powers and actually became intelligent, adding a whole new element to the story. However, in the case of more standard items, players often assume they can purchase them at store in town and do not spend time narrating this part of the story. Nevertheless, outfitting a character can also add to the emotional immersion that connects player and character. While the *Player's Handbook* provides the option of a starting package with standard equipment for each new player, Mazzanoble (2007) relates this option to "sitting on a bench outside of JC Penney with the elderly husbands waiting for their wives to finish shopping" (p. 67). Some players may opt for pretty standard equipment, but those who really become involved emotionally with their characters may find outfitting them an important part of the game.[4]

Whether or not they enjoy outfitting them, players often do become attached to their characters to a degree not often seen in response to traditional narratives. Fine (1983) observed that players often responded with anger or resentment to their character's problems or death (p. 222). In a post to a blog titled "gamer_chicks," a user posed this question: "In your gaming groups, have you ever had such an intense/amazing/tragic/touching event happen that people start crying in the middle of the game — in-character or out?" In the fourteen responses that bloggers gave to the question, there was unanimous agreement that TRPGs provoked this type of emotional response. Furthermore, the situations presented always involved situations such as death or trauma in a character's life. One respondent explains that she cried when, her "character's mentor/love interest sacrificed himself to save the party." Other players also mention the death of players. One blogger tells the story of a conflict between their character and the group:

> My Mage (another man) was in love with a villain (partly a past life thing) who returned his feelings, but all the other characters HATED the guy. My player character walked a fine line, staying loyal to his companions while staying faithful to his lover, but hiding his real emotions. When they finally figured it out, they cornered him and called him on it. He had to explain how he felt and how it had all happened, and try to talk them out of killing their enemy. That got me, and some of the other players too.

To these experiences, I add my own experience with the situation presented at the beginning of this chapter. Although many moments in the Sorpraedor campaign led to strong emotions, the strongest emotional scene for me was the confrontation between Whisper and David that resulted in David's death. Although these feelings did not negatively affect our out-of-game relationships, there was a great deal of anger and frustration exhibited during gameplay over this development in the story.

Social Immersion

While spatial, temporal, and emotional immersion are connected to both the storyworld and the game world, none of them hold up if social immersion is not present. The importance of the social setting in the TRPG was a point brought up repeatedly by my survey participants. Of the 40 respondents to provide a written response explaining why they enjoyed multiple types of role-playing, over half (26) explicitly mentioned the social interaction involved in the TRPG. One player notes, "The face-to-face [game] serves a social purpose as much or more than the game itself, at least in my demongraphic." Another states, "It's an activity that helps me become belonged in a small community, and lets me be creative with other people, which is a valuable resource to me."

The social setting can reinforce or interfere with other types of immersion in the TRPG. Goffman (1961) observed that face-to-face games involved a sort of mutual emotional commitment that could either be added to or detracted from based on the other participants' level of engrossment. He states that a player not being as involved in the group activity "can discredit the identity imputed to him as someone who is able and ready to immerse himself in an encounter and can weaken for the others their own involvement" (Goffman, 1961, p. 42). Although Goffman's (1961) analysis predates TRPGs, the way the social situation affects immersion in the game is similar. During the RPGA session I observed, one of the participants was particularly distracted by her need for dinner. She spent a good amount of time pursuing local take-out menus, often needing to be reminded that it was her turn or even asking another player to take her turn for her. Her lack of immersion in the social situation appeared to affect the intensity of the game as a whole. Since many TRPG gaming sessions last six hours or more, incidents such as this, phone calls, computer distractions, or the like are not uncommon; however, this type of distraction can lessen the immersion in both the game and the story for the group as a whole.

The shared experiences of the group members may also increase the level of emotional responses, such as laughter, to situations in the story that recur. For example, the incident in the orc adventure where Maureen carved an "M" into her dead assailant's body later became an inside joke for the group. David, at the time, had commented that he could not tell if the marking was an "M" or a "W"—whether it stood for Maureen or Whisper. While this incident led to David's increased suspicious of Whisper that ended with the confrontation I have told here, the reference to "Is it an M or a W?" continued to come up in the game, even after both Maureen and David were no longer active characters in the game. My fellow players liked to throw this little inside joke out there any time my character did anything suspicious, and it resulted in laughter from the group as a whole. Goffman (1961) calls such moments of shared emotional response "flooding out" as the emotion of the group can no longer be contained (p. 56).

The "gamers_chick" blog posting also mentions moments when not just one player but an entire group was reduced to tears over a particularly emotional situation. When these times are not shared, they can prove embarrassing, and one player relates retreating to the bathroom for a private cry during a role-playing session. However, another blogger responds, "I had such a phobia of that before it finally happened, and WHEN I finally cried in front of the group I was SOOOO embarrassed! But now all the males in our group have cried or at least gotten teary-eyed at some point or another." The emotional immersion of the group setting also seems to increase over time and is thus more prevalent in long-term campaigns than in games that last for only one session. The longer I played Whisper, the more the tension increased at moments that were crucial to her survival as a character. Likewise, the longer the group stayed together the more common experiences they had to relate to each other. Thus, emotional immersion exists both because of players' relations to characters within the story and in response to the social connections among players as they respond to the story.

Social Motive

Comments from both gamers and scholars show a connection between the fictional world of the narrative in the TRPG and the actual world (AW). Not only is the connection between these two worlds key for an enjoyable role-playing experience, but we also begin to see that there is a social purpose behind the TRPG. What is the purpose that ties together the social group of TRPG players? What is the exigence that calls them together to perform this specific activity? Bitzer (1968) explains that an exigence is "an imperfection," something that needs to be fixed in some way (p. 6). In terms of rhetoric, the exigence must be of social rather than individual concern; Miller (1984) states that "exigence must be seen [...] as a social motive" (p. 158). She goes on to explain that "exigence is a set of particular social patterns and expectations that provides a socially objectified motive for addressing danger, ignorance, separateness" (Miller, 1984, p. 158). But what does this have to do with role-playing? Bebergal (2004), a journalist and gamer, explains that for his group of friends, TRPGs were a means of "creating narratives to make sense of feeling socially marginal." He also reminds his readers that *D&D* can help them make stories from the world around them, stories that can lend clarity to current political and cultural situations (Bebergal 2004). Murray (1998) points out that games, like narratives, offer "interpretations of experience" and that they are rituals used to "enact the patterns that give meaning to our lives" (143). Similarly, Mackay (2001) sees TRPGs as a means of bringing unity to the lives of players (p. 116). Games and narratives both "reflect our desire and sorrows with the heightened clarity of the imagination" (Murray, 1998, p. 274). It seems that scholars recognize that the exigence to create and control narratives is defined by the social motivation to connect with others and impose meaning on the world.

Similarly, scholars of both narrative and rhetoric have discussed the power of storytelling, in general, to make sense of experience. W.R. Fisher's (1984) article "Narration as a Human Communication Paradigm: The Case of Public Moral Argument" builds on MacIntyre, who argues that it was not reason but storytelling that separated humankind from animals. Thus, Fisher (1984) claims that narrative is the dominant paradigm for interpreting and understanding experience (p. 1). Similarly, Jerome Bruner (1991) sees narrative as "an instrument of mind in the construction of reality" (p. 6). Ochs and Caps (2001) stress narrative as a "sense-making process" rather than a "finished product" (p. 15). Narratives, then, seem to have direct relevance to society and the way that we interpret the world around us. They seem to serve a rhetorical purpose. However, the TRPG consists of fictional narratives, not personal stories about the AW. Current narrative theory has not always distinguished between fiction and non-fictional narratives and for good reason. Walsh (2007) points here to the influence of Hayden White and the argument that all narratives (White focuses on histories) are to an extent inherently fictional (p. 39). Yet, one might argue that the need for fictional narrative is not one of making sense of the world but about escaping from it. TRPGs have also been heralded for their escapist qualities. When players are immersed in a fantasy world, they may feel like they can escape from the AW. Certainly the world is fictional and the experiences depicted in the story, such as casting spells or speaking with orcs, are not directly analogous to real-world experiences. Murray (1998) explains that "a good story puts us safely outside ourselves" (p. 100). Fine (1983) explains that TRPGs do just that. They create a "world set apart from the everyday world" (p. 183). However, it seems to me that the position of narrative as meaning-making versus narrative as escapism do not have to be seen in opposition. Fine (1983) admits that even *D&D*'s fantastical events "are grounded in the physical world" (p. 183). Mackay (2001) agrees that TRPGs establish an "alternate reality" but that this reality is "derived from patterns established in the artifacts of popular culture" rather than actual events (p. 81). Escapism is a powerful draw of the TRPG, but in order for a world of fantasy to make sense, it must in some way connect to the AW.

Returning to possible-worlds theory, I offer an explanation of the connection that fictional narratives might have with the AW. Ryan (1991) explains that the principle of minimal departure states that when we create an alternate possible world (APW), we tend to interpret it based on our assumptions about the AW (p. 51). For example, in order for us to understand the entangle spell that David casts on the orcs in the Blaze Arrow story, we must assume that without the spell, orcs move freely about the earth in a manner much as we walk about ours. Because this assumption is in play, we are able to comprehend the idea that the entanglement spell prevents the orcs from moving normally.

TRPGs offer a particularly interesting test case for the principle of minimal departure because of the way they shift so quickly between real and imagined worlds. While we apply the principle of minimal departure to the characters in the fictional world (including the narrator), Ryan (1991) states that even in the case of first person narration we are able to differentiate the author from the narrator. As an example, she explains that if John Smith wrote a tale about a gnome named John Smith, the reader would not simply picture John Smith as a gnome but would understand that the gnome is a character separate from John Smith, the author (Ryan, 1991, p. 59). While a traditional narrative may allow the reader to separate author and narrator clearly, this separation becomes more complicated in the TRPG setting where the creator of the character is right in front of you, pretending to be a character that has, quite possibly, a different race or a different sex. Although Mary originally played the character of Maureen, she later switched to the male character, Gareth. However, the group as a whole continued to refer to Gareth as a "she" and at the very least decided that Gareth was a very effeminate male character. Boundaries between player and character are blurred in the TRPG, in part due to the lack of a physical or visual text. This sometimes leads to over-applying the principle of minimal departure. If I were to read the description of Cuthalion created by Mark, I would realize that Cuthalion is, in fact, much shorter and older than Mark himself. However, when I picture the character of Cuthalion, it is very difficult to picture anything except Mark with more elvish features, such as pointy ears. Similarly, seeing Mary's character as female over extends the principle of minimal departure in a way that does not happen with visual or print-based texts. What we see here, then, is that rather than being an internal logic of the APW, the medium of storytelling affects the way that we apply the principle of minimal departure and the degree to which we apply it.

Furthermore, the principle of minimal departure helps us explain why narratives, even fictional ones, might inform our views of the AW. If the way to understand the fantasy world is by placing it in relation to the AW, this process can easily be reversed and the fantasy world can be used to make sense of the AW as well. Schott (2006) gives an example of this from the game Oddworld. He cites one player's connection between events in the game and the way African American slaves were treated (Carr et al., 2006, p. 141). This example shows the reversal of the principle of minimal departure where the player is able to apply something in the APW in order to understand something in the AW and explains previously cited claims that games can lead to greater political awareness. We can begin to see, then, why fictional narratives might still meet Bitzer's criteria for a rhetorical situation of causing change in the world.

However, just because games hold this potential for increased understanding of the AW does not mean that the primary motivation for playing them, or the rhetorical situation that they respond to, relates to this understanding. For me, the point that TRPGs respond to such an exigence seems too clean, too simplified. It seems too much to argue that TRPGs always bring players a greater understanding of the world and their place within it. They are, after all, games — mostly played for entertainment. The above claims seem to benefit the educators in us, looking for value in a popular text. We want to show that it is valuable to learning, that it can be useful in our classroom, that it improves our lives.[5] While this perspective is not altogether bad, it undercuts the way that TRPGs are actually engaged with in society. While there is often some truth in "socially marginalized" stereotypes, many gamers have successful careers and families.

Many exist far more in the mainstream of society than we might imagine. Furthermore, the game may not directly add any insight into events in the AW. Rather than arguing that gamers emerge from their TRPG experience as more socially adjusted, politically aware individuals (although they might), I argue that TRPGs allow players to access their creativity and tap into the power of narrative. This power is a unifying purpose that allows us to separate the TRPG from other genres of both narratives and games.

Direct application of role-playing events to the AW may or may not happen, but some gamers find that through escaping to a fantasy world they are able to find comfort in their everyday lives. One survey participant mentioned that TRPGs helped them "be a better person then I could possibly be in real life." Nephew (2006) argues that "role-playing allows the player to escape a sometimes harsh reality into a dreamworld in which they can re-assert their personal power and individual sense of worth" (p. 125). When I interviewed Mark from the Sorpraedor campaign he shared with me that just before joining the Sorpraedor campaign, he had suffered a personal tragedy. He felt that playing *D&D* provided him an escape to a world that was better than our own world — or if not better at least more within his control. Unlike the situation in his real life, Mark felt that in the gaming world our party of adventurers was equipped to handle whatever challenges were thrown our way. Even after years of gameplay and friendship, I had no idea that Mark had experienced the tragedy he mentioned until our interview. It did not come directly into the game, nor did Mark try to deliberately work out personal feelings though Cuthalion's in-game actions. However, the sense of control that he had over the game world and the immersion he experienced in Sorpraedor allowed for a powerful escape from the AW.

Immersion in the setting, plot, characters, and social setting all work together to meet the social exigence of bringing together players to form a narrative. Narrative, as a rhetorical device, is used to bridge separateness and to provide a better understanding of our world and our lives. Role-playing, in a more general sense, may be used in counseling or educational settings to help participants understand situations in new ways. The application of the TRPG — as a genre of entertainment — may not be so direct. Nevertheless, the very ability to escape to a world over which one has some control, where one can set things right and be a hero, is itself a powerful social force. Thus, a social motive that involves connecting with people to make sense of the actual world is not actually at odds with the notion of escapism.

While all of these factors are important to the TRPG, it is important to recognize that they are not all generalizable. As I have noted, gaming sessions that are isolated events do not evoke the same kind of immersion as those of longer running campaigns. Without this in-depth immersion, the players may not feel the same type of escapism or connection with their lives that might be true for long-time gamers in a common social group. In addition, the gaming style of a group or particular player may lead them to be more immersed in one aspect of the game than another. These differences in style may also affect the story as it evolves from the gameplay. For example, although it was a one time adventure, when I DMed *Speaker in Dreams* (Wyatt, 2001) I provided a story hook for a player that I knew would be interested in her character's backstory. I told her that her character's mentor was in the town where the adventure took place and that she was there to visit her. The NPC who I determined was the mentor was the victim of a kidnapping in the story and thus this bit of backstory both changed the trajectory of the adventure and added to the story. Similarly, Scott created a backstory for a character named Blaine that would later enter the Sorpraedor campaign. Blaine's true lineage, unknown to his player, was connected to one of the key nobles in the Sorpraedor world. However, this particular player was not the type to be overly immersed in the character. Therefore, unlike the story of Mary and Maureen, this particular point in the story was left unexplored.

Some gamers and gaming groups may be more interested in progressing the storyline, while other may want to explore territory, and others may be primarily interested in developing their characters. The degrees of immersion in each of these areas vary. However, what does seem to apply to TRPGs as a whole is the potential for each of these kinds of immersion. That potential may go unrealized in a particularly unsuccessful gaming session where players do not bond, fail to follow clues that lead them in interesting directions, or allow themselves to be drawn in by any number of distractions. For example, when I attended NC State Game Day, the one-time TRPG session was not immersive at all for me. In this case it was merely social pressure and etiquette that caused me to continue playing, much different forces from those that maintained my attention in the Sorpraedor campaign. Stories in other mediums may fail to immerse their audience as well. A reader may skip ahead in a book or stop reading altogether. Thus, the failure of any particular text to be immersive should not lead us to discount the potential for immersion in any given medium.

I have outlined here the many ways that TRPGs may be immersive, but not all of these immersive qualities pertain to the story. Dice rolling is more a matter of gameplay than story, although the outcomes of dice rolls do affect the outcome of the story. In addition, social connections may cause gamers to be emotionally immersed in a gaming session even if they do not feel a particular connection to their characters. However, the key immersive factor in each of these categories seems to be the control that players feel. Co-creator of *D&D*, Gary Gygax is quoted as saying that the appeal of role-playing is that average people, who may not have power in their own lives, "become super powerful and affect everything" (as cited in Kushner, 2003, p. 6). It is this sense of control that ultimately meets the rhetorical exigence of the TRPG.

7

Levels of Authorship — How Gamers Interact with Texts and Create Their Own

I have argued that one of the key features of the tabletop role-playing game (TRPG) is the narrative agency experienced by players. As I have previously discussed, agency is not always a component of interactivity. Readers may interact with a text, like a gamebook, without having agency over that text. Yet, just as interactivity does not presuppose agency, agency does not presuppose authorship. In her study of on agency and authorship in role-playing games (RPGs), Jessica Hammer (2007) explores the complexities of agency and authorship in both tabletop and online role-playing games. She defines *agency* as the "capacity to take action" and *authorship* as the "ability to enforce and judge the results of those actions" (p. 72). Similarly, Murray (1998) notes that there is a difference between playing "a creative role within an authored environment" and having "authorship of the environment itself" (p. 152). This distinction is key as we begin to talk about the way that gamers interact with other texts. I argue that in the TRPG, gamers always play a creative role, but they may also have an opportunity to actually author their own environment and narratives.

Although a distinction between readers and authors is important, it is also problematic. Post-modern theory has shown us that all readers, to an extent, are responsible for authorship. This view has been particularly advanced by the reader-response school of criticism. For example, Stanley Fish (1982) maintains that reading is always an interpretive act; therefore, a text does not fully come into being until the reader becomes involved. The classic Fish example is that of words written on the blackboard as a homework assignment for one class that the next class interpreted as a poem. Thus, for him the second class created the poem from the context of the words (it was a poetry class)—nothing in the form inherently made them a poem (Fish, 1982, p. 329). This view has parallels to our earlier look at genre, where we saw that different audiences might interpret the same text as different genres. The author-reader dynamic is problematic in studying traditional texts, let alone games.

There is nothing inherent in any one medium that shifts this dynamic. Rather the relationship between author and reader is defined in terms of the way that we interact with texts. Roland Barthes (1977) distinguishes between *works*, which are objects of consumption (p. 161), and *texts*, which can be "experienced only in an activity of production" (p. 157). Fish's (1982) critique might very well turn every work into a text. Still, in seems that certain forms of media encourage the reader to step out of a traditional consumer role more so than others. In the TPRG, the Dungeon Master (DM) has an ability to modify the text in a way that just isn't present in most computer-mediated environments. In some ways, this is an affordance of the medium of the TRPG. Face-to-face gaming allows for players' imaginations to dictate the situation rather than the code of a computer environment. Yet, one might envision a situation, such as the TRPG run through a blog or other online environment, in which the DM might have the same degree of control.

In fact, the Sorpraedor group frequently used a message board and email to interact outside of regularly scheduled gaming sessions. These additional forums added significantly to the story and character development possible in the game. While individual character and player needs can be addressed in face-to-face arenas, and sometimes were by the DM taking a player to another room for confidentiality or passing them a private note, these moments would take time away from the group as a whole. Using email allowed the Sorpraedor group to engage in these type of interactions without interrupting the entire group session. However, the DM still maintained his relationship with the group members rather than being limited by the use of computer technology. Thus, I agree with Aarseth (1997) when he states that "the politics of the author-reader relationship, ultimately, is not a choice between paper and electronic text, or linear and non-linear text ... instead it is whether the user has the ability to transform the text into something that the instigator of the text could not forsee or plan for" (p. 164).

Like Aarseth, Murray (1998) indicates that the author-reader dynamic changes only when the text can somehow be steered in an unintended direction. Again, Fish might argue that a reader will *always* steer a text in an unintended direction. In my interview with Mark from the Sorpraedor group, he indicated that he was working on writing a fantasy novel and explained that he saw a parallel between the reaction the DM often gets when players pick up on a minor detail and pursue it and the initial reactions he got to his fantasy manuscript. In his novel, Mark described a sign that hung over a village. Upon receiving his first bout of reader feedback, he was surprised that several readers asked very specific questions about the sign. This example reminded me of my previous example from the Sorpraedor campaign where Alex (playing David) focused on the details of the labels on the scroll tubes at Blaze Arrow, a detail that Scott threw in off the top of his head that was not initially important. In both cases, the reader focused on something that the author had not intended.

However, in a more traditional textual relationship, the reader's interpretation of the text would only change for that individual or group of individuals. Because Mark was blogging his manuscript and asking for feedback, he was able to change the story based on feedback. However, if his novel had been published and printed, the detail of the sign would only be envisioned within the mind of the individual reader, not changed in the actual physical text.[1] Again, this is much like Carr's (2006) example of playing an evil character in a computer role-playing game (CRPG) that did not adequately account for alternate paths — the "evilness" of her character existed in her own mind, but the physical artifact, such as the visuals of the game, did not change. Murray (1998) argues that unless "the imaginary world is nothing more than a costume trunk of empty avatars, all of the interactor's possible performances will have been called into being by the originating author" (p. 152). Yet, "a costume trunk of empty avatars" is very much the way TRPGs can be run, and this is what allows for a less traditional relationship between author and reader. The details of the story of the TRPG game are not directly found in rule books, modules, or campaign settings; rather, they are formed in the course of the gaming session. As we have seen, characters are created almost exclusively by the players, and players cannot only choose pathways for the narrative but also create pathways. These pathways need not be anticipated by the DM or the game designers. Therefore, we must ask: Who, if anyone, can then be considered an "originating author" — the game designer, DM, or player?

Jessica Hammer (2007) offers a taxonomy of authorship for role-playing that begins to shed some light on this question. She argues for three levels of authorship: primary, secondary, and tertiary. Primary authors, according to Hammer (2007), have authorship over the system and the setting; they create the rules and the storyworld (p. 71). Secondary authors create the story; the scenario encountered in the gaming session. Tertiary authors form the text that emerges from the gaming session (Hammer, 2007, p. 71). To return to Murray's (1998) metaphor of the costume trunk, Hammer (2007) explains that "if the primary author creates the sets and costumes, and the secondary author provides the characters and a script outline, the tertiary authors are the ones who bring the story to life" (p. 71). When first looking at these definitions, the division of authorship might seem clear in the TRPG. The game designers could be seen as primary authors, creating rule books and campaign settings. The DM of a home campaign who creates his or her own setting might also be in this category. In general, though, the secondary author role seems to be filled by the DM — a DM will present the encounters that the players respond to and have control over what actions enter the narrative of the gaming session. The tertiary authors are the players themselves — the ones responding to the scenarios and bringing life to the story by creating the text through gameplay. These definitions provide us with a basic understanding of the three levels of authorship in the TRPG. However, rather than being static, these roles are in constant motion. As Hammer (2007) notes, we must continually assess "who is acting as world-builder, who as story-builder, and who as story-player" (p. 72). In this chapter, I look at the way that participants in the TPRG interact with multiple texts and how their positioning in relationship to those texts continually shifts, redefining their role within the taxonomy of authorship.

In this chapter I focus primarily on authorship in the homemade game of Sorpraedor. I look specifically at the way that Scott, as DM, interacted with other texts; both those created by the gaming industry and those created by players in the game. For this analysis I use Scott's notes, my own notes from the game, interviews with select players, and email exchanges between Scott and other players. These email exchanges took place outside of the game itself, but were another place where the players were able to exercise control over the gaming environment and story. In fact, Mary had entire subplots for Maureen that took place outside of normal gaming hours. I also look at the way the player interacts with multiple texts, including those created by the DM and the gaming industry as well more general references to popular culture. Finally, I also include information from game designers, authors, and Role-Playing Gamers Association (RPGA) members that add to the complexities of authorship in the TRPG. This analysis will show how the TRPG allows for rethinking the author-reader dynamic.

The Multiple Roles of the Gamer

In the TRPG, the shift in the author/reader relationship takes on two levels. The players take the game in directions the DM could not have anticipated and the DM takes the game in directions the game designers could not forsee. While a computer game designer may not be too fond of the hacker that cracks the code of a computer game (such behavior may indicate a flaw in their design), TRPG designers welcome this sort of interference. Monte Cook explains that one of the great joys of being a game designer is hearing the creative ways that DMs have used his material to go in their own directions (personal communication, June 30, 2009). He says, "It's fun in a way that I think is unique to this medium because I wrote a novel and I hear back from readers, they are all going to have had the same experience, because the story was the same, but when I hear back from players, their experiences are all going to be different." Cook does not expect his materials to be used in one way by DMs but notes that a good DM will really make a module his or her own. Similarly, Gygax maintained the importance of the DM in having final say over what was in the rule books or modules. In an interview with Fine (1983), he said that when he would DM, he would not allow players to argue a ruling with him by pointing to a rule in the book: "I say, "Who cares? I just told you otherwise. It doesn't make any difference what the book says'" (as cited in Fine, 1983, p. 111). Even the writer of the original rules acknowledges that the DM needs to adapt them based on the individual game and situation.

As someone who both writes text and changes existing texts, the DM straddles the line between author and reader, and between primary and secondary author, frequently shifting between multiple roles. According to Fine (1983), the DM is often considered "God," "storyteller" or "playwright" (p. 73), all of which convey that authorship is a role of the DM. One of the participants in my survey writes, "I have found tabletop games to be better for intimate storytelling. I enjoy playing games that offer a great deal of player authorship. I like to simultaneously be actor, director, and author." Mackay (2001) also adds actor, director, even editor to the list of DM roles (p. 6). DMs may indeed begin their own stories and worlds, although these worlds will shift based on the players' actions. Although DMs cannot possibly plan for all possible actions that players may take, they can certainly anticipate those that are most likely. Fine (1983) notes that the DM accepts decisions made by the players, but will also shape them in the direction of the story he or she wants to tell (p. 88). In this way, the DM often acts as a director. Mackay (2001) refers to the DM's role as a continuity editor. The DM is the one who determines whether character suggestions become a part of the world and is the one who is responsible for maintaining the consistency of that world (Mackay, 2001, p. 30).

The DM must manage these multiple roles and balance the rule books and pre-written modules along with player needs. DMs often do extensive planning for gaming sessions, but everything is subject to change at a moment's notice depending on what the players do. Scott had several different plans laid out for the Blaze Arrow adventure (see appendix). Although we ended up following one fairly closely, the group could easily have abandoned the mission all together and instead sought after the strange cloaked assailants who threatened the group at the very beginning of the session. Fine (1983) also commented that DMs could not plan too much in advance because they needed to continually change the story and the world in response to the characters' actions (p. 194). The DM occupies a middle position between game designer and player and is called on to collaborate with both primary and tertiary authors.

The participants as well as the DM, then, do have a measure of authorial control over the narrative. However, in the majority of instances it is the exchange between the participants and the DM (not one or the other) that causes the "collective creation of a story" (Mackay, 2001, p. 7). The DM may have final authorial say, but the participants are hardly a passive audience. They actively shape what happens next. At points where the players take over the position of author, the DM could be considered another member of the audience; for, while he or she has control over the stories being produced, he or she is often the one addressed by players' contributions to the stories. Fine (1983) observed that the DM accepts decisions made by the players but "shapes them in directions that he believes are profitable and constructs a good 'story' which he can control" (p. 88). Yet, the DM's control is never absolute as he or she must continue to respond to the input of the players. As we've seen, in order for the TRPG to fulfill the purpose of creating a narrative, the entire group must share this goal. It cannot be executed by an individual. Authorship is in constant motion as narrative control shifts among the game designers, DM, and players.

From Literature to Gaming

As noted in the introduction to this book, fantasy literature (particularly the work of Tolkien) was highly influential in the emergence of fantasy role-playing. Fine (1983) notes that shared knowledge of fantasy books and films often connects players (p. 35). Likewise, players sometimes base their characters on those from fantasy literature. For example, let's look at the character of Cuthalion from the Sorpraedor campaign. Mark was highly influenced by Tolkien's work and based his character on "The Silmaril-lion." He was struck by the character Beleg Cuthalion from this Tolkien story. As Mark describes it, Beleg Cuthalion was a truly noble ranger who protected the elven border. Beleg became friends with a human warrior, Turin, who ended up committing evil acts because of a cursed sword. Despite this, Beleg saw the good in his friend and remained loyal, even though Turin eventually killed him. Mark was drawn to the tragedy of this story and the nobility of the character Beleg Cuthalion. However, Cuthalion in the world of Sorpradoer is not Beleg Cuthalion. Instead, Mark wrote his own story in which Beleg Cuthalion once rescued an elven town from orcs, and the village was so impressed with the elf that many of them trained to become bowman themselves. Upon reaching adult-hood, the elves in this village competed for the name Cuthalion, which had basically become a title. Mark explains that his character's true name is Ivelios but that only his village would know that name — to the rest of the world he would go by his title after the famous elf— Cuthalion.

As an isolated story, one might be able to argue that the story of Cuthalion is a work of fan fiction. Like works of fan fiction, which "rework and rewrite" a primary text by "repairing or dismissing unsatisfying aspects, [or] developing interests not sufficiently explored" (Jenkins, 1992, p. 162), Mark incorporates a key character from Tolkien's work and tells an untold story about this character saving an elven village from the orcs. However, the main difference between fan fiction and Mark's writing is that this story is only the backstory for Mark's character Cuthalion, not a part of the narrative told during the actual gaming session. In the world of Sor-praedor the original Cuthalion is never even mentioned, and it is Mark's Cuthalion that takes center stage. This Cuthalion took on a life of his own and his views quickly shifted from the Tolkien world to the world of Sor-praedor. This shift is apparent in the way that Mark describes his reaction to the Blaze Arrow adventure:

> Until the day the party chose to speak with the seven entangled orcs
> near Blaze Arrow, Cuthalion hadn't ever tried to parley with orcs. He
> didn't think it was possible. To hear that "civilized" orcs existed was an
> oxymoron. To actually see an orc give his word, then work very, very
> hard to keep it was an astounding shock to Cuthalion's sense of reality...
> Like many [Tolkiensian] elves, he "follows" a god, rather than worship-

ping one. But he felt so strongly off-beat about his role at Barrenstone, that he went to the temple of Ehlonna to do penance for the "sin" of negotiating peace with orcs and ogres, rather than killing them. The vision of Ehlonna reassures him that what he did was genuinely good, and reinforces his brave new world view.

We see here a shift in Cuthalion the character (and likely in Mark the player) from the expectation inherent in the Tolkien worldview. There is the expectation that orcs are evil and uncivilized. Scott liked to challenge these sorts of assumptions in the world of Sorpraedor, and we see that Mark is adjusting to that shift. This commentary on Cuthalion's response to the Blaze Arrow story was written as a response to an email that Scott sent Mark describing Cuthalion's vision from Ehlonna, his god. This vision reassured both Mark and his character that the actions that had been taken were fitting in this new world. Thus, Cuthalion transitions from the world of Tolkien to the world of Sorpraedor and truly takes on a life of his own.

In addition, Mark continued to be influenced by other pop culture texts as he continued to develop Cuthalion. To an extent, he did want to remain true to the Tolkien universe, and used both the movies and the books as influences for Cuthalion's character. However, other texts were influential as well. At one point, Mark decided that he was no longer completely happy with Cuthalion as a bowman, and he thought long and hard about how to incorporate more hand-to-hand fighting skills in Cuthalion's repertoire. When I interviewed Mark, he said that part of his impetus for changing Cuthalion was that he had just watched the Conan the Barbarian movies and really wanted to incorporate some of that fighting style into his *Dungeons & Dragons (D&D)* character. However, when looking at what kind of hand-to-hand weapon Cuthalion might acquire, Mark turned back to *Lord of the Rings*. In an email to Scott, he explains that he re-watched the *Lord of the Rings* movie and discovered that "in reality there's one of almost every kind of sword used by the elves *except* the longsword." Thus he rules out the use of the longsword. Like the DM's choices, however, Mark's choice is not just a matter of a certain look or feel that he is trying to capture from movies he has watched, it is a choice that must work for the gaming group as a whole. Mark also rules out the bastard sword because Alex's new character has one, and he doesn't want to "steal his thunder." In addition to adapting the character to new images from pop culture that appeal to him, Mark adapts the character in a way that will work for his real life gaming companions. Mark is not animating Cuthalion in a world that is primarily authored by someone else, but is authoring his own character based on influences from popular culture.

From Gaming to Literature

As we saw in chapter 3, sometimes *D&D* games also influence published novels. *The Temple of Elemental Evil (Temple)* was one example of this. There are two different types of influences at work here. On the one hand, we have novels that are specifically published for an audience of gamers. These books are usually printed by a gaming company, such as Wizards of the Coast, and the author may be restricted by needing to keep the book in the published game setting. As we saw with *Temple*, a savvy *D&D* player could figure out what spells from the rule books were cast and perhaps even what skills the different characters possessed. Another type of influence, however, is the less direct influence of *D&D* on fantasy literature. Just as it influenced countless games in terms of its mechanics and rules, the settings and monsters of *D&D* have influenced modern day fantasy writing.

One well-known author of *D&D* fantasy books is R.A. Salvatore. Salvatore writes in the *Forgotten Realms* universe as well as other settings and is best known for his characters Wulfgar and Drizzt Do'Urden, who were created when he wrote for TSR, Inc. In an interview with Rebecca Goings (2001), Salvatore talked about his experiences writing *D&D* novels. Some of the challenges writing for a gaming company come for Salvatore in having to make his characters conform to the *D&D* world and rules. He explains that he rarely uses wizards as key characters because of all the rules that surround them. He also explains that sometimes gamers want the characters to line up perfectly with the game, and sometimes character sheets with statistics are created for his characters the way they would be for a player character within the game — something he finds frustrating. Because of these limitations, Salvatore also writes books set in his own world (the Demonwars series) rather than *Forgotten Realms* (as cited in Goings, 2001). When asked if he ever writes up a book based on a gaming session, Salvatore's answer is a resounding "no." "I can't stress this enough," Salvatore says, "I keep the books and the games separate" (as cited in Goings, 2001).

There definitely seems to be some important differences between writing for a fantasy role-playing campaign and writing a fantasy novel. A few years after the Sorpraedor campaign, Mark decided to shift his career from a job in the technology industry to become a fantasy author. I talked with him about this shift and about the differences between running a character like Cuthalion in a *D&D* campaign and writing his own novel. As a long-time *D&D* player, Mark said that when he first started building a world for his fantasy novel, he thought back to his gaming days. He started from the rule books and materials he had used to play *D&D*, which he said was a great way to get started in building his own fantasy world. However, he found that certain things about the gaming structure were limiting when writing a novel. The main difference Mark brought up was that in a TRPG it is important for characters to gain levels and experience; for the genre to function as a game, that progression is necessary. While a character in a novel may grow and change, they don't necessarily get new skills and abilities by facing the challenges in the story. For example, Mark mentioned that while he wanted magic in his fantasy world, he saw it as something more innate to his characters rather than something learned through experience. He gave the example of a goblin that could turn invisible. Unlike in *D&D* where that character would then win a battle, get experience, and go up a level, Mark liked the idea that he would always have just that one magical trait rather than gaining new ones. To deny a player in a TRPG the ability to add more spells as they went up in level, though, would take away one of the fundamental game mechanics that keeps players interested.

Just as Mark used the initial *D&D* rules as a springboard for creating his own fantasy world, he used events that he experienced as a player as inspiration for events in his own writing. Mark recalled a particular incident in the Sorpraedor campaign that stuck out in his mind. The party had been walking through a swamp, when they came upon a hag. For some reason the hag focused her attention immediately on Cuthalion, hitting him with both hands and grabbing a hold of him. Although I did not initially recall this moment from our campaign, it stuck out in Mark's mind because Cuthalion almost died in the attack, and he realized that his character was not very capable when it came to hand-to-hand fighting. Mark explained that in the fantasy series he is writing, he has a female villain who has some special powers, and that when he was thinking about how this character might behave, he recalled the scene with the hag from the Sorpraedor campaign. He determined that he will write a scene where she turns into a hag and attacks the bowman because he really liked the vivid image that the incident from Sorpraedor left in his mind.

There is a key difference between the writers who write up the story of a particular gaming session (like my Blaze Arrow story in the appendix) and Mark writing his own fantasy novel. Just as Mark's use of Tolkien as an inspiration for Cuthalion's character in the Sorpraedor world goes beyond typical fan fiction, his use of the Sorpraedor campaign in his later fantasy writing is inspiration, not adaptation. As I will explain in more detail in chapter 8, fan fiction writers work more clearly from an existing text and rather than using a text purely as inspiration, they work to inhabit the worlds and write about the characters in the original text. Although Salvatore's books may continue to exist within the *D&D* universe, Mark's fantasy novel does not.

Furthermore, when looking at the influence of gaming on literature, levels of authorship are complicated. If a novel is based off of a role-playing game, such as is the case with *Temple*, should we consider the game designers' primary authors and the novel writers secondary authors? Sometimes TRPGs are based off of storyworlds such as *Star Trek* from the TV series. If we see these authors of a TV series that a TRPG is based on as primary authors, and the game designers as secondary authors, it would seem the reverse would be true. However, I would argue that in both cases these authors are to be viewed as primary authors. Both authors create the framework for the game or the novel. Even if the same world is used for a game or novel, both the novel author and the game designer have control to change that world as they see fit for the new medium.

Gaming Modules

In addition to inspiring novels and stories, campaigns often inspire adventure modules. However, the relationship between modules and novels is quite different. In my interview with Monte Cook, he explained that he often tested ideas for his rule book or module by playing them with his gaming group. Likewise, the original *Temple* module comes from Gygax's personal gaming group (C. Broadhurst, personal communication, July 1, 2009). In the module itself, Gygax seems to digress and talk about his personal campaign a bit in his notes for the DM. When he talks about the world of *Greyhawk* setting, he explains, "This epic adventure formed the basis for a mini-campaign within the larger *Greyhawk* campaign. It wasn't exactly a side show, as it turned out, but the adventuring began that way" (Gygax & Mentzer, 1985, p. 28). Although I was not able to interview anyone from the original *Greyhawk* campaign, this line seems to indicate that the players within that campaign may have steered things toward a certain direction so that *Temple* became even more important than Gygax had originally envisioned. They aren't given authorship credit for the publication of the module, but the players no doubt guided Gygax's creation of the *Temple* story.

The RPGA provides a particularly interesting example of how players affect the writing of modules and the creation of storyworlds. Under 3rd edition *D&D* rules the RPGA games took place in the *Greyhawk* universe, but since 4th edition, they now happen in *Forgotten Realms*. Players from a small home campaign, like Sorpraedor, often influence the DM as he or she creates the story and world but the RPGA boasts members from around the globe, and players may not consistently meet with the same group or have the same DM. Yet, in order to maintain consistency in this world, the members that write modules must be aware of what has happened before in that game universe, and DMs must stick more closely to the written module than they would in a home campaign. Creighton Broadhurst, who was in charge of the core modules for the *Living Greyhawk* world, explains that if a DM ventures too far off the pre-written adventure, players might get confused in subsequent RPGA adventures (personal communication, July 1, 2009). In addition, players report the results of the module to the RPGA and based on the most consistent result, RPGA leaders determine the official conclusion to an adventure. In this way the actions players take in their gaming session affect the way the game in the larger community progresses. Broadhurst explains, "This official result affects the region in which the adventure is set and in the case of the *Forgotten Realms* may influence future products" (personal communication, July 1, 2009). Writers for RPGA modules often come from within the RPGA community rather than being outside game designers. Players, DMs, and game writers all work together to provide a coherent story within this larger group.

Unlike the modules that Cook and Gygax wrote based on their own long-standing games, RPGA writers must continually produce modules that will be used by the group. Adventures are released on a weekly basis (www.wizards.com). These modules may not come from campaigns that are already complete but will help shape the larger campaign world of the organization; a world that multiple authors, DMs, players, and module writers continually contribute to. The RPGA writer must also be aware of the feedback from players and the way they are taking the adventure, but these players will not just be from an individual group. Rather, these players come from a collective that has played that adventure in many smaller groups with many different variations. Since *Living Greyhawk*, Wizards of the Coast and the RPGA have begun to adapt the way things are run to incorporate even more player feedback. Answers to adventure questions are collected from those that have played a particular module so that future writers will be aware what types of activities are happening throughout the campaign world. Although shared-world campaigning originally discouraged the DM from making adjustments, the RPGA now boasts that "DMs are now empowered to adjust adventures to accomplish this task, just like they would in their home games" (Tulach, 2008). It appears that the increased amount of feedback collected from the RPGA has enabled Wizards of the Coast to produce modules that more directly respond to the wants and needs of their players. While it is tempting to say that the module writers are the primary authors of RPGA adventures, what they write is based in part on the results reported by the players.

The main difference in how a DM in a home campaign might make use of a module is in terms of the way he or she incorporates that module along side other texts. Rather than use the text as is, the DM building a home campaign often samples from various modules to create his or her own world and story. In terms of the Sorpraedor campaign, it is difficult to trace the influence and use of gaming modules. Unlike the core rule books, modules are often published by various authors and companies, and often these smaller companies do not last. One of the key settings in Sorpraedor was the city of Gateway, which came from the module "Gateway: City of Living Water" by Darrin Drader and Tony Bounds. This module was published in 2001 by Dark Portal Games. It was one of the many that took advantage of the Open Gaming License to publish D&D adventures using the d20 system. However, Dark Portal Games went out of business and what used to be a free PDF on their website became difficult to obtain. In addition, Scott found it difficult to remember exactly what parts of the Sorpraedor adventure he had taken from which source and what had made up completely from whole cloth. When questioned about the Blaze Arrow adventure, he thought that it was mostly spontaneous; however, he later mentioned that he did remember reading a module that may have influenced the gaming session but could not recall the details. This lack of distinction between text created by the DM and text created by game designers shows just how problematic the idea of authorship is within the TRPG, particularly in a home run campaign. The DM will take a snippet here, and idea there — a name, a map, a character — and will incorporate these into his or her own world. This sort of "textual poaching," to use Jenkins's (1992) word to describe the way that fans rewrite TV shows, is common and acceptable in home TRPGs.

Unlike fan fiction writers, who take the text in a direction that the

TV producers and writers don't necessarily support, TPRG modules are meant to be adapted in this way. As previously discussed, they are written more like technical manuals than novels. These various sections help illustrate that modules are indeed manuals rather than stories themselves. They follow a fairly rigid formula that begins with an introduction, adventure background, synopsis, and adventure hooks (www.wizards.com). After the summary of the key parts of the adventure, the adventure hooks are designed to get the players interested in starting the adventure and give their characters a reason for being there. Often these hooks anticipate that the players have been together for a while in a regular campaign setting. After the adventure hooks, the writer of the module outlines encounters. *Encounters* are any actions that take place in the game. Often these are combats that occur where the players fight a monster, but they can also be key locations where players must interact with a Non-Player Character (NPC) or gain an important clue.

Of course, the players can always take the encounters in a different direction. A module may detail how a monster will fight in combat and be designed for such a combat to occur, but the players may decide (like we did with the orcs at Blaze Arrow) to negotiate, and the DM may have to come up with a completely different response from what is dictated in the module. When I DMed the *Speaker in Dreams* module, I found that the text in the module gave me tips for combat and the skills and abilities I needed for the NPCs to fight; however, it gave me no insight as to how to initiate the combat or what to do if the players did not engage in combat. As an inexperienced DM, who naively thought I could just follow what was in the book, this lead to an awkward moment where the characters entered a room, saw the NPCs, and stood there. Unsure how to get things started, I had the NPCs immediately become threatening and tell the characters to leave or else. This signaled to the players that a combat was the intended outcome of entering that room, but did not prove for a very interesting story. A good DM must take an authorial role at this point, come up with dialog, and engage the characters and players in the encounter. Interestingly, module writing has shifted from the early days of *Temple* where Gygax and Mentzer organized the module by location rather than encounter and included many superfluous locations where no encounters would take place. Either method gives the DM a great deal of flexibility. When extra locations that do not have encounters included, the DM can exercise creativity to make these locations interesting or to add encounters. When the module is organized by encounters, the DM may need to add additional locations to complete the world and answer player questions.

For Scott, the *Gateway* module served more as a location for his own story than as a story of its own. This particular module was designed more as a setting and was organized around locations in the town of Gateway. Scott took the map from the module along with the general description of the city and incorporated them into the world of Sorpraedor. For example, the city in the module is powered on water turbines, has a large population of nobles, and several powerful thieves' guilds. These elements were all key in the city of Gateway in the Sorpraedor campaign. For example, a larger story element within Sorpraedor was the growing discontent of the gnome population. Within Gateway, Scott decided that the gnomes were the one responsible for maintaining and running the water turbines that powered the city. Thus, as tensions increased within the gnome community, the city gradually began to fall apart. The gnomes went on strike, and eventually refused to operate the turbines altogether. The player characters were involved in this plot only to a small degree, although they could have pursued it more if they had chosen. Instead, the party pursued one of the key underground guilds, the Obsidian Brotherhood, which was based loosely on the Scarlet Sashes from the Gateway module. In this way, the DM must author many possible stories, but be willing to go whichever direction the players choose. In our case, the party was scarcely aware of the gnome problem — despite a series of clues and hints provided — until the entire city of Gateway shut down, and we were forced to leave. Because the players did not choose to pursue this plotline, it was authored more solely by the DM than through collaborative effort; however, other plotlines were authored more by players.

Re-writing Rule Books

Although modules are often used in both home campaigns and RPGA gatherings, the game rule books always serve as a key text that the players and DM interact with. Three main rule books are needed to play *D&D*. These books include the *Player's Handbook*, *The Dungeon Master's Guide (DMG)*, and *The Monster Manual*. The first is necessary for players in the game while the DM will likely use all three books. As new editions of *D&D* have been released, these books have been changed and updated, but the same three books remain essential. *The Player's Handbook* contains information needed to create and run a character, including character classes, spells, feats, skills, and even possible deities for characters to worship. *The Dungeon Master's Guide* is what a DM will need for running a campaign, including information on how to distribute experience points, create NPCs, and treasure that can be purchased or gained as rewards. *The Monster Manual* is also a tool for use by the DM that gives stats for various monsters that the players may fight in the game. In addition to these three core books, there are a large variety of additional materials available for both the DM and the player. For example, a player may acquire a book that is specific to the character class he or she wants to play. I used a book called *Tome and Blood* (Cordell & Williams, 2001) designed for magic users that listed additional spells and additional classes that my character could eventually gain. Likewise, a DM might use a book that details a campaign setting, such as *Forgotten Realms*.

Again, we might say that the writers of the rule books are primary authors, but as I have noted, these rule books are not the final say on the way that the game is run. The DM has control (authorship, if you will) over the campaign world and the rules used in his or her game, and this is particularly true of a home campaign where the DM can institute new rules. Rather than use a pre-made campaign settings (as one would in the RPGA), Scott created Sorpraedor himself, and he wanted certain things to be true about the world that did not line up perfectly with the rule books. In terms of being a continuity editor, the changes he made to the rules were also important to maintaining the realism and consistency he wanted in his world. To explain the way the DM, the rule books, and the players interact, I turn to an email exchange between Scott and Mark. This exchange occurred after Mark had been playing in the game for approximately a year and half. At this point, he began to feel frustrated at the amount of treasure his character received and asked Scott to explain his philosophy on this point. Mark writes:

> Realize that a real discrepancy exists between where Cuthalion is, and where I expected him to be in terms of wealth and magic items... This discrepancy exists because a smaller amount of treasure is being handed out than I had anticipated, and the free market economy you created is eroding the value of what we do take away. Cuthalion is a 9th level character — almost 10th level. 9,000 GP shy of where the v3.5 DMG would put his wealth as a 9th level character.

Mark refers here to his expectations for his character, and it seems clear that these expectations come from the *DMG* rule book. His character has significantly less in the way of gold pieces (GPs) than if he were to start a character at 9th level and take the recommended amount of gold from the rule book. This discrepancy concerns Mark because he feels that players might be encouraged to discard a character they are currently playing and start over with a character that has more gold; something he considers doing with Cuthalion. An inconsistency like this would not happen in the RPGA where it is important that characters of a certain level are equal to other characters of that level in case the player moves to a different adventure with a different DM.

However, Scott's response to Mark clearly shows how and why a DM might change rules from a book to fit a specific campaign.

> Part of my philosophy for the world is that magic isn't uncommon, not by any means, but it *is* special. Wars are fought over it, entire races die in pursuit of it, eons of conquest and feuding have been wagered on acquiring and taming it.

In the world of Sorpraedor, Scott does not envision that any character can just walk into a store and buy the powerful magic item that the player sees in the *DMG*. In fact, to maintain consistent logic within the world, he made certain items particularly difficult to obtain. Mark had wanted to purchase a special type of arrow designed for killing undead creatures. He inquired about it at a local merchant and was told that it was not readily available and would have to be created specially for him, costing 500 GPs more than the listed price for such an item in the *DMG*. Mark baulked at the exorbitant price, to which Scott responded:

> I am not trying to penalize a character for thinking, planning, and being smart and figuring out anything, I am just accounting for the rarity of an item. Take, for example, your idea of buying undead slaying arrows because you think a vampire is in control of the city. Don't you think the vampire would be rather irate if his smiths were cranking out undead killing stuff? So, prices will be higher to compensate cost.

We see here that Scott does use the rule books, but that he also changes things as is fitting for his world and his campaign.[2] He does acknowledge that undead slaying arrows exist as an item that can be found both in the rule book and in his world. However, since a vampire is in charge of the city, Scott makes it more difficult to obtain this item. His change to the rule book not only is consistent with the world of Sorpraedor, but no doubt signals to Mark that he is correct about the leader of the city being a vampire. The fact that the merchants don't seem to carry items for fighting undead also signals to Mark (playing Cuthalion) that the people in the city know that their leader is one of the undead, and that they have perhaps had unpleasant encounters with him in the past.

In addition, Scott's response to Mark on the issue of the game being light on treasure shows that he also adapts the game to fit the players and their needs. Dividing up treasure can be problematic for any gaming group. Rather than being assigned to any one player, the DM usually lets the entire party know what riches are discovered in an adventure and leaves it up to them to divide the spoils. After much deliberation, the Sorpraedor group decided that the total value of all the items would be divided evenly among the players, and then they could decide to either take that gold piece sum or "buy" one of the items found in the treasure from the group. This method worked well in terms of equitable distribution but made it so that it was unlikely that a really valuable magic item would remain in the group since the chance of any one player being able to afford an item were slim.

All of the decisions on how to divide treasure were made through negotiation among the players in the group, and the DM did not vote or express an opinion on how this should be done. However, he did compensate for the decision made by the players in the way that he handed out treasure. Scott explained to Mark:

> The way the party divides treasure means that if I put a +3 flaming sword in the haul, even if one of the group wanted it, they couldn't afford it as their share unless I made everything else in the haul worth 32,000gp each as well. So, I put items that *could* be powerful in a haul, so that if someone takes the right item, it will grow with them.

What Scott alludes to here is a type of item he created called leveled items. He got the idea for this modification from an official Wizards of the Coast publication, *Dragon* magazine, but made his own items specific for the characters in the Sorpraedor campaign. These items would gain powers as they went, as characters do. Usually when characters meet a challenge in the game, they are awarded experience points. Characters gain experience points and new skills, but items are not usually malleable like this. However, leveled items can be given some of a character's experience points and can also level up and gain new features. By adding these items to the game, Scott was able to give the party a seemingly low powered item in a haul, but that item might feel special to a particular character and might become more powerful with time. This prevented the players from simply selling all the best magic items. For example, Whisper was obsessed with dragons and found a pair of dragonskin gloves. These gloves did not seem overly valuable at first, but my character was instantly attracted to them and took them as her share of the treasure. As she gave experience points to the gloves, she was given choices such as whether she wanted them to be thicker and more protective or whether she wanted them to help her do damage. In this manner, I was able to work with Scott to create a powerful magic item for my character that would be unique and not available in any rule books. Adding these items to the game also allowed Scott to adjust the typical rules to make magic items more accessible within the method of treasure distribution decided upon by his specific gaming group; but to also make magic more special as per his philosophy for the world of Sorpraedor. Had my gloves been found at full power either in a treasure horde or a magic shop in Sorpraedor, I would likely have not been able to afford them. Because Scott was working with five players rather than an entire community, as seen in the RPGA, he was able to adjust these rules to fit our game and his vision for the storyworld.

Collaborative Storytelling

The DM works from published texts, such as modules and rule books, but must also accommodate different types of players with different styles of gaming and somehow pull together a coherent adventure. While Broadhurst explains that the author of an RPGA module "can't make any specific assumptions about the party mix and so cannot design encounters which require a specific power/class/race/etc to overcome" (personal communication, July 1, 2009), the home DM knows exactly who his players and characters are and can allow them to influence the story more directly. As I mentioned, the dragonskin gloves were created solely with my character in mind. The DM will steer players toward things that he knows will interest them. This level of attentiveness is most common in on-going campaigns where the DM knows the players and their characters well; however, this might happen on a more general level in other gaming session, such as guiding the wizard in the party toward the magic item. In so-doing, we see the DM in the role of director and producer rather than sole author. A good DM must allow the players a chance to participate and author their own characters and parts of the world, but he must still direct these activities to fit in with the world and story he has authored.

In the world of Sorpraedor, Mary was particularly involved in authoring Maureen's story, in part due to her gaming style and in part due to her absences from multiple gaming sessions. A player missing a gaming session can cause a hole in the coherence of the game, one that the DM must carefully mend. When Mark missed a session he left Cuthalion in the hands of other players, but when Mary missed out, she worked collaboratively with Scott, over email and in person, to devise an alternate plotline for Maureen. Maureen's unique storyline started from her conception as a character. Mary decided that her character, a rogue, was in jail at one point and worked with Scott to come up with the specifics of the backstory. In a personal email, she expressed this idea to Scott, explaining that she hoped her character could have escaped from a prison and have evil enemies pursuing her. Scott replied with some ideas on how to work this into the already existing Sorpraedor campaign:

> There is a rogue's guild (or four) in the city of Gateway. One of them in particular is very displeased with Whisper and her party. What better place for someone on the run to go, but to people who also are hated by your nemesis? Perhaps you even used to be a part of this organization and you can only leave feet first, unless you are a resourceful rogue who manages to escape.

Thus, Scott folded in Mary's idea for a character backstory with already existing parts of the Sorpraedor world. Adding a pre-existing relationship between Maureen and the Obsidian Brotherhood gang, added to the interest of the group in this particular plotline. A player and character with an individual stake in a particular event or plot can thus steer the party in a particular direction.

Individually oriented plots like this can also give players more of a chance to narrate their own stories. Mary (playing Maureen) ended up knowing a great deal of information that the party as a whole was not privy to. In chapter 3, I noted that much of the plot and storyline behind *Temple* was written in the module, but not presented as text for the DM to read aloud. Thus, it was up to each DM what information to reveal to players and when. By giving Mary her own plotline, Scott turned some of this power over to her. She knew key information that she could share with the party when (and if) she pleased. Because the game continued over the course of many sessions, this power could more easily be turned over to a player than if all of the information needed conveyed in a short 4–6 hour time span, as might be the case for a one-time RPGA adventure.

Mary chose to narrate only small bits of the story to the group. She also used the opportunity to develop an individualized plotline as a chance to engage with adult themes that might not have come up as frequently in regular face-to-face gameplay. She requested that her character be a victim of torture and become involved in drug use. Scott responded with a narrative email telling the story of Maureen's capture and imprisonment, complete with the torture of being forcibly tattooed. He told Mary clearly that she could share as much or as little of this story as she wanted with the group. Maureen showed the party her tattoo, but did not explain the entire story that Mary and Scott had worked together to create. As a result, the group spent a good deal of time trying to figure out if the tattoo was magical and if the Obsidian Brotherhood were using it to spy on the party. It also raised suspicion among the group as to where Maureen had come from and just what she had been up to. In the story of Blaze Arrow, we see the party capture and interrogate a would-be assassin who has attacked their camp. Whisper assumed, as did I, that this attacker was sent by one of her previous enemies, and interrogates the prisoner about Thaddeus, the drow. However, the captive responds that he was sent by Soren, a name I did not recognize. This name was unknown to any of the party except for Mary (playing Maureen). Soren was her connection in the Obsidian Brotherhood and the one who had tortured her in prison. Rather than reveal this plotline, Maureen killed the prisoner, leaving the rest of the party somewhat baffled.

The example of the warning from Soren shows how the DM can manage multiple plotlines designed for individual players and how individual players can assume a degree of authorship over these plotlines. Mary could have explained to us about her imprisonment and could have revealed to the party who Soren was. Instead, she remained quiet, maintaining her own control over her character's story rather than offering if up for group consumption. Although the example of Maureen's individual story is quite pronounced, it was not uncommon for Scott to give different clues to different party members, giving them the choice of which parts of the story to share with others and, thus, which storylines to follow as a group, individually, or not at all.

Defining the Author–Reader Relationship

As I have shown from these multiple examples from the Sorpraedor campaign, the DM does not maintain one simple relationship with the text of the TRPG but must actively engage in role shifting as he or she prepares for and runs a gaming session. The same is true for the player. The DM and players are readers when it comes to rule books and modules. In fact, they may consume these texts in a rather traditional manner by reading them thoroughly and may memorize a good deal of information from them. However, the reader dynamic is turned on its head once the DM incorporates these texts within actual gameplay. When confronted with a group of players, the DM is expected to know the rules but is also expected to modify them as needed to fit the needs of the group and the story. When Mark challenged Scott on the amount of treasure available in the Sorpraedor world, he seemed satisfied with the response he received.

Mark did not seem to mind Scott's lack of adherence to the rule books as long as there was a reason for adapting them within the individual game rather than simply ignoring or being ignorant of the rules.

Mackay (2001) notes that the game system "establishes the setting, tone, and direction of each narrative" yet the DM steers that narrative (p. 47). The particular narratives that come out of using a module or campaign setting may be unanticipated by the writer of that text. Yet, these materials are designed to be taken in different directions and to be used as tools, so the DM ultimately performs the function that is expected by the game designer, who creates the rule books and modules not as stories themselves but as manuals to guide the DM and players in creating a story. It is only when we try to compare this relationship to more traditional texts, such as novels or even television shows, that the author–reader dynamic truly seems disrupted.

Both game designers and DMs can function as primary authors. Monte Cook explains the odd relationship between being a game designer and being a gamemaster or DM:

> The biggest difference between a game designer and a gamemaster is that the gamemaster knows the players, knows the way their characters are and can react to those kind of things. It's kind of weird writing an adventure for publication. It's like you're creating a story, but you don't know who the characters are [M. Cook, personal communication, June 30, 2009].

Using the tool set of modules and rule books, the DM creates something new — authors a new world with new stories and characters, and in doing so they must respond to the needs of their specific players. The players could then be seen as the readers. Mackay (2001) says that this is the most common relationship between the DM and players, but that shifting between frames can cause a break between reader and author (p. 134). In terms of my model from chapter 5, we can see that the DM may surrender authorial control when a shift occurs from narrative speech to narrative planning speech where he will let the players interact with each other to determine a course of action. However, when we shift back to the narrative frame, the DM is again in control. As Mackay (2001) notes, the players may control actions, but the DM controls the results of those actions (p. 94). Fine (1983) also explains that the DM can re-roll dice or otherwise alter events, thus preserving the notion of him as author over the text created in the gaming session (p. 113). The players have agency, even tertiary authorship, but the DM maintains primary or secondary authorship in these cases. The players, as readers, break the standard author–reader relationship by taking the narrative in a direction not anticipated by the DM. Yet, like the game designers, an experienced DM is one that thinks on his or her feet and is not surprised by players going somewhere or doing something unexpected. Once again we find that rather than rebellious readers taking a text somewhere it was not intended to go, the players fulfill what is their expected role within the genre of the TRPG.

A better analogy for the DM–player relationship might be that of a director and actors. A director may come prepared with a script, but the actor may add some dialog of his or her own or portray the character in an unexpected way. Another way to see this relationship would be to see the group — both players and DMs — as collaborative authors with the DM having editorial control over the final text. All authors contribute to the text, but the editor decides the final shape of that text. Yet, none of these metaphors are a perfect fit for the DM–player dynamic. While directors and actors and editors and writers work together for a coherent text, DMs and players may hide things from each other. Often the information is all threaded through the DM, but sometimes players may keep certain facts about their characters private. Mary could have envisioned her own tortured past for Maureen and let this affect her actions in the game but not have told anyone, even the DM, the details of this past. In fact, this is probably more true of an RPGA game where a player shifts among DMs but keeps the same character. The player does not have time to fully explain the backstory or to work as collaboratively with multiple DMs as Mary did with Scott. Such an example, however, might be seen as too far removed from the gaming session to actually be included as a part of the text. A more common scenario is one in which the DM knows each piece of the story but players do not share bits of information with each other, or the DM withholds information from the entire group. Doing this can increase the suspense of the game and can lead to a richer story.

Finally, Murray (1998) offers one last metaphor for the role of the DM — that of a bard. She explains that if we reconceptualize authorship in terms of a bard, we can "think of it not as the inscribing of a fixed written text but as the invention and arrangement of the expressive patters that constitute a multiform story" (Murray, 1998, p. 194). A bard, by Murray's (1998) description, chooses bits and pieces of stories to create his or her own (p. 188). A bard also responds to a live audience, noting which direction of the story they are interested in hearing. In fact, one can imagine that a bard might even allow members of the audience to take over parts of the story and tell them, although not in the same way we see in the

TRPG. The metaphor of the bard also seems fitting, and somewhat ironic, because it is one of the character classes available in *D&D*.

Whatever metaphor we chose to represent the relationship between the DM and players, we clearly see that the TRPG does not follow the traditional notion of the author and reader. We also see that DM and player roles change depending on the type of game and game setting. A home campaign is not the same as an RPGA campaign, yet in both we see an interaction with texts that is productive. While it is difficult to define who is the author and who is the reader, we can see that acts of authorship continually occur in relation to the TRPG. When a game designer sits down to write a module, he or she does so as an author. When the DM creates his or her own world, he or she does so as an author. In Hammer's (2007) terms, these are both acts of primary authorship. However, when a player creates a character complete with a full narrative backstory, he or she also does so as a primary author. When the DM takes that character backstory and uses it in their campaign setting, they become secondary authors, just as when they take settings from published works by game designers. Likewise, both DMs and players work together as tertiary authors to bring the world they have created as primary or secondary authors to life. According to Aarseth (1997), "the reader is (and has always been) a necessary part of the text, but one that we now realize can (or must) perform more than one function" (p. 74). While it is often argued that digital texts are reason for a revolution in reader–author–text dynamics, the TRPG offers a clear example of how this dynamic is not new, although it may be more prevalent in a digital world. The TRPG as a text is collaborative; it is multi-vocal, but it is not just the text that must take on multiple voices. The players — including the DM — must simultaneously play the role of the reader as well as the primary, secondary and tertiary author.

8

The Culture of TRPG Fans

Throughout this book, I have looked at the ways that tabletop role-playing games (TRPGs) foster narratives. In chapter 5, I divided the actual gaming session into three spheres that access different worlds and are governed by different logic. Of these spheres, the final sphere was the social sphere, and it is the one that I turn to in this penultimate chapter. As we have seen, social interaction is often the least important to developing the story and has the least degree of narrativity. It is, nevertheless, a key reason why players engage in TRPGs. It also contributes to the sense of agency they receive from their participation. However, my model only looked at the social sphere within individual gaming sessions, not at the larger social sphere of the gaming community. Fans of TRPGs form their own niche group in society and often meet at gaming stores or larger gaming conventions. The significant of the TRPG is not only textual: it is social and cultural.

Gaming culture has recently become a part of the scholarly discussion of fan culture, or *fandom*. Although fans engage in a variety of activities, which may include role-playing, the genre that has garnished the most attention is fan fiction, where fans write their own stories based on TV shows or other artifacts of popular culture. In order to explain what attracts people to gaming as a particular subculture, I compare gaming to the subculture of television fandom, as presented by Henry Jenkins in his book (1992) *Textual Poachers*. Aarseth (1997) mentions Henry Jenkins's work on fandom as another example of textual transformation (p. 164), and the type of productive interactivity that is seen in TRPGs is very similar to the activities Jenkins discusses. It was in fan communities (specifically fantasy and science fiction fans) that *Dungeons and Dragons (D&D)* first became popular, and it has retained its popularity in these communities (Mackay, 2001, p. 16). In fact, Crawford and Rutter (2007) suggest that gaming in general should be considered as a part of studying fandom (p. 271). Can TRPG players be considered just another group within the larger fandom subculture or does it represent its own culture?

Perhaps gaming is a part of fandom as a whole. Certainly, we see gaming tracks at fan conventions along side science fiction and fantasy TV film stars. But we must keep in mind that a variety of fans exist. To call fandom one coherent community is misleading. In this chapter, I begin by looking at gamers as members of participatory culture and by comparing the way they interact with texts to the way that fan fiction writers interact with texts. I explore what it means to participate in fandom culture, and gaming culture. Ultimately, I show that this participation is varied, and outline a typology of different types of fans and gamers.

Subcultures, Fan Cultures, and Consumer Culture

In his article "How 'Dungeons' changed the world," Bebergal (2004) explains that those who play TRPGs feel marginalized by society, thus pushing them to form their own subsociety. Fine (1983) sets up his *Shared Fantasy* book as a study of the subculture of the TRPG. According to Fine (1983), a subculture must be distinct from other groups in society, must have common activities, and share cultural elements (p. 25). In addition, a subculture must have a network of communication for its members and both the members and those outside the subculture must recognize it as a separate group (Fine, 1983, p. 26).

Fine (1983) applies these criteria to tabletop gamers, and despite some changes, they still seem applicable. He estimates in 1979 that the TRPG base was 500,000 people, enough for its own subculture (p. 27). Wizards of the Coast estimates that as of 2006, four million people in the United States play *D&D* each month, with the worldwide numbers being even higher (www.wizards.com). This number also does not include gamers that play other TRPGs besides *D&D*. It seems, then, that there are still plenty of people to make up a subculture and, in fact, the hobby is more mainstream than at the time of Fine's study. Fine (1983) went on to note that playing the game is, itself, the activity shared by members of this culture. He also shows that common references and terms indicate that *D&D* players share cultural elements (p. 29). I would argue that this shared cultural reference has gone beyond terms to include lore surrounding adventures such as *The Temple of Elemental Evil (Temple)*. Even if they have not played the game themselves, adventures such as this one form a common cultural background for players. In terms of communication, Fine (1983) mentions magazines and conventions as two of the main methods open for gamers to communicate with one another (pp. 32–33). These are still important aspects of communication between gamers, but the Internet has expanded these to include message boards, blogs, and other online forums. The two main magazines about *D&D, Dungeon* and *Dragon*, are now only available online. Finally, in keeping with Fine's (1983) claim that members of a subculture distinguish themselves as such, I have already shown that both players of TRPGs and members of the larger gaming community distinguish the TRPG as separate from other types of gaming. All of these factors seem to indicate that Fine was correct in calling tabletop gamers a subculture; however, is this subculture the same as fandom and fan fiction subculture?

Both fan fiction writers and gamers use different tools — fan fiction and gaming sessions — but both respond to the dominant mainstream culture and react against the view of texts as objects of consumption. Jenkins (1992) and Mackay (2001) both refer to Roland Barthes' (1975) idea that re-reading is "not consumption but play" (p. 16). In the case of television fans this re-reading often takes place quite literally as fans continually re-watch episodes of their favorite series. Some fans then use incidents and characters in the series to write their own stories, called *fan fiction*. Gamers may return to the same game time and time again, but re-playing a TRPG adventure would be so different from session to session that I am hesitant to call this re-playing at all.

Instead of considering it re-reading or re-playing, Mackay (2001) proposes a Barthean-type process in which role-players created a new reality "derived from patterns established in the artifacts of popular culture" (p. 81). Like fans, gamers take bits and pieces of popular culture, such as the fantasy worlds of J.R.R. Tolkien, and re-appropriate them to create their own narratives. As we saw in the previous chapter, in the Sorpraedor campaign, the character Cuthalion was based on Tolkein's "The Silmarillion," but still took on his own life in the Sorpraedor world. In addition, the new role-playing games that have come about in the last thirty years often use a pop culture setting and are often based on popular television series or movies such as *Star Trek* and *Star Wars*.

In a way, TRPGs based on popular media are gamers' way of interacting with these worlds, understanding them, and appropriating them as their own. Both gamers and fan fiction writers reject the sort of aesthetic distance that comes from simply reading or listening to a story (that is, from consumption) and instead seek their own narrative control over the text. Jenkins (1992) explains that for many fans, rejection of aesthetic distance is a rejection of authority. Instead of simply accepting the texts as they are presented, fans feel they have the right to offer their own interpretations. They "enter the realm of fiction as if it were a tangible place they can inhabit and explore" (Jenkins, 1992, p. 18). TRPGs offer popular fiction worlds, with the full possibility of exploring and inhabiting them during the gaming session but, furthermore, they offer players the ability to completely transform and control these worlds.

Mackay (2001) states that role-players aren't consumers because the TRPG is a process-performance. He explains that "the role-playing game exhibits a narrative, but this narrative does not exist *until* the actual performance" (Mackay, 2001, p. 50). Although players buy products, such as the rule books, the outcome of their games (the narrative that is created through gameplay) rarely becomes a consumer product. Similarly, while fans may invest in buying paraphernalia associated with their fandom, the texts they create through fan fiction remain unpublished and are freely exchanged among members of the group. Although they are consumers in the sense that they buy products, fans and TRPG gamers do not consume these products. Rather, they use them to actively produce texts of their own.

A key difference between fan fiction writers and TRPG players, however, is the nature of the texts they create. Fan fiction writers use the original text, such as the *Star Trek* television series, to produce a new text — their work of fan fiction. On the website www.fanfiction.net, one can find gamers writing *D&D* fan fiction that is based on their own gaming sessions, much like my writeup in the appendix. As we saw in chapter 7, the lines blur between fan fiction and fiction that is simply influenced by another text within pop culture. I would not consider Mark's use of Tolkien to ultimately be fan fiction (though his initial story might be) because he continued to develop the character in a world that was not the world of Tolkien. Likewise, some *D&D* fan fiction writers base their work on their own campaigns and characters. A www.fanfic.net user, Mute Bard, explains, "I am in the process of turning game sessions into Prose narrative. *D&D* is perfect for telling a story, as even the author doesn't know what is going to happen until it actually does" (www.fanfiction.net). Although this story still takes place in the setting created by the Dungeon Master (DM), this type of writing seems distinctive from fan fiction in general because the writer of the fiction is in direct contact with the DM and shapes the story and characters through game play, rather than beginning from a more static text. Whether or not *D&D* players choose to later write a fictional story based on their gaming encounters, they still contribute to the creation of stories during the gaming session.

However, some of the stories on www.fanfic.net are based on *D&D* novels and characters created by other authors rather than actual campaigns. For example, a user named Tizai explains, "I had decided to base my next few stories on the *Eye of the Beholder* trilogy for a couple of reasons: I thought that the stories must be told and I have found only one other story (based on *Eye of the Beholder 2*)" (www.fanfiction.net). This type of fan fiction works from a preexisting text and, thus, these writers seem to fit more clearly under the label of fan fiction. In addition, it is important to recognize the difference between published *D&D* novels and fan fiction. Jenkins (1992) explains that fans expect something different from the published texts and often complain if they find them too "fannish." While R.A. Salvatore's *D&D* novels add to a more complete textual universe, they are different than fan fiction in part because of the way they enter the economic system. Rather than being freely available and exchanged fan to fan, these books are sold by the gaming company for gamers to read and consume. As we have seen, these books are also not based directly on an already existing text; even if they make use of *D&D* rules, those rules do not already contain a narrative.

Furthermore, TRPGs as a genre are highly influenced by popular culture, and there are game settings and rule systems based entirely on television series. However, there is a difference between an actual role-playing game that has been based on a TV universe and fans simply acting out roles from a TV show. Both are examples of role-play, but the second case is not actually a TRPG. In the case of an informal role-playing group based on *Buffy the Vampire Slayer*, Hammer (2007) explains that series creator Joss Whedon is the primary author and the fans are secondary authors (p. 72). However, her example is from fans participating in role-playing not a role-playing game. In an actual TRPG based on a television series, there is the author of the series but also the author of the game rules based on the series. In such games, it is rare that the players run the exact characters from the television series in a TRPG. TRPGs differ from fan fiction where the writer may add additional characters but usually centers the story around characters from the original work. Instead, gamers create their own characters within the universe. Fan fiction writers may focus more on minor characters from the show that they feel have more of a story to tell or on repressed or forgotten stories that they feel are subtexts in the show. However, a fan fiction writer's relationship to the text is different than that of TRPG players, even when the game is based in a TV universe.

Another difference between fan fiction and gaming is that while fan fiction may remain unpublished, it is, nevertheless, consumed by other members of the fandom who read it as a complete text of its own. On the other hand, TRPG stories are often not represented in any physical form. Even when I did write up the adventure at Blaze Arrow, my write-up of the orc adventure was done with the purpose of informing Mary what she had missed in her absence from that gaming session. It is one of only several stories from our Sorpraedor campaign that has been written down, and even these were never intended for an audience beyond the Sorpraedor group. Similarly, when Monte Cook bases gaming modules on his own home campaigns, every detail of those stories is not represented in the module; rather, the module acts as a guide for creating new stories in those worlds. In part, this is because TRPG stories are rarely complete, rather, they continue from session to session. Moreover, it is impossible to replicate the complexity of the interaction that occurs in each frame of the TRPG in a written story. Mackay (2001) explains that players continue to play out of a "desire to return to the *presence* of emotion" that disappears when the game stops (p. 85). The desire to return to the story that can never end, that can never be consumed, keeps TRPG groups going for years. Mackay (2001) sees this ongoing process as one that "suspends the desire to consume the texts (i.e. commodities) of the spectacle of popular culture" (p. 131). The audience, if they can be characterized as such, resists consumption in favor of production. Because the world and characters of *D&D* are created in the minds of the players, there is no physical text to consume.

The ability to create texts that cannot be reproduced or commodified is important to gamers. Bebergal (2004) shows that in *D&D* imagination is key, not pre-written modules and rule books. He comments that looking around at his child's room full of toys, he wants to shout, "I created worlds with nothing more than a twenty-sided die!" There is a strong sense of power and ownership involved in creating something that can exist only in a person's imagination; something that can never be read or consumed by others. Gamer Simon Andrew states, "it's great being part of an underground world which baffles 90 percent of people you talk to" (as cited in Waters, 2004). While some gamers want to share their stories with the world in forums like www.fanfiction.net, other gamers pride themselves on creating worlds and stories that are incomprehensible to those outside their gaming group. As members of a subculture, TRPG gamers connect through their shared desire to produce texts. Because immersive qualities of TRPGs give players a sense of belonging to a storyworld and interactive qualities give players the sense of actively contributing to this world, players see their gaming as a process of production rather than consumption. By engaging in this type of creative and productive behavior, gamers create a culture of their own that rejects notions of texts as consumed objects.

Post-Subculture: A More Complicated View

While *D&D* seems to fit neatly into the notion of a subculture (even a fandom), more current studies have challenged the binary between dominant consumer culture and the championed notion of non-consumer based subcultures. This critique has come both from sociology and cultural studies. The idea of post-subculture and post-subculture studies relates to the post-modernist concern with ideas being reduced to binary oppositions. Rupert Weinzierl and David Muggleton (2003) argue that "the subculture concept seems to be little more than a cliché, with its implications that both 'subculture' and the parent culture against which it is defined are coherent and homeogenous formations that can be clearly demarcated" (p. 7). People do seem to create categorizations for themselves and others; as I have noted, different types of gamers have been known to distinguish themselves from each other. However, a more critical look at any of these communities shows that they are far from homeogenous. For example, there are tabletop gamers who are more focused on combat and ones who are more focused on story and character. The same is true for computer gamers. Some Massively Multiplayer Online Role-Playing Game (MMORPG) gamers focus on the cooperative, team-building aspects of the game while others prefer to engage in player-versus-player combat. None of these communities are homogeneous; which is a limitation of looking at genre from the perspective of audience. Nevertheless, I argue that homogeneity is not necessary for coherence. TPRG players are able to bond together because of common interests and goals while still maintain diverse approaches to the game.

Earlier studies of subcultures tended to not only see these populations as homogenous but to herald their rejection of mainstream capitalist culture. Stahl (2003) explains that an early view of subculture was that it "took objects from the dominant culture and transformed their everyday naturalized meaning into something spectacular" (p. 27). We can see this view present in Jenkins (1992) early work on fandom, and despite *Textual Poachers* place as a key text in media studies, it has been challenged on this same ground. In their edited collection on fandom, Gray, Sandvoss, and Harrington (2007) explain that early fan studies were overtly political. They "sided with the tactics of fan audiences in their evasion of dominant ideologies, and set out to rigorously defend fan communities against their ridicule in the mass media and by non-fans" (p. 2). By doing so, scholars of fandom maintained the binary between fans (who were creative and rebellious) and mainstream culture (which was consumer-based and non-productive) (Gray et al., 2007, p. 3). As a result, fandom studies focused on those fans who participated in activities such as fan fiction and ignored other fans, particularly those who may seem to be more in line with dominant cultural ideologies (like sports fans) (Gray et al., 2007, p. 5).

Gray, Sandvoss, and Harrington (2007) explain that a second wave of fandom scholars has been more careful about falling into binary thinking and has sought to explicate fandom's role within the dominant, capitalist system. The work of Matt Hills (2002) falls in this category. Hills (2002) explains the paradox of studying fandom; that within it exists "both anticommercial ideologies and commodity-completist practices" (p. 28). Fans may follow a philosophy that resists consumerism, and many may engage with texts in a more productive manner but they nevertheless buy products. Many fans are collectors of specialized merchandise, and these fans may or may not be the same fans who also work to creatively produce texts of their own. In fact, Hills (2002) recognizes that some of those within the dominant power structures, particularly some TV producers, have come to recognize the value of fans and appealing to them (p. 36).

A part of this shift is also the shift of post-modernism: as we become an increasingly specialized society, the specialized niche audience of fans becomes increasingly important. A producer no longer has to appeal to every family watching prime time TV, but can focus on an audience that tunes in to a specialty cable channel to see a particular type of show. In addition, producers who are particularly popular with fans (such as Joss Whedon) have made moves to directly appeal to them. During the writer's strike of 2008, Whedon released "Dr. Horrible's Sing-Along Blog" online to fans, free of charge. While it later was released as a DVD as well as a soundtrack and other products, the initial video was shown without financial gain. In addition, fans were asked to participate by sending in their own themed videos, some of which were then released as special features on the DVD.

This sort of shift to appeal to fans and involve them more directly in the development of more mainstream texts has been a focus of what Gray,

Sandvoss, and Harrington (2007) call third wave fandom scholarship. This wave involves a broadening of perspective to include "a wide range of different audiences reflecting fandom's growing cultural currency" (p. 8). While Jenkins's (1992) study may already seem somewhat dated in light of these new views on fandom, some of the ideas expressed in *Textual Poachers* and throughout Jenkins work are not necessarily incompatible with this more post-modern view of fandom. In particular, I would argue that it is not fandom that has changed as much as it is mainstream culture. The way that fans interact with texts has become more acceptable, and even mainstream. This sort of response to texts is not new. Fandom did not originate with the Internet, or even with television. Pearson (2007), for example, studies fans of Sherlock Holmes, Shakespeare, and Bach. Yet, Internet technologies have furthered fandom in a way that was previously unfathomable. Although it is problematic to assume coherence among audience groups, it seems safe to say that with the Internet and social networking, dominant culture has shifted to interact more directly with texts. It is not only fans who now Twitter or update Facebook status messages while watching a favorite TV show, or even something as mainstream as the presidential debates or the Super Bowl. More often these practices also relate directly back to the mainstream. Shows, particularly news shows and reality TV shows, may ask audiences to go online and vote on issues while they are watching. While not practiced by every viewer or every demographic within the audience, engaging with texts in a more active manner is becoming more mainstream. Fan culture may, to an extent, still exist as a subculture yet more and more, mainstream culture is becoming participatory.

The Rise of Gaming in Popular Culture

As we remember from chapter 2, *D&D* served as an antecedent genre for many computer games. However, as computer games have become more and more common, the perception of gamers has moved from that of a subculture to mainstream culture. This shift has been well documented by scholars. Dovey and Kennedy (2006) explain in their book *Game Cultures* that "in the past a taste for fantasy literature, comics, *Dungeons and Dragons* role-play and technological gadgets all marked the subject as outside dominant 'respectable' taste cultures" (p. 76). They found that these particular interests were common among early computer game designers and that as they made gaming into big business, the view of the game designer shifted to be in the center of dominant culture rather than on the sidelines (Dovey and Kennedy, 2006, p. 76). There is no doubt that computer gaming has transformed the way that gaming is perceived in popular culture. It now permeates our lives, from simple games like *Bookworm* on a cell phone, to exercising on the Wii Fit, to fully immersive MMORPGs like *World of Warcraft*. However, just because gaming has become mainstream does not mean that all modes and genres of games are equally accepted. Although certain homogenous groups may assert power, mainstream culture is no more homogenous than a subculture.

We need look no farther than the academic literature on gaming to see that tabletop games, which are often all thought to be synonymous with *D&D*, continue to be labeled in more marginal terms. From Murray's (1997) slap at "12-year olds playing *D&D*" to the more subtle metanarrative of progress found in scholarship on computer gaming, there is a clear move to position *D&D* as earlier, more primitive than computer gaming. Dovey and Kennedy (2006), for example, spend some time establishing the connection between game designers and their childhood love of *D&D* (possibly without intent) to establish it as a less mature game that inspires children to go on to better and more mature games. While it is very possible that many designers (and others) were exposed to *D&D* as teens or children and did not continue to play as adults, there are countless others who have kept the hobby even as new technology has emerged. Again, an antecedent genre is not necessarily less advanced than the genres the draw upon it.

Furthermore, there have been a great number of advances in games that are not computer-mediated, including TRPGs. For example, the d20 system for TRPGs that emerged in 2000 has changed and improved the game mechanics behind role-playing.[1] The system simplifies rolling dice in TRPGs so that a 20-sided die is used for the majority of rolls. Wizards of the Coast viewed this move as a response to solidify the fading TRPG market in the early 1990s by standardizing TRPGs with, then, varying methods for play (www.wizards.com). This move also is significant for the relationship it established between Wizards of the Coast, who controls *D&D,* and other game design companies. While there was skepticism in the companys' choice to trademark the d20 system, Wizards of the Coast provided the System Reference Document (SRD), and the Open Gaming License (OGL) to "allow royalty free, nonexclusive use of the game system at the heart of *Dungeons and Dragons* by anyone who wishes to do so, for both commercial and noncommercial works" (www.wizards.com) This move to standardize systems and share among gaming companies is a far cry from TSR, Inc.'s notorious reputation for litigious pursuits. The earlier owners of *D&D* were known for pursuing even the smallest copyright infringement, especially in the later years as the company was beginning to fail.

Despite a shift in the traditional business model, *D&D* fans still gather in traditional consumer spaces, such as stores. As Fine (1983) notes, it is important for fans to be able to connect with one another, and because TRPGs are played in person, there must be physical places where these connections can take place. Two main sites exist for TRPG fans to connect with others. There is the local gaming store and the gaming convention. Although these sites are ultimately designed for profit, they also function against dominant consumer trends. Local gaming stores are very rarely chain stores. While most stores exist mainly for shopping (the backbone of consumer activity) gaming stores are sites for gamers to hang out, meet each other, and play games. Some gaming stores may charge membership fees, but many allow players to game there for free. They rely on the purchase of products needed for the games, such as dice, rule books, or even snacks, but do not charge gamers simply to be there and game. In addition, gaming stores often hold tournaments and special events for players to participate in for prizes. These prizes can be provided by the gaming store or from the larger gaming company. For example, Wizards of the Coast holds worldwide game days when new products are released. At these days, participating gaming stores get modules specially released for the event as well as prices and other sample products.[2]

Conventions are another gathering place for gamers. The largest of these conventions is actually the birthplace of *D&D*, GenCon. GenCon was created by Gygax in 1967 and has been an annual gathering place for gamers ever since (www.gencon.com). Originally GenCon was for war gaming enthusiasts, and this is where Gygax met up with Arneson to hear about his new approach to gaming. Today, GenCon is the brand name associated with multiple conventions that take place worldwide. However, the most well known of these is currently held each August in Indianapolis and boasts 27,000 attendees each year (www.gencon.com). Their website describes GenCon as "a consumer and trade experience dedicated to gaming culture and community." With a four-day pass to the convention costing approximately $75, the convention gaming experience seems to be slightly more commercial than the local gaming store that may allow gamers to congregate for free. In addition to gaming, GenCon has vendors who sell gaming products, an art show, a writers' symposium, and other special events. Players do have the chance to play games and to purchase products; however, they also have opportunities that are not as readily available in consumer culture, such as interacting with authors and game designers. For example, game designer Monte Cook held a session at Gen-Con 2009 titled "Designing Dungeons with Monte Cook." In addition, gamers and game designers can interact in numerous online forums. Gen-Con has its own message boards, as does Wizards of the Coast. These boards also often post updates from conventions for those players that cannot attend in person. Although fans go to these locations to spend money on gaming, they also go to game, to meet game designers, and to connect with others. GenCon is focused exclusively on gaming, but other conventions include gamers along side other fannish activities.

How Fans Interact with Texts

Although post-modernism has lead to a flattening of binary oppositions, I would still argue that some of the original claims about subcultures and fandom apply to the culture surrounding the TRPG. As I have explained, I do not believe that all *D&D* players are socially marginalized or that they play *D&D* in order to rebel directly against cultural norms. However, the text created during a TRPG session is still far less consumable than a text created by most videogames. There is a difference between games that can be continued, such as TRPGs, MMORPGs, or even simulation games such as *The Sims* and computer games that reach the point where all quests have been completed, the entire map has been explored, and the player can go no further. The later products have been consumed, whereas the former can never be.

In addition, the way the audience interacts with any given text is variable. As third wave fandom studies have acknowledged, there are different types of fans. In fact, there is a good chance that everyone is a fan of something at some point in their lives. However, I would argue that all fans are not a part of the subculture of fandom. There still exists a subset of fans who respond to texts in certain ways. This distinction may be more problematic in our current cultural milieu, but we can't deny that however artificially constructed it is — there is a difference between sports fans with season tickets and TV fans who dress up as their favorite characters at a convention.[3] Socially, these groups are not equal, nor is their involvement with the object of their fandom the same. A sports fan who simply attends games may be no different than a TV fan who tunes in weekly to watch the series. Each may hold a certain level of participation, but as that participation becomes more and more involved, fans move more and more toward the fringes of mainstream culture. What we might be able to argue is that a sports fan who engages actively in a fantasy football league might be similar to a *Star Trek* fan who plays the *Star Trek* role-playing game. Both of these fans go beyond the act of participating by tuning in. What I am arguing for, then, is a definition of fandom that is based not on interests but on the way that audiences engage with texts. Fandom, in the sense I mean it here, consists of those fans who Dovey and Kennedy (2006) call "prosumers," those who are "the consumer as producer" (p. 15). They do not watch a show, read a book, or play a game and simply move on to the next episode or the next show. Instead, they take what they have consumed and expand on it through writing, creative game play, art, or interaction with others. Thus, fans may be involved to a lesser or greater degree in this subculture of fandom.

This difference can be seen in gaming as well. There are gamers who quickly run through a game to pass the time and there are those that actively engage in the worlds, characters, and stories created by games. New games such as *World of Warcraft* have certainly allowed players more of an opportunity to engage actively and creatively with the text of the game; however, even earlier games allowed for a more fannish response. *Doom*, which was created in 1993, included a game editor for players to make their own changes (Dovey and Kennedy, 2006, p. 14). In fact, many games now include the opportunity for the player to create a map or scenario. Even those that don't have built in options for modifications no doubt have hacker followings that go against the intended use of the game to make their own changes and cheats. In addition, gamers post walkthroughs online where they explain all the different moves and possibilities to beat the different in-game challenges. Regardless of the degree that a particular genre or medium affords a productive response, there will always be an audience that responds to a text by engaging with it in a more productive way. In keeping with Jenkins (1992) exploration of fandom, we might call this productive response a "fannish" response. It may be that those who desire this sort of interaction are more drawn to texts that more easily afford it, such as TRPGs or MMORPGs, but the response can be found in relation to any type of text.

Even though the TRPG may attract those who desire to interact with texts in this productive manner, it is, again, misleading to think of this audience as homogenous. Even within the Sorpraedor group, Nick ran a fairly standard fighter character and was focused on making his character better for combat, while Mary actively engaged in her own character's storyline outside of normal gaming time. Nick was more of a consumer of the game; he was there to fight a monster, gain a level, and move on. Mary was there to create her own story; one that the majority of the group did not even become privy to. However, I am hesitant to call Mary a fan of *D&D* and Nick not. In fact, Nick had a stronger loyalty to *D&D* as a gaming system than Mary, who was interested in playing TRPGs in any system. Nick also was more actively a purchaser of *D&D* merchandise. He was more familiar with the many different rules, character classes, and monsters from the rule books. Mary was far less concerned with these particulars and only owned the basic essentials for playing the game. In terms of belonging to a subculture, neither Nick nor Mary attended conventions, frequented gaming message boards, or were actively engaged outside of the Sorpraedor group with gaming culture. When Mary went to law school and Nick had another baby, these concerns took precedent over gaming and were reasons for them to leave the group.

Are Mary and Nick typical *D&D* fans? It is difficult to define what might be typical, although it is easier to do so in terms of community demographics than style of play. While Fine (1983) was much better able to define the small subculture that existed in 1979, it is far more difficult collect data on the typical player when the culture is now so widespread. However, the Wizards of the Coast market survey gives us some insight into what might be more typical now than at the time of Fine's study. Fine outlines several characteristics of gamers. Some of these are demographics such as age and sex. According to Fine, in 1979, it was rare to find a *D&D* player over the age of 35; young teens were far more common (Fine, 1983, p. 39). Wizards of the Coast found that by the late 1990s, 34 percent of tabletop gamers were between the ages of 25 and 35, while 23 percent were between the ages of 12 and 15 (Dancey 2000). These statistics show that *D&D* is not only maintaining its audience, it is still recruiting new members. In terms of sex, Fine (2001) estimated that only 3.8 percent of the DMs at GenCon in 1979 were female (p. 41). Based on an interview with Gary Gygax, he estimated that only 10–15 percent of the total market at the time was female (Fine, 1983, p. 41). This number has increased some, and Wizards of the Coast estimated that 21 percent of their 2000 market was female (Dancey 2000). Women seem to have become more involved in TRPGs, but the dominant market still appears to be male. Neither Fine nor Dancey show any statistics on ethnicity or race. However, Fine (1983) also looked beyond demographics in defining the typical gamer. He found that most gamers believed themselves to have active imaginations, were highly educated, and were interested in sci-fi, fantasy, or history (p. 47).[4] These statistics may give a picture of the diversity (or lack thereof) in terms of the demographics of a subculture, but they do very little to help define the different ways that *D&D* fans interact with texts. Thus, we must look further in order to answer the question of whether or not Nick and Mary are typical *D&D* fans.

A Typology of Fans

When confronted with the dual nature fans as consumers and producers, Hills (2002) asks if the contradiction can ever be resolved. He says that "the best we can hope for is a theoretical approach to fandom which can *tolerate* contradiction without seeking to close it down prematurely" (p. 29). In this vein, I propose a series of traits to help define a typology of fandom audiences. These traits are to be used as sliding scales rather than binaries. They have been developed initially with the gamer fan in mind, but I believe they may be applicable to other fans as well. Further research is needed in order to determine which traits might be more dominant in TRPG fans, but I believe we can safely say that there will be fans at all positions along the spectrum.

The first trait is the fan as *producer* versus the fan as *consumer*. As Hills (2002) notes, most fans are both producers and consumers, yet, I argue that they are most likely to fall on one end of this scale more clearly than another. Fans who consume focus on very actively reading or watching their fandom. Thus, the word "consumer" may be a misnomer in that it evokes the idea of passivity. A consumer is actually quite active; however, that activity involves quickly moving through a variety of texts rather than using a text as a springboard for other activities. Furthermore, consumer often has a negative connotation, often because of the binaries set up in fandom studies. However, I argue that those who approach their fandom with a more consumerist perspective are not less creative than productive fans, they simply interact with their object of fandom in a different way. Within the TRPG community, a consumer fan would be the kind to buy all the rule books, have a great deal of knowledge about the different types of monsters in the game, remember all the different specialty equipment that might be acquired, and study all the traits that might eventually be added to a character. This alone may take a great deal of time and skill; however, the fan who memorizes rules may be less willing to shift them or produce their own rules. The TRPG consumer may run out and grab the next new module to play through it with a gaming group. This fan may or may not also be productive as well; however, their focus is more on consumption of goods related to their fandom. A productive fan is less interested in the details of the gaming product and more interested in the way they can use that product for their own creative ends. These fans may be more interested in creative additions to their characters, such the gnome in the Sorpraedor campaign who wanted a talking bunny for a hat, than with beating the next quest. In the TRPG, the productive fan will be most interested in the story and character creation that comes from the gaming session rather than the details of the rules from the books.

Another trait is whether a fan is more *loyal* or more *open*. By this, I intend to distinguish between fans who are particularly loyal to a text and its canon and those who have broader interests. Nick, for example, would be a loyal fan of *D&D*. He played *D&D* for years, through multiple editions, and is likely to continue playing *D&D* over other choices. Mary, however, would be an open fan. For her the TRPG was the vehicle for her productive creativity, and it did not matter whether that TRPG was *D&D* or whether it was a part of a different system in a different setting. It may seem that loyal fans are more likely to be consumers while open fans are more likely to be productive. However, that is not always the case. For example, one can envision the difference between a loyal *Star Trek* fan who writes a good deal of *Star Trek* fan fiction, but who is concerned with the way that fan fiction fits with the canon of the *Star Trek* universe and whether or not their portrayal of the character is true to the original work. This player is productive, creating his or her own texts, but also loyal. Contrast this with a fan fiction writer who prefers to write a story that features a love affair between Captain Kirk from *Star Trek* and Princess Leia from *Star Wars*. This fan would also be productive — engaging in a creative way with texts and creating their own. However, this fan is less concerned about one particular fandom and is open to crossing between fandoms. As a result, they are probably also less concerned with keeping canon.

The final trait I propose is the *community-oriented* fan versus the *individual* fan. Again, this is a sliding scale. TRPGs, for example, must have a community of sorts since they must be played with a group. Thus, they may not attract fans completely on the individual end of the scale. However, there are degrees to which the player is involved within the larger gaming community. A TRPG fan may be social with one steady gaming group or he or she my attend conventions and meet a number of players. Likewise, a more community-oriented gamer might participate in online forums talking about *D&D*. The same can be said for other fan-based cultures. Whether or not fans attend conventions or connect online with others, or whether they only write stories for themselves will determine their position in relation to this trait.

The Future of Fan Studies

The criticism against early studies that saw fandom and subcultures as groups that responded against the dominant consumer culture are not completely unfounded. However, current studies should move to a more audience-centered view of fandom and of gaming. A given fan may consume texts by purchasing new modules and may choose to focus on detailed rules rather than character creation. Yet, that same fan may ally him or herself with the subculture of gaming by attending conventions and interacting directly with game designers on a message board. There are not only many aspects to fandom, there are many traits that vary in any given fan.

In general, we might be able to say that participatory culture — culture where we produce and consume, where we participate more actively with texts — is becoming more mainstream. It is becoming harder to separate a sub culture from a mainstream one. Nevertheless, we must also acknowledge that not all current media or entertainment industries allow for the sort of relationship between user and text, between author and reader, gamer and designer, as does the TRPG. While fan fiction may have increased dramatically in popularity, there is nothing within the medium of television or film that prompts viewers to interact productively. According to Winkler (2006), "gaming requires one to engage with the game and with other players, thereby simultaneously mediating and constructing one's experience," which he sees as a key difference between the gaming and the film industry (p. 151). Furthermore, Winkler (2006) argues that the computer gaming industry is different from the TRPG industry because it is more often run by large corporations and the games are sold at large chain retailers (p. 143).[5] Even with a blurred line, TRPGs can still be seen more as a subculture than as a dominant culture. In addition, the form itself requires players to be more productive than other forms. Even if Fletch was a big consumer in the world of Sorpraedor, buying up all the best items from the *Dungeons Master's Guide* rule book and taking all the best skills, Nick was still the creator; the producer behind the scenes of Fletch. While some texts appear more static and less likely to receive a fannish response, there has always been an audience that takes a more productive and creative approach to these texts. Likewise, there are texts, like the TRPG, that have always encouraged a fannish response to begin with.

9

Conclusions, Definitions, Implications, and Limitations

A central concern in this book has been one of definition. With so little scholarship currently available on the tabletop role-playing game (TRPG), we must first ask how we should define and study it. The question is a complex one. I have shown that TRPGs cannot be subsumed under the study of other games, particularly computer games, nor should they occupy a position of prior and inferior text. As computer games continue to evolve as a medium, they too need to be studied on their own terms. Even computer games that might have been based on *Dunegons and Dragons (D&D)*, such as *Baldur's Gate* and *Dungeons and Dragons Online,* have significant differences from both the original TRPG genre and from each other. Yet, the justification for the study each of these texts is the same as the justification Aarseth (1997) gives for studying adventure games:

> They present an alternative mode of discourse; a different type of textual pleasure. By investigating this we may be able to extract knowledge of a more general kind, which may tell us something about discourse itself and which we could not have learned from our previous, more restricted horizon [Aarseth, 1997, p. 109].

Even genres that die out, such as the text-based adventure game or the gamebook, at one time offered us a new form of discourse. These texts still offer us the chance to learn more about the progression of genres and how texts influence each other. Too often we focus on the newest example of a genre, the latest technological advance, and we forward a myth that each new change constitutes a more advanced form of discourse, a new literacy that requires us to change our methods for studying texts. Our theories of authorship, readership, and texts in general suddenly seem to fall short, and we seek new methods, new theories to explain each new phenomenon. While advances in technology and the emergence of new genres and new media may indeed challenge our current definitions and call for new theories, I argue that these changes are neither as extreme nor as sudden as we might imagine. In fact, we find that our notions of authorship, of interactive narrative, of genre, are all challenged by the TRPG, a genre that is neither new nor makes use of digital technology.[1] D&D, the first TRPG, began in 1974 at the very onset of post-modernism and well before the Internet offered possibilities for massive collaborative storytelling. What strikes me about Murray's (1998) text as well as Ryan's (2003) study of virtual reality is the unyielding desire and hope that new technologies will afford us opportunities for interaction, authorship, and agency that I see already available in forms like the TRPG. While digital environments continue to progress toward games with increased opportunities for building social communities and authoring both stories and storyworlds — opportunities that seem particularly present in genres such as the Massively Multiplayer Online Role-Playing Game (MMORPG) — we must not be so focused on our futuristic utopian visions that we forget to look at our own backyards. We might say that this book has been a study of Kansas, not of Oz. This perspective offers both new insight and new questions. Like any study, it is also limited. As I conclude this book, I wish to take a closer look at both the implications and limitations of the work that has been done here and the work that is left to do.

New Definitions

Throughout the course of this book, I have compared TRPGs to scholarship about traditional narratives, traditional games, gamebooks, cybertexts, fan fiction, make-believe games, and virtual reality. Of all these genres, TRPGs fit most closely with make-believe games in the form of oral discourse, with computer role-playing games (CRPGs) in terms of the gaming rules, and with fan fiction in terms of purpose. As my model in chapter 5 shows, the levels of interaction in a TRPG, from off-record to narrative speech, are analogous to those Cook-Gumprez (1992) identified in make-believe play. To these types of speech, my model also added the game sphere to account for the more complex interaction surrounding game rules, such as dice rolling. Like make-believe, though, the form of the TRPG is one where players frequently shift among multiple levels of discourse. This structure is far more open than the tree structure found in adventure games, gamebooks, and even some videogames. Because some

CRPGs directly adapt *D&D* rules to a digital environment, we see some strong similarities between videogames and TRPGs. These similarities primarily have to do with the gaming rules, such as the way characters gain experience and level up, or the mechanism of hit points to keep track of how much damage a character has received in battle. However, in purpose, the TRPG is perhaps more closely related to fan fiction. Both gamers and fan fiction writers engage with popular culture in order to create their own texts. The sense of agency and authorship that players feel is one of the main reasons they cite for participating in TRPGs. All of these genres have commonalities with the TRPG, and with the level of intertextuality gamers engage in, this comes as no surprise. Some TRPG players have become computer game designers, some write fan fiction, and most have active imaginations. However, despite the connections between the TRPG and other genres, players keep coming back to the TRPG. They continue to play it while still participating in other games and other genres. Thus, a definition of the TRPG must stand on its own. It must be defined by its own characteristics and not simply on its relation to other texts. This definition is one that many scholars have failed to articulate, who instead never move past comparison. Most studies focus on another type of text with only a quick mention of the TRPG as an antecedent genre. Others, such as Hammer (2007), deal specifically with role-playing games (RPGs), but do not separate TRPGs from CRPGs, live action role-plays (LARPs) or other types of role-play. Instead, Hammer (2007) argues that three elements are present in every type of role-playing — collaboration, narration and improvisation (p. 69–70). Certainly these are important aspects of the TRPG, but they are not its only defining features.

Mackay's (2001) definition fits the TRPG as a genre of its own, separate from other types of games.[2] His notion of the TRPG as "an *episodic* and *participatory* story-creation *system*" (p. 4) accurately describes both the form and the purpose of the TRPG as a genre, that includes a group of players using the gaming system to produce a narrative. However, it does not account for the rhetorical purpose that sets this communicative event apart from other rhetorical responses. If we view exigence and genre in terms of rhetorical theory, there must be a social, rather than artistic, motive for engaging in the TRPG. It is only by looking at the view of genres as rhetorical — the view of Miller (1984), Swales (1990), and Russell (1997) — that we are able to account for the on going success of the TRPG; and social motive must be key to our new definition.

I thus propose expanding on Mackay's (2001) definition. In my view, the TRPG can be defined as *a type of game/game system that involves collaboration between a small group of players and a gamemaster through face-to-face social activity with the purpose of creating a narrative experience.*[3] By game/game system I wish to convey the importance of the system of rules behind a TRPG. While role-playing can exist in a number of settings, without these rules, that role-play does not consist of a role-playing *game.* Childhood make-believe, for example, might be role-play that creates a narrative experience, but it is not a role-playing game. Even if participants in such role-play activities decide on rules for their activity, there is not a gaming system that guides this freeform role-play as there is in the TRPG. A key part of this system, that must be present in order to qualify as a TRPG, is the presence of a gamemaster. The gamemaster may be referred to as a Dungeon Master (DM), a storyteller, a referee, or something else, but is always the person who has the final say within a gaming session. In addition, the game must be primarily collaborative rather than competitive. The players may seek to defeat monsters and challenges presented by the DM, but they work together to do so. Likewise, players may sometimes be at odds (as was the case with David and Whisper) but the point of this confrontation is not ultimately competition. Alex and I pursued the conflict between our characters because we both enjoyed playing them the way we felt they would act, not because we wanted to beat the other player at the game. One could even argue that the conflict between Whisper and David shows how Alex and I worked collaboratively to tell an interesting story. Finally, in order to fit the genre of the *tabletop* RPG, face-to-face social interaction must exist. This interaction may be supplemented by online activities (as it was with the Sorpraedor group), but as we have seen, this in-person social interaction is a key reason players present for engaging in the TRPG. The medium of face-to-face interaction also allows for a degree of narrative agency that is currently not easily attainable in computer-mediated games, and this agency adds the narrative experience players enjoy. Although my definition is similar to Mackay's (2001) definition, I focus on the narrative experience rather than narrative form. As we have seen in chapters 4 and 5, the form of the TRPG may not fit with some definitions of narrative, but the game, nevertheless, creates the experience for the players of participating in a narrative. This definition, thus, allows us to see the ways in which TRPGs differ from other genres not only in terms of form but also in terms of rhetorical purpose.

Limitation of Genre: Different Player Perspectives

Although I have defined the TRPG in rhetorical terms, it is important to note the limitations of genre theory, particularly when it begins to focus on audience rather than form. As Russell (1997) notes, the same texts may function as different genres depending on the rhetorical purpose and audience that they address (p. 518). He offers *Hamlet* as an example. When used as a script by actors, the rhetorical purpose is different from when literary scholars analyze the play or it is taught in a literature classroom. Each instance involves a different activity system, and therefore forms a different genre (Russell, 1997, p. 518). At first glance, the idea of gamers who focus on different aspects within the same game seems reminiscent of Russell's example of *Hamlet*, functioning as a different genre within different activity systems. However, do these differences in game play really represent different systems? Are there really unified communities with unified style of play that can be used to define genres? Certainly that is possible. For example, MMORPGs sometimes have an option for competitive rather than cooperative play. In his analysis, Kelly (2004) defines the group of player verses player (PvP) gamers as an entirely different community than regular MMORPG gamers. However, my experience with TRPGs shows that different types of players exist even within one group. One player in a group may be enjoy acting out his or her character while another may just want to fight battles (what is commonly called "hack and slash" gaming). Is it possible for each player in a group of six to experience the game as a different subgenre? At what point does the concept of genre cease to be useful?

Fine (1983) notes that "*D&D* players can be divided into two groups, those who want to play the game and those who want to play it as a fantasy novel" (p. 207). From my research, including the descriptions given by other gamers, the desire to play TRPGs as fantasy novels seems to be the force that has kept this genre alive in spite of computer games that are far more accessible and may even use the *D&D* gaming rules and structure. This return to more basic storytelling elements has made the White Wolf games popular, and the changes in the 3rd edition of *D&D* confirms the popularity of this way of playing TRPGs.[4] However, it should be noted that the genre conventions discussed in this book may not fit every TRPG gaming experience and that different styles of play may affect the way players experience the genre.

Several taxonomies are currently used by gamers to explain the differences in styles of play. In fact, it is a common topic on gaming forums to form theories that explain the different styles of play. One of the most common theories is the Threefold Model that came from a series of online discussions. In July 1997, Mary Kuhner came up with the term the "three-fold model" to explain the model that emerged from the rec.games.frp. advocacy forum in the mid–1990s (Kim, 2008). John Kim offers an explanation of this model on the www.darkshire.net website, last updated in 2008.[5] The model suggests three types of game play — the dramatist, the simulationist, and the gamist. A dramatist is someone who is primarily interested in a good story and the forward progression of a narrative. A simulationist is most concerned with a realistic story, where characters act in a way that makes sense within the framework of the storyworld. The primary difference between these two types of players is that the drama-tist will use whatever rules or character building tools are available through the game in order to create a better story, whereas a simulationist will pre-fer to make decisions based solely on the reality of the storyworld, pre-tending to ignore the game world completely. A gamist, on the other hand, will be most interested in meeting challenges in the game, whether those are puzzles to solve or combats to win (Kim, 1998). This model has become popular, and in fact, there is a wealth of "RPG theory" such as this, writ-ten by gamers and game designers that is available freely online on web-sites such as www.darshire.net or www.rpg.net.

Dancey's (2000) market survey uses a similar model for looking at different gaming styles. By asking gamers to rate a series of qualities on a 1–5 scale, Wizards of the Coast developed a model that divides gamers into four categories: the character actor, the storyteller, the thinker, and the power gamer (see figure 4). Game designer Sean K. Reynolds reported on this model on his website in 2003, and explains the gamer types as fol-lows.

Character actors enjoy the theatrical aspects of the game and mak-ing decisions that are fitting for the way they think their character would actually behave. Thus, character actors seem most analogous to simula-tionists in the threefold model. Storytellers are most concerned about the progression of the narrative and what will happen next. They initially seem similar to the dramatists of the threefold model, but Reynolds (2003) explains that they "will look for a non-rules answer to inconsistencies or anachronisms in the game experience," thus, there is still an aspect of sim-ulationist here. The thinker may like to find clues in the game or the best ways to maximize their character, making heavy use of sourcebooks. Finally, the power gamer prefers a combat-oriented style and usually plays a character to whom they have little attachment. Thinkers and power

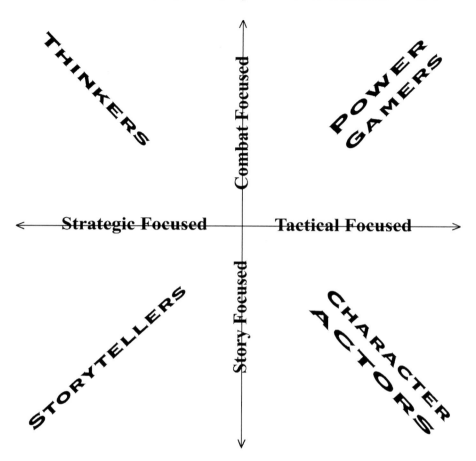

Figure 4: Role-playing game players (adapted from Sean K. Reynolds with permission)

gamers come closest to the gamist perspective, both drawing heavily on the challenging aspects of game play rather than the narrative aspects of the story and characters. Dancey's (2000) market survey showed the market fairly evenly divided among these game types, with approximately 22 percent in each category and another 12 percent falling somewhere in the middle (as cited in Reynolds, 2003).

With these different gaming styles, it is tempting to say that the TRPG no longer represents one genre, but has splintered into multiple genres based on different gaming styles. However, I am hesitant to draw this conclusion because my research shows that the majority of participants still give the same general reasons for playing TRPGs. In addition, because different kinds of gamers often exist within the same gaming group, the type of game play seems specific to individuals rather than to texts. For a text to be a different genre, it needs to be recognized as such by a group rather than an individual. In Russell's (1997) example, groups in different activity systems use the same text differently but there is still coherence among those groups. It is unlikely that one student in a literature seminar will see *Hamlet* as a script and come to class performing it while another will see it as literature to read for a homework assignment. These students may all interpret the work differently, but they will read it as the same genre because they are reading it within the same context, just as Stanley Fish's (1982) linguistics seminar recognized the names on the board as a homework assignment and his poetry seminar interpreted them as a poem.

Although I maintain that the TRPG represents one genre, despite multiple styles of play, I must acknowledge the way that my definition of this genre may be influenced by my own style of play. As a player I fall clearly on the half of the graph consisting of character actor and storyteller. One of the reasons the Sorpraedor campaign ran so well was that the majority of the players were interested in a style supporting storytelling and character acting.[6] This style combined simulationist and dramatist elements and, thus, I may have overstated the role of narrative in TRPGs at large. While Nick seemed to represent a more gamist perspective, most likely that of a thinker, I was unfortunately unable to follow up with him for the type of in-depth interview I conducted with Mark. While the blog postings and survey responses I've incorporated here support the idea that narrative is overall an important aspect of the TRPG, the gamist perspective is underrepresented and should be taken into account more in future research.

In addition to the various types of players, as I have noted, there are various ways to play a TRPG, from an individual session in a game store or at a convention to ongoing home campaigns such as Sorpraedor. These different types of gaming session may lend themselves to different types of play. In addition, not all gaming sessions will be successful, in that they will not all meet the needs of the players or create a narrative experience. For example, my experience as a player in a one-time TRPG at the NC State Game Day involved a different method of playing TRPGs. As I previously mentioned, this game did not immerse me. I cared little for the characters (which were pre-generated) or the setting and, quite frankly, was anxious for the game to end. Early in the session I offered a suggestion that might have quickly achieved the goal that had been set out for our party, but it was frowned upon, and the DM did not allow it to succeed. Mackay (2001) also found that TRPGs played in the context of the gaming convention were often more restrictive and adhered more closely to the rule books than on going gaming groups (p. 102). He explains his own frustration in not connecting with these convention-based gamers and mentions that it is only when the same group of players meets with the same characters several times across conventions that players begin to create the sorts of narratives that he sees in longer lasting gaming groups (Mackay, 2001, p. 102). Both Mackay (2001) and I struggled with convention role-playing because we came to it with the expectation of creating a narrative through social interaction. Instead, the games we encountered were more gamist in their orientation, where the goal seemed to be to exert skill in combat and defeat the monsters rather than to create an in-depth story. Nevertheless, my data from the Role-Players Gaming Association (RPGA) suggests that gamers who continually attend these sessions are able to add to a more communal narrative because reported results influence the design of additional gaming modules (C. Broadhurst, personal communication, July 1, 2009). Thus, I argue that while convention gaming may not completely satisfy my own expectations for a narrative experience, it may still be seen as such by those gamers who participate in this arena.

Finally, I have done here what many genre studies do — taken one instance of a genre as representative of the genre as a whole. While survey data again contributed a more varied perspective to the study, the majority of this book has offered *D&D* as the exemplar of the TRPG genre. To some extent, this move is justified in that *D&D* was clearly the first example of the TRPG genre and is arguably still the most recognizable and popular TRPG. However, it is important to note that multiple other examples of the TRPG exist, and a further exploration of these games is necessary in future research. In addition, the Sorpraedor campaign may not be particularly representative of *D&D* campaigns. In fact, by the end of the campaign, Scott had begun not only to create his own setting but also more of his own gaming system. It has been suggested to me by other *D&D* players that the simulationist approach our Sorpraedor group preferred is better suited to other TRPGs, and perhaps this is why Scott ended up modifying as many of the original rules as he did. Nevertheless, Dancey's (2000) data shows that character actors and storytellers are equal in number to power gamers and thinkers, and one wonders if the gamers who fall more in line with these styles are more likely to modify the rules as our group did. It would also be interesting to see if certain types of gamers tend to gravitate toward different TRPG systems, if storytellers and method actors prefer diceless systems over more combat-oriented play. While I have offered an initial analysis of the TRPG as a genre, there are still many points that need further investigation.

Future Directions for Narrative, Game, and Rhetorical Theory

Throughout this book, I have argued that TRPGs defy certain binary oppositions. They are neither wholly games nor wholly narratives but use structures of both games and narratives. They are neither wholly immersive nor wholly interactive but, rather, both immersive and interactive. They both involve consumerism (buying rule books, etc) and rebellion against it (creating stories with no physical form). They complicate our understanding of the relationship between authors and audiences, and our definitions of these terms. Furthermore, the study of the TRPG challenges our disciplinary boundaries as such work does not clearly fall under the purview of any one disciplinary framework. I thus offer some suggestions for different disciplines based on the implications of my study.

For genre and media studies, I suggest further inquiry into the way that stories are formed across media. Jenkins has been a primary voice within media studies on fandom and its impact on culture. He joins with Janice Radway in criticizing "the tendency of academics to regard audiences as constituted by a particular text or genre rather than as 'free-floating' agents who 'fashion narratives, stories, objects and practices from myriad bits and pieces of prior cultural productions'" (as cited in Jenkins, 1992, p. 36). While stories may be shaped by media, audiences exist outside of media and create their view of texts from experiences in multiple media. As we have seen in chapter 3 with *The Temple of Elemental Evil*, the same story is often re-envisioned in multiple forms, from a tabletop module to a videogame to a novel. The story does change based on the affordance of the medium, but rather than bringing this story to a new audience each time, it is often the same audience that engages with these multiple versions. It is fans who are most likely to seek out multiple version of a text and who are most likely to build their own version. Future studies should focus more on how these texts work together to form the experience of a fan rather than how they work against each other.

For those in narrative studies, my study suggests the need to look at narrative as an experience rather than a form. As the study of narrative continues to expand beyond its structuralist origins, it is important to look at narrative not just as a cognitive framework, but as a social one. Rather than asking if a certain text is a narrative, we might shift the question to ask if a certain text offers the audience a narrative experience. And we might go on to define what such an experience might look like. In this case, I have shown that the structure of the TRPG incorporates multiple levels, which have varying degrees of narrativity. However, the immersion that players feel in the TRPG provides them with a narrative experience. When I hear players talk about their gaming sessions, I rarely hear them recounting the off-record speech and the conversation they had about the latest movie coming out. Instead, they tell tales of what happened in the gaming session — how they beat the monsters, how they found the clue they needed, how they saved the world from evil. The actual text of the TRPG session is ephemeral. It exists in the moment of face-to-face inter-action and then vanishes. Yet what is preserved are stories — write-ups like the Blaze Arrow narrative that show no signs of the complex interaction involved in creating it. While we could study these narratives that exist after the fact as we would any other story, I believe there is something to be gained by also studying the experience of collaboratively creating that narrative through game play.

Likewise, I believe game studies, as an emerging discipline, has much to gain by focusing on the experiences of the players rather than the structure of the game. A perspective that focuses on audience experience rather than formal characteristics will allow game studies scholars to bring in important theory from narrative studies and other disciplines while continuing to form a discipline of their own. It is possible to claim a unique status for games while still acknowledging their narrative characteristics. My study on the TRPG shows that they exist as their own genre, with their own form, but that they do not exist in a vacuum. TRPGs emerged from both a literary tradition and a game tradition and both draw from and influence fantasy literature as well as other types of games. Thus, I feel it is needlessly limiting for ludologists to study only videogames. This perspective does not fully account for the historical progression of games or for the many games that exist outside of computer-mediate environ-ments. While videogames may represent the most mainstream form of gaming, TRPGs as well as LARPing, board games, card games, and minia-ture wargaming all continue to be popular.

Finally, I offer some possible directions for research in my home dis-cipline of rhetoric and writing. Just as in games studies, I have seen a tendency here to focus on the way authorship has changed because of digital technology. I challenge us to look beyond this to texts like the TRPG which challenge views of authorship in media (like oral communication) that have always been within the purview of rhetorical studies. I do not feel that we should ignore the influence of digital environments, but too often I see us making assumptions that these are the only environments that challenge traditional views. In addition, the TRPG is a prime example of collaborative writing and although I have not dealt with it here, pedagogical applications are sure to arise from further studying of the way gamers work together and write collaboratively. As one of my survey participants explained, "Eventually, though, I began to want to tell a story with my characters, and as I blossomed into a writer, I found that telling a story using roleplaying media was what I most enjoyed doing." What potential do games have for developing the writing abilities of those involved, for making them "blossom" as writers? Furthermore, the TRPG offers an interesting opportunity for both technical and creative writing scholars to connect. Game designer Monte Cook calls TRPGs an "interesting mix of both technical writing and fiction." Although the modules he writes are designed for players to come up with a creative story, he notes that when actually writing the modules "you intentionally break all the rules they tell you in a creative writing class" (personal communication, June 30, 2009). Though I touched on this connection over the course of the book, it is one that merits further exploration.

Despite the lack of attention it has historically received from scholarly audiences, the TRPG is a text that offers a wealth of possibilities for study both within disciplinary traditions and in terms of interdisciplinary research. In fact, academic work is not all that different from playing a TRPG. We each work within our own disciplinary structures, our own rule books, if you will. We have both agency within and authorship over those frameworks, as we adjust the rules to best fit the stories we wish to advance. Our individual narratives fit together to form larger stories, and it is our need to tell these stories that drives us to continue researching and theorizing. While this analogy may take things a bit far, what I wish to convey as I close is the need for collaboration and for continued research. Mackay's (2001) study on the TRPG has been cited frequently, particularly his definition of role-playing. However, many of these later studies have appropriated Mackay's work to their own study of MMORPGs and computer games. While this potential exists, and these studies may offer important insight, they also represent the continued view that the TRPG is only valuable as a precursor to later games. Thus, the TRPG continues to occupy a marginal status within both society and academia. I have presented here one view of the TRPG as a genre and as a forum for narrative experience, but I am only one voice. What if a ludologist, a narratologist, a rhetorician, and a media specialist all came to the table to study the TRPG? What new insights would we discover on this culturally influential genre? Like the DM who presents a situation to her players and then asks for their contribution, I present to other scholars my current study, but then I turn and ask, "So, what do you do?" Where will you take the research from here?

Roll initiative.

Appendix: The Orc
Adventure at Blaze Arrow

This is a write up I did of two gaming sessions that took place in Jan-
uary–February 2003. I took detailed notes during the sessions, includ-
ing writing some dialogue down word for word. Other dialogue and
details I filled in as best I could from memory. I composed this tale
and posted it on the Sorpraedor Yahoo list on 3/18/03 as a synopsis for
my group members and to inform Mary, who was absent during these
sessions, what she had missed. I added a few clarifying remarks and
deleted a few bits of extraneous information for the present use.

How the Gang Defeated the Orc Army Through Cunning
and Diplomacy

The magistrate of Gateway had informed us that the outpost Blaze
Arrow had not been heard from in over a week. A new bastion of guards
had recently been sent there, but had never checked it. Considering all of
the talk of attacks along the borders, the magistrate was understandably
worried and sent us to investigate. Fletch, David and I headed in that
direction. Maureen vowed to catch up with us as she had some "personal"
business to attend to.

On our way out of Gateway, another ranger approached us. This one
was an elf who called himself Cuthalion. Given my past experience, I
wasn't keen on another elf, or another ranger, but Cuthalion soon proved
useful as he captured some wild birds for our dinner. David returned from
the hunt with bunnies, which may very well satisfy a halfling appetite, but
was not enough for the rest of us.

Other than a large ant snapping at us, our journey was uneventful.
The main path veered to the East, but we needed to continue across the

hills to Blaze Arrow. Concerned that Maureen would have trouble finding us if we went much further, we made camp and settled in to eat the feast our rangers had prepared.

Not long after we drifted off to sleep, we were disturbed by a caltrop being thrown into our camp. We readied our weapons and called out into the darkness, but there was no response. As David and the wolf crept out into the woods to check it out, Fletch was struck by a tickle. We heard the familiar giggle of Maureen.

"Maureen!" I exclaimed, "Don't scare us like that!"

Maureen sighed. "Would you all like some almonds? David?"

David grumbled, "You take the second watch. Now." He returned to his bedroll.

Maureen shrugged her shoulders and agreed to watch camp. So, we all snuggled back into bed, only to be awakened once more. Maureen had spied three figures in black robes approaching us. As David readied his sling, two arrows whizzed past Maureen and Cuthalion. The figure in the rear hurled a sack into the camp, which landed at my feet. I immediately began to investigate by poking it with my rapier. The sack seemed to be made from a fine cloak and was closed by gold-woven cord. I cut it open and two heads rolled out. I jumped back in shock ... it was the half-elven twins, Mirador and Mardowin! In addition to the heads were two hands tied to a long black arrow, and a scroll tube with the markings of Erbin, the god worshiped by those evil religious zealots we had encountered in Gateway. I wondered immediately what Maureen might be up to and grabbed the scroll tube and stuck it in my cloak. My thought was to see what it said before she did.

I found that Maureen had charged one of the assailants with her rapier, and he appeared to have fallen. By this time, Maureen and the others were chasing one of the other attackers, and I saw my opportunity to get some information without the others finding out. But Maureen must have had the same thought because she returned to the body as well. The guy was unconscious, so I sacrificed one of my healing potions in hopes of getting some useful information from him.

As he came through I challenged him, "Who sent you?"

He spat at me. Without hesitating, Maureen cut off his ear and asked again, "Who sent you?"

The prisoner glared at us, "You know who sent me — the one who will be your death."

Maureen went for his other ear, but I stopped her. After all, we needed him to be able to hear us. She cut off his finger instead and asked, "Why were you sent?"

"To deliver a warning. Had they wanted you dead, you would be dead."

"Did Thaddeus send you?" I asked, trying to make my connection between the mysterious man I encountered in Travensburg and the Obsidian Brotherhood, the underground group that we fought in Gateway.

He scowled, "Thaddeus is not my master."

"But you know him?" I prodded.

"Of course, I know him."

"So, who *is* your master?" Maureen proceeded.

"Soren. He will come for you." At which point the prisoner faded into unconsciousness. We decided to end his suffering, so I gave Maureen my dagger to slit his throat. Much to my shock, she also carved her initial in his chest.

We returned to camp to find Fletch still there. The rangers were still in pursuit of the enemy, and knowing what a powerful enemy it was, I decided it would best to warn them and sent Poe, my raven familiar, to tell them to come back to camp. Meanwhile, Maureen offered us a much-needed drink.

The rangers returned to camp and asked about the attacker we had pursued. We hadn't thought much about how the party would respond to our interrogation of him, so we quickly said that he had been taken care of. They asked if we had searched the body, and I admitted that we hadn't.

David immediately wanted to check it out. At which point, Maureen and I stood in his way and tried to convince him it was of little importance. But this only piqued his and Cuthalion's curiosity, and they seemed in none too good a mood to begin with. So, they went and searched the body and were quite unhappy to find him with an "M" carved into his chest.

They returned to camp and demanded to know who these attackers were, who the heads were, and what was going on. At this point I had no choice but to trust my new party members. Maureen and I explained who the Obsidian Brotherhood were and our various dealings with them. Maureen even showed the group her tattoo.

Cuthalion thought that perhaps the tattoo was a tracking device that had allowed the Obsidian Brotherhood to find us so easily. I recalled the snake tattoo that was on one of the members of the Brotherhood we had captured back in Gateway and how the tattoo had come alive and strangled him when we began questioning him. I decided to detect magic on the mark. The brand did indeed radiate magic for a second and then faded. As I detected the magic, the magic amulet I wear grew warm and throbbed but the sensation faded as the magic faded.

"It's definitely magic!" I exclaimed as I looked suspiciously at Maureen, "How do we know you're not a spy?" For that she did not have a very satisfying answer.

Cuthalion instructed us in ways of interrogating prisoners less violently and as he spoke, the nature of Maureen's actions began to disturb me, and I trusted her less and less.

I felt more uncomfortable with Maureen around. I figured she probably wasn't a willing spy but that the tattoo could very well be a scrying device and that she might inadvertently be allowing the enemy to hear or see us. So, I suggested privately to her that she return to town and seek out my magician friend, Ingie, to attempt to remove or deactivate the tattoo. She agreed. I sent Poe with her, instructing him to take her to Ingie and if anything went wrong to find Ingie or return to me.

In the morning, the rest of the party proceeded to Blaze Arrow. Now that Maureen and her possible spying device were gone, I relayed the rest of my adventures to my new friends. Then, as a show of honesty and good will, I whipped out the scroll tube and opened it in front of them for all to see. Unfortunately that didn't turn out to be such a good idea.

The scroll tube opened with a hiss. Inside, I found a scrap of very old parchment that crackled with age as I unrolled it. As soon as I looked at it, a flash of light came from the paper and struck each of us, and we heard the following words:

> A curse upon you all in the name of ERBIN! For your meddling, you have now been marked so that any follower of the great god will know you for what you are. When we find you, your death will be most exquisite. You will be dragged to our new temple when it is completed, and you will be punished in the name of ERBIN. We will find you when we are ready for your death, but if we find you or any of your party here in Gateway again, you will not live to regret it. So sayeth the high priest of ERBIN!

The voice and glow faded and both the scroll and the tube crumbled to powder.

Well, the party was not real happy that I had shared *that* bit of information with them, and there was a bit of bickering back and forth. I detected magic on us, and found that there had indeed been some sort of magic cast upon us, though it seemed of a more clerical nature than arcane. We decided there was not much to be done about it at that point and proceeded to Blaze Arrow.

We were nearly there when we came up a hill to see a bunch of orcs hiding in a grove of trees. I put two of them to sleep with a spell, and

Cuthalion shot arrows at them. Fletch also started attacking and killed several. David killed one. We noticed that the orcs had a symbol on their shields that looked like a bloody hand and Fletch identified them as a local tribe called "The Blood Fist Tribe."

David rode over the hill to find many more orcs and smoke coming over out of the Blaze Arrow tower. The halfling thought quickly, knowing he would be no match for so many large orcs, and used his spell power to entangle the lot of them.

Luckily, Cuthalion speaks orc and could communicate with them. First he insulted them, "You sylvan unicorns, what are you doing here?"

An orc responded, "Trying to get rid of Skullbash." Fletch recognized this as the name of one of the other local orc tribes.

"Why are you taking out Skullbash? And why at this time?"

"Smatter was destroyed. We go for vengeance." Fletch told us that Smatter was an orc village off to the west, about a week away.

"How do you know it was Skullbash that took it out?" The elf continued his questioning.

"We saw them."

"Who's in the tower?"

"Us."

"Who told you to take the tower?"

"Chief Grumbach." Fletch informed us that Grumbach was the leader of the Blood Fist tribe and that he was an ogre who had decided to take up farming.

Cuthalion proceeded, "How long ago did you take the tower?"

"This morning. He told us take tower. Don't want to raise alarm on way to Skullbash."

"Where is Skullbash?"

"Over mountains." Fletch confirmed that this is where he had heard the Skullbash tribe lived, up in a series of rugged mountains that most traders avoided because stone giants lived there.

"Why would humans tell Skullbash you were coming?" Cuthalion continued.

"Humans no like us."

"Is Chief Grumbach in the tower?" The orc shook his head "no." "Where is Chief Grumbach?"

"Me tell, you no kill?" We agreed. "Orders were take forts, meet chief in Barrenstone."

"What about Black Tower?" Cuthalion inquired about the other outpost.

"Other group there."

We discussed amongst ourselves the political repercussions of the situation and decided that if at all possible it would be best for humans to stay out of this orcish war.

Cuthalion once again spoke to the entangled orcs, "Send this message to Chief Grumbach — tell him to find a way not to involve humans in this conflict. If you do, we will kill both tribes. Get your people out of both towers. One of you go ... the rest stay." David released the entanglement and six orcs stayed, sitting and glaring at us, while the one we had been speaking with went to the tower.

Eight orcs came out of the tower and seven started to the east. The leader returned. "Ok, we go tell Grumbach," he said, "Meet other orcs and tell message."

Cuthalion smiled, "Tell Grumbach you made a wise choice." The orc nodded and headed off with his comrades.

We ventured into the now empty tower to find several piles of bodies. It appeared as if some orc bodies had undergone ritual cremation while 12 humans lay about haphazardly. One ballista was in pieces, the other loaded and pointed at the gate while its operator lay among the dead. The smell of burning orc profaned the air, reminding us of the battle that took place only a few hours before. The gate was broken, but the tower was intact.

Cuthalion closed the remaining working gate as we entered and headed for the top of the tower; Fletch accompanied him. David and I looked for the message box the magistrate had told me about. We found it on the second floor and the key I had been given fit perfectly. The box opened and inside were three tubes: one labeled "Gateway," one labeled "Black Tower," and one that was unlabeled. Next to the tubes there were paper and ink for writing messages.

I immediately sent a warning off through the Black Tower tube. "About 40 orcs are headed your way. We've sent seven to tell them to turn back."

I slide the message down the tube and a whooshing sound carried it away. I then composed a message to Gateway, "Orcs took Blaze Arrow, 12 dead. Orcs after Skullbash group in the mountains near Barrenstone. We told them to leave humans alone. So far they have complied." As I dropped this message in the tube it made a sputtering sound like it had gotten stuck.

I looked at David. We decided to send a "test" message to the Black Tower tube asking them to confirm receipt. About three minutes later a note arrived back saying the message was received. I replied that the tube to Gateway seemed not to be working and asked them to forward my message and ask the magistrate to reply directly to me.

While we were waiting for a response, David began examining the machine. He discovered that the label for Gateway was loose. "Perhaps it has been switched," he suggested.

We decided to try a test message through the third unmarked tube.

Almost immediately we received a letter back, "Message received. What status?"

I repeated the story once again and told them the tube had been mislabeled. The operator on the other end replied that they had been attempting to connect the tubes to Barrenstone but so far had been unsuccessful.

Well, we were of course suspicious as to why the labels had been changed — that someone was purposely trying to screw up communication. David decided to ask about the guard rotation, "When was the last rotation? When can the next rotation come?"

The response came, "A day or two ago. They didn't report in when they got there."

We wondered if they had arrived and if not who the dead men in the tower were. "How many were in the rotation. Could we get a roster to identify the bodies?"

"10–12 people." That matched the number dead. "We are sending new people now. Will take one week. How bad is damage?"

"One ballista and one gate destroyed," we reported.

"What is the status of the second outpost? When will the orcs arrive there?" Gateway questioned.

We discussed the possible timetable. "About an hour. Warn Barrenstone too. We're on our way to Black Tower."

We decided to send a message to Black Tower as well as Gateway to tell them we were on our way. However we added that we might not make it in time due to our injuries. We didn't have any injuries, but David and I thought we might need more time to solve the mystery of the switched labels.

However, no more evidence presented itself and the group agreed to head off for Black Tower. We figured we would have to work it out carefully so that we could defend the tower if needed, but not make the orcs that were going to call for peace think we didn't trust them. David volunteered to sneak ahead and find the orcs. He returned shortly explaining that there were orcs ahead in the trees having an argument that he could not understand. The argument appeared to be between the orcs we had sent and the orcs we had not yet encountered.

Cuthalion agreed to accompany David so that he could interpret what the orcs were saying. Fletch and I waited, trying to determine how long we should stay put before thinking something had gone astray. At last, the two rangers returned, and Cuthalion announced that the majority of the orcs had been swayed to meet up with Grumbach. David suggested we bypass the tower alltogether and start heading for Barrenstone in case the orcs decided to attack there, because it was their meeting spot. But the rest of us were worried about the few dissenting orcs that were sure to attack Black Tower.

We snuck quietly toward the tower. Unfortunately, I always seem to trip when I'm trying so hard to move silently through the brush. The orcs heard me, and we took off running for the gate. We made it to the tower and explained the situation to the guards inside.

David asked the lieutenant to take us to the message box, and he did so without hesitation. The labels appeared to be in firmly in place; communication here had not been compromised. Fletch and Cuthalion reported that the orcs had retreated.

We communicated with Gateway, and Lieutenant Parros received his orders. He was to leave three men to man the ballista while he and the remaining nine followed us to Barrenstone.

As time was now quite short, we decided to run toward the town, taking only short breaks to rest. It was a tiresome journey, but we made it intact and appeared to have beaten the orcs. We immediately located the town official and informed him of the situation.

Cuthalion and David again decided to check on the situation with the orcs. I'd been practicing the art of invisibility and offered to make them both invisible. I called the energies around me, recited the words, and suddenly Cuthalion and David were gone. Fletch and I waited in town for them to return and convinced Lieutenant Parros to start evacuating the town.

After more than a bit of nervous waiting on our part, Cuthalion and David returned. They were again visible but in one piece.

"I spoke with Grumbach," the elf explained. "I told him that the magistrate knows what he's been up to and that we have plenty of soldiers in the village to challenge him; therefore, if he attacks the village he would be greatly weakened for his battle with Skullbash. I asked him what his reason for wanting to take the village was."

"What did he say?"

"He said he wanted prisoners as bargaining chips and to carry goods and supplies. So here's the deal ... he's willing to bypass the town in exchange for twenty pack animals to carry his things. He's going to come to the gate in 12 hours for our decision."

"Well, the town is nearly evacuated now. I don't know what they'll think of this," I explained, and added, "It was Fletch's idea to go ahead and evacuate."

Fletch shrugged his shoulders in his easy-going manner and said, "It needed to be done."

So, we went about the task of finding any pack animals that had been left behind and chasing after the villagers that had taken theirs and convincing them to give them back. It turned out with everyone so scared of the orcs it wasn't as difficult a task as we anticipated. We reassured the townspeople we would have twenty-five pack animals sent from Gateway to replace their twenty, and they thought it was a fair deal. Having gathered the livestock, we settled down in a few of the abandoned houses for some rest. It had been a very long day.

We were awakened by the news that some eighty orcs were headed for the town gate. I wiped the sleep from my eyes and combed my hair and headed out to see. We brought the cattle out from the gate and met the orcs. Cuthalion greeted them in the orc language, but we did not see Grumbach.

Out of nowhere, the voice of the ogre returned the orcish greeting in our own common tongue. With a lopsided grin, Grumbach's shiny black teeth appeared, as did the ogre himself. He towered above even the tallest orcs by several feet. His light blue skin and white eyes contrasted his black hair and teeth and a pair of vestigial horns adorned his brow. I noticed his fancy club and thought that my old friend Boris would be quite jealous for it was nearly five feet in length and quite shiny. I couldn't quite tell if it was made of metal or of wood.

Cuthalion presented the livestock as our gift of peace, and Grumbach told his men to take the animals. Then he turned to us. "What stops me from taking the town, too?" he asked.

I exchanged a nervous glance with my friends, but Cuthalion did not waiver. He replied defiantly, "Us."

Grumbach laughed, but it was a friendly laugh. He didn't believe us, but he respected our courage. "Maybe we meet some other time," he said.

Cuthalion responded, "And when will you be returning through here?"

Grumbach replied, "It should not take long to kill Skullbash. Three weeks."

"Then we will tell the humans not to disturb you on your return," Cuthalion replied with all the diplomacy of his elven ways.

Grumbach once more flashed a blacked grin, and the orcs continued on without incident.

Giddy with the joys of success, we headed back toward Black Tower where we sent a message relaying our accomplishments to the magistrate.

The magistrate returned a note, "Congratulations. Twenty-five horses and cows seems a small price to pay for the safety of Barrenstone."

Although none of us were injured, we decided we would like a cleric to meet up with us and have a look at the curse before entering Gateway. However, due to the nature of the communication and our fears that it would somehow be compromised, we simply requested that a cleric meet us outside of Gateway to attend to our injuries. Naturally the magistrate had no problems arranging this.

As promised, a half mile outside Gateway a jolly old cleric named Celegorm met us along with four guards who spouted the diamond district emblem. We explained our situation to Celegorm, but unfortunately he was not a skilled enough cleric to help in the removing of curses. The guards insisted that we were to come straight to the magistrate upon our return, and though I was nervous about entering town with the curse still upon our heads, we had little choice but to follow.

As we walked through town, it seemed everyone was looking at us. A ragged old man stared intently and then ran off suddenly, as did a young boy. But we made it to the magistrate without incident.

Once in his chambers, I introduced my new comrades to Eldonerand, the honorable magistrate of Gateway. He was pleased to meet them and thanked all of us for overcoming the orc situation.

"I am working with the council to deal with the possible problem when the orcs return," he told us.

David stepped up, "I was wondering, sir, did the last group of guards at Blaze Arrow report in? We found that the message array there had been mislabeled."

The magistrate looked somewhat concerned, "Hmm ... we will look into that. Any ideas?"

"Oh, nothing specific," David responded, "I just found it odd."

"Indeed."

"There is one more thing I wish to speak with you about, magistrate," I interjected. I proceeded to tell him my concerns about the curse that had been cast upon us. "Would it be possible to get an escort to the temple of Heironeous, where they may be able to help us?"

"Why certainly! This is most unfortunate."

"Yes. I think that we should lay low for awhile, magistrate."

"Yes, yes. Certainly. The council will be meeting soon, and I will put in a request that you be rewarded for your efforts."

"Thank you, sir."

After finishing our pleasantries with the honorable magistrate, we were escorted to the temple of Heironeous where I was recognized and well received. We were placed in the hands of an experienced cleric by the name of Brother Timothy. After telling our story, he smudged us with incense, sprinkled us with holy water, and muttered some prayerful words.

"There is indeed a blackness that touches you," he said. "I have seen many curses in my time, but nothing quite like this, nothing this powerful. Yet, it does not seem to be impairing you."

"Then there is nothing you can do?" I asked mournfully.

"I am afraid this is beyond me," he replied, still quite perplexed.

"Then, perhaps a blessing upon us, Brother Timothy?"

"Of course, of course." He blessed us but refused to accept any offering in exchange. "It is an honor to help you," he said with a courteous bow in my direction.

My friends insisted on stopping at the temples of their various gods since we were in the temple district. Every stop made me increasingly nervous, for everywhere we went people were staring at us. But the others seemed not to notice and accused me of being paranoid.

At last I relaxed a bit as we entered the familiar surroundings of the Topaz District and Scalamagra's Tower. The bouncy blonde-haired Ingie greeted me warmly, and once more I introduced my comrades. Poe flew from the back room and landed securely on my shoulder. "'Bout time," he squawked.

Ingie chuckled, "He's missed you."

We inquired about Maureen. Ingie informed us that she was going to remove the tattoo, but that didn't seem to be the thing to do. She suggested that Maureen try the temple, but had not heard back from her. "I believe she was staying at the Weary Wanderer Inn," she informed us.

"Thank you, Ingie." I led the party out of the shop and to the Weary Wanderer Inn where we were given Maureen's room number. We headed there to meet up with our friend and tell her of our most recent adventures.

Chapter Notes

Introduction

1. See essays by Waskul, Schut, Nephew, Marsh in Williams et al., *Gaming as Culture: Essays on Reality, Identity and Experience in Fantasy Games* (2006).

2. See essays by Hendricks in Williams et al.,*Gaming as Culture: Essays on Reality, Identity and Experience in Fantasy Games* (2006).

3. Interestingly, while tabletop role-playing games (TRPGs) emerged from wargaming, wargaming has also shifted as a genre. *Warhammer*, in particular, outlines a backstory for the different armies involved. In some cases, players of war games report the results of their battles, and these results then go toward the continued development of the game and story surrounding it. However, I would still consider *Warhammer* a wargame rather than a role-playing game (RPG) because of the focus on whole armies rather than individual characters.

4. Board games have grown extensively in recent years, and more studies need to be done to fully theorize what forms this medium as well.

5. *Dungeons and Dragons* (*D&D*) is probably one of the more rule-bound TRPGs. The rules of 2nd edition *D&D* were particularly complex; however, one of the goals of 3rd edition was to simplify the rules in order to get back to the original fantasy elements of the game (Rausch). Currently, 4th edition is out

and the rules have been changed again to be more simplified. However, all the editions are still in play depending on the particular gaming group.

6. I do not consider a narrator in a computer role-playing game (CRPG) to be a gamemaster because the voice-over is preprogrammed and not a live participant in the game. As online games are expanding, however, some may include another person acting in the role of the gamemaster (GM).

7. I use dungeon master (DM) over GM in this study to show that I focus on *D&D*. Although many of my arguments about the DM's role may be applicable to the GM in other games, I look specifically at *D&D,* which refers to the gamemaster as the dungeon master.

8. Massively multiplayer online role-playing games (MMORPGs) may also have invitation-only groups. However, a researcher could still buy the game and go home and immediately begin playing it. It may involve a great deal of game play before the researcher gains the social status to observe a guild in an MMORPG, but he or she can begin playing the game alone. A TRPG research cannot. However, a quick pick-up game of a TRPG may be easier to study as any gaming store will likely hold *D&D* session that anyone can join in.

191

Chapter 1

1. Each of these terms is problematic; however, I am not focusing on the role of the author in adventure games, so I offer these three terms as a way to refer to one concept — that of the force behind the creation of the story.

2. I find it interesting that the game states that the word is not in "your vocabulary," thus making the user seem like the one who is limited not the game itself. For instance, *stroll* is in the vocabulary of the user, if he or she typed it in, but the use of second person shifts the burden on the user to come up with the right words to access the narrative.

3. To the best of my knowledge, early text-based adventure games did not always have the save game features that make this more possible in current computer games.

4. I remember playing a text-based game, *Sherlock Holmes*, as a teen and being continually frustrated when the computer said something to the effect of "Holmes, your brain is Swiss cheese" when my commands were not understood. I gave up in frustration and never completed the game.

5. Although this study was the most recent one that was publicly available, it is already outdated. The study was conducted before 3rd Edition *D&D*, not to mention the most recent 4th Edition. It is likely that the numbers have changed with these new changes in the game. In fact, I did not start playing the game regularly until after 3rd edition, when the rules became easier for me to follow. In addition, this statistic does not take into account the many other tabletop role-playing games (TRPGs) besides *D&D*. Thus, it is safe to say that the number is currently higher than this data suggests.

Chapter 2

1. The 2nd edition of *Dungeons and Dragons* (*D&D*) was called *Advanced Dungeons and Dragons,* or *AD&D*.

2. Of course, the dungeon master (DM) has the power to have never created the door in the first place but, like the player, once he has articulated the presence of the door, it exists and cannot easily be retracted just because the players interact with it in an unanticipated way.

3. This is true for other types of texts as well. For example, one person may view a film as more of a thriller, picking up on the suspense aspects of the plot, whereas another may see it as a drama and be more attune to the characters' emotions. However, it seems that games, and in particular role-playing games (RPGs), are more likely to invoke different experiences due to their more overt participatory nature.

Chapter 3

1. This could be an author, a narrator, a dungeon master (DM), a game designer, even a user, but it is someone who takes a role in the development of the text.

2. This type of comment is common in all Dungeons and Dragons (*D&D*) modules, though when I observed the Role-Playing Gamers Association (RPGA) game one member commented that it was a line that had recently been added to all RPGA modules. He noted that in the past, RPGA games had not been allowed as much flexibility.

3. The DM may have a more complete view of the story and characters because he or she will be familiar with the details of the module. However, this does not mean that the DM will be privy to all the characters' motivations as players may also have secret agendas.

4. While the original Gygax and Mentzer module came out when an earlier edition of *D&D* was standard, both the new module by Cook and the computer role-playing game (CRPG) follow 3rd edition *D&D* rules.

Chapter 4

1. She includes in this list Espen Aarseth, Gonzalo Frasca, Markku Eskeline, and Jesper Juul (Ryan, 2006, p. 183).

2. Ryan (2006) points out that some games do follow a more prescribed order, while others have an open structure (p. 186).

3. Aarseth is talking specifically here about the hypertext story *Afternoon*; however, his analysis also fits with his view of adventure games.

Chapter 5

1. Special thanks to Brian Epstein who took the time to give me this clear description of possible-world theory in personal communication on July 13, 2009. Possible-world theory is far more complex than this, but the basic idea here will help inform the explanation of the theory in this chapter.

2. Of course, those that are skeptical of whether or not we can directly access reality may also call current reality a possible world.

3. Ironically, Punday (2005) states that "fictional worlds cannot be considered possible worlds strictly, since fictional worlds are created by an author" (p. 129). Punday cites Howell's 1979 article here, a forerunner in possible-world theory. However, he does not challenge the concept of the author evoked in this piece. Punday does go on to talk about fictional worlds referencing possible worlds but does not discuss the way readers rather than authors may form these worlds. These lines between authors and readers are particularly blurred in the tabletop role-playing game (TRPG).

4. Certainly an author can never know how his or her writing may be interpreted; however, in traditional texts, the reader does not change the direction of the text the way a player in a TRPG can. Even in a hypertext story where the reader may read the story in different or-ders, the reader still does not add to the text, merely navigate it in a different order. I return to this point extensively in chapter 7.

5. I acknowledge that this audience may be a personal one, such as the audience for a diary written only for a future self to read.

6. The players may be able to turn the table on the dungeon master (DM) to an extent by using alternative rules such as action points. Action points allow players extra bonuses. For example, a player may suggest in the game frame that their character use a rope to cross a chasm. The DM may then require a skill check, asking for a dice roll. Let's say the player roles a 1, which is the lowest roll. The DM may then narrate "your character attempts to swing on the rope, but his grasp fails and he falls into the chasm." At this point, a character with an action point to burn may say, "Wait! I want to use my action point. My character does successfully make it across." In this case the player would be able to take what the DM has narrated and basically un-write it and replace it with a different outcome. Yet, action points are an alternative rule, and even when they are used, their number is limited. Furthermore, I would argue that the DM always has the power to tell the player that the use of the action point is not allowed in that circumstance, thus holding final control over the narrative. Of course, social pressure comes into play here as well. A DM that makes a particularly unfavorable ruling may be subject to social pressure on the part of the players to retract this decision and thus alter the narrative.

7. This speech is referred to in the story in the appendix but is not included because the story was written from the point of view of Whisper, who was not present when the speech was delivered. However, other speech in the story is represented, many times word for word, as it was delivered in the gaming session.

8. Experience points are rewarded to players for successful activities. Usually

this involves combat, but in some games, DMs will grant experience for outstanding success in other areas. Because Sorpraedor was more focused on narrative and character development, this focus was reflected in the rewards given to players.

9. Occasionally players may run more than one character. This has happened in my experience when a player needed to be absent from the campaign and had another player play his character. It has also happened when only a very small group has been able to get together, such as a game with only two players. I would hypothesize that in these cases the players would also be more likely to use 3rd person.

Chapter 6

1. This set of miniatures started as a collectible miniatures game, and interesting throw back to the wargaming genre. However, after several years, the game ceased to be officially supported by Wizards of the Coast, who found that the main market for the miniatures consisted of those playing the tabletop game. At this point, they have continued to release the figures, but not the stat cards needed to play the miniatures game. Interestingly, a community of players (with Wizards of the Coast's blessing) has continued to produce stat cards for these new figures. This game would be an interesting study by itself, but unfortunately falls outside the bounds of the current project.

2. The scale of many miniatures is 28mm:6ft.

3. I give more information on both of these backstories in the next chapter on authorship.

4. Interestingly, these two do not always seem to go hand in hand. For example, I was far more interested in Whisper's backstory than the items she was carrying while I found that other players really enjoyed outfitting characters with-

out really knowing much about their personal histories.

5. Many colleagues have asked me about the pedagogical value of this work, and while I do think there might be something to be gained by thinking about role-playing in these terms, pedagogical implications are not the goal of this current study because of the reasons listed in this chapter.

Chapter 7

1. The reader could, however, write his or her own text in response, such as in the case of fan fiction. However, this still does not alter the actual text.

2. This type of attention is more likely to happen in a campaign where the DM creates his/her own world and has an ongoing relationship with the players. It also indicates a simulationist sort of approach where realism in the storyworld is privileged over game rules.

Chapter 8

1. Naturally, some would argue this was not an improvement, and some gamers continue to play with 2nd edition Dungeons and Dragons (D&D) rules before the d20 system was implemented.

2. I attended Worldwide D&D Day at my local gaming store on May 23, 2009. This day was for the release of the 4th edition Monster Manual 2 rule book. I received a special edition miniature and played a module that had been released specifically for that event.

3. This point was brought home to me during the course of writing this book when I attended DragonCon in Atlanta the same weekend as a major football game. Unfortunately, football fans were reported yelling slurs at, and even throwing eggs at convention goers. It is socially acceptable to wear the football jersey of a favorite team while walking down the street, but it is not acceptable to wear a

corset and fairy wings. This difference in social status makes me hesitant to consider sports fans in the same light as other fans; however, I acknowledge that this community is also not homogenous.

4. Fine also found that the majority had a strong opinion about war, but not necessarily a common opinion. Some were former military officers, some pacifists. This particular statistic is interesting, but seems more relevant to the time of Fine's study in the Vietnam era.

5. This is changing to an extent as some *D&D* books are now found at chains such as Barnes and Noble. However, it is only at a local gaming store or a gaming convention that one will find a variety of tabletop role-playing game (TRPG) products, and it is rarer still to find a gaming group playing a TRPG at a large chain store.

Chapter 9

1. I have been surprised at the number of scholars who, upon hearing about my book, have assumed that *Dungeons and Dragons* (*D&D*) and tabletop role-playing are examples of digital technologies. Gaming has become synonymous with digital technology and digital literacy, so much so that I have even seen texts, such as Hammer's (2007) piece that incorporate to face-to-face games talked about in terms of "videogame" theory. Ludology and its explicit focus on videogames only serves to further this notion. It is my hope that this study helps shatter the myth that all gaming is computer gaming.

2. Interestingly, Hammer (2007) objects to Mackay's definition because it is not broad enough to include massively multiplayer online role-playing games (MMORPGs) (p. 69), while Mackay clearly criticizes other definitions as being so broad as to apply to "an online MUSH

... a murder-mystery game, or a game of cops and robbers" (p. 4). Unlike other authors, he seeks a definition that is specific to the tabletop game.

3. This definition may initially seem to fit live-action role-play (LARP) as well. Players still distinguish between TRPGs and LARPs, but there is a fine line between character acting in TRPGs and the sort of acting that takes place in a LARP. I hypothesize that one of the main differences between these genres would be the number of people involved in any instance. While conventions may have rooms full of TRPG players, they are still broken into small groups for game play while LARP usually involves large groups. However, additional research is needed in order to fully explain the relationship between these two genres.

4. At the time of this writing, *D&D* 4th edition has been out for a year, and there is still a great deal of resistance by players who argue that the new rules do not promote storytelling in the same way that 3rd edition did. However, it is still too early to tell what effect this new edition will have on the genre. It may become the preferred method of play with only a small handful of gamers sticking to 3rd edition (or earlier), or it may be that it is less successful and more rule changes will quickly come about.

5. Kim appears to be the originator of the threefold model, although the original listserv is not currently accessible, making it difficult to pinpoint the origins of the model with any certainty. Kim reposts some of the original messages on his website, but does not make it clear who said what in some of the original postings. This problem is a common challenge with online source material.

6. Both Mark and Mary have also commented on it being one of the best groups they have ever played with.

References

Aarseth, E. J. (1997). *Cybertext: Perspectives on ergodic literature.* Baltimore: The Johns Hopkins University Press.

Barthes, R. (1975). *S/Z: An essay.* (R. Miller, trans.) New York: Hill and Wang.

_____. (1977). "From work to text." (R. Miller, trans.) In *Image music text* (pp. 155–164). New York: Hill and Wang.

Bawarshi, A. (2003). *Genre and the invention of the writer.* Logan: Utah State University Press.

Bebergal, P. (2004, November 15). "How 'Dungeons' changed the world." *The Boston Globe.* Retrieved December 1, 2004, from www.boston.com/news/globe/editorial_opinion/oped/articles/2004/11/15/dungeons_and_dragons_we_love_you/.

Bitzer, L. (1968). "The rhetorical situation." *Philosophy and Rhetoric, 1,* 1–14.

Bolter, J. D. (1991). *Writing space: the computer, hypertext, and the history of writing.* Hillsdale: Lawrence Erlbaum.

Bruner, J. (1991). "The narrative construction of reality." *Critical Inquiry, 18,* 1–21.

Carr, D., D. Buckingham, A. Burn, and G. Schott (2006). *Computer games: Text, narrative and play.* Cambridge and Malden: Polity.

Cook, M. (2002). *Book of vile darkness.* Renton: Wizards of the Coast.

Cook-Gumperz, J. (1992). "Gendered contexts." In P. Auer and A. DiLizio (eds.) *The Contextualization of Language* (pp. 177–98). Amsterdam: John Benjamins Publishing Company.

Cordell, B. R., & Williams, S. (2001). *Tome and blood: A guidebook to wizards and sorcerers.* Renton: Wizards of the Coast.

Crawford, G and J. Rutter (2007). "Playing the game: Performance in digital game audiences." In J. Gray, C. Sandvoss and C. L. Harrington (eds.) *Fandom: Identities and communities in a mediated world* (pp. 271–284). New York: New York University Press.

Dancey, R. (2000). *Adventure game industry market research summary (RPGs) V1.0.* Wizards of the Coast. Retrieved October 24, 2004, from www.seankreynolds.com/rpgfiles/gaming/WotCMarketResearchSummary.html.

Devitt, A. J. (2004). *Writing genres.* Carbondale: Southern Illinois University Press.

Dovey, J., and H. W. Kennedy (2006). *Games cultures: Computer games as new media.* New York: Open University Press.

Drader, D., and Bounds, T. (2001). *Gateway: The city of living waters.* Anchorage: Dark Portal Games.

Dungeon Master's Guide: Core Rulebook II. (2003). Renton: Wizards of the Coast.

Fanfiction.net. Retrieved August 2009, from www.fanfiction.net/.

Fine, G. A. (1983). *Shared fantasy: Role playing games as social worlds.* Chicago: University Of Chicago Press.

Fish, S. (1982). *Is there a text in this class? The authority of interpretive communities.* Cambridge and London: Harvard University Press.

Fisher, W. (1984). "Narration as a human communication paradigm: The case of public moral argument." *Communication Monographs, 51*, 1–22.

Fludernik, M. (1994). "Second-person narrative as a test case for narratology: The limits of realism." *Style, 28*(3), 445.

Flynn, B. (2004). "Games as inhabited Spaces." *Media International Australia Incorporating Culture and Policy, 110*, 52–61.

GenCon LLC. Retrieved August 2009, from www.gencon.com/.

Goffman, E. (1961). *Encounters.* Indianapolis: The Bobbs-Merrill Company.

Goings, R. (2001, July 2). Interview With R.A. Salvatore. Retrieved August 15, 2009, from www.3rdedition.org/articles/viewer.asp?ID=29.

Gray, J., C. Sandvoss, and C. L. Harrington (2007). *Fandom: Identities and communities in a mediated world.* New York: NYU Press.

Gygax, G., and F. Mentzer (1985). *The temple of elemental evil.* Lake Geneva: TSR Hobbies.

Hammer, J. (2007). "Agency and authority in role-playing texts." In M. Knobel and C. Lankshear (eds.) *A new literacies sampler* (pp. 67–94). New York: Peter Lang.

Hendricks, S. Q. (2006). "Incorporative discourse strategies in tabletop fantasy role-playing gaming." In J. P. Williams, S. Q. Hendricks, and W. K. Winkler (eds.) *Gaming as culture* (pp. 39–56). Jefferson: McFarland & Company, Inc.

Herman, D. (2004). "Toward a transmedial narratology." In M.L. Ryan (ed.) *Narrative across media: The languages of storytelling* (pp. 47–75). Lincoln and London: University of Nebraska Press.

Hills, M. (2002). *Fan cultures.* New York: Routledge.

Jamieson, K. (1975). "Antecedent genre as rhetorical constraint." *Quarterly Journal of Speech, 61,* 406–415.

Jasinski, J. (2001). "Genre." In *Sourcebook on rhetoric: Key concepts in contemporary rhetorical studies* (pp. 268–276). Thousand Oaks: Sage.

Jenkins, H. (1992). *Textual poachers: Television fans and participatory culture.* New York: Routledge.

_____. (2002). "Game design as narrative architecture." In N. Wardrip-Fruin and P. Harrigan (eds.) *First Person.* Cambridge: MIT Press. Retrieved June 20, 2009, from web.mit.edu/cms/People/henry3/games&narrative.html.

Juul, J. (2001). "Games telling stories?— a brief note on games and narratives." *Game Studies, 1*(1). Retrieved October 10, 2003, from www.gamestudies.org/0101/juul-gts/.

Kasavin, G. (2003, September 22). "The temple of elemental evil review." *Gamespot.* Retrieved September 19, 2009, from www.gamespot.com/pc/rpg/greyhawkthetempleofee/review.html.

Katz, D. (2004). Gamebook history. Unpublished Manuscript.

Keller, D. (2007). "Reading and Playing: What Makes Interactive Fiction Unique." In J. P. Williams and J. H. Smith (eds.) *The players' realm: Studies on the culture of video games and gaming* (pp. 276–297). Jefferson: McFarland & Company..

Kelly, R. V. (2004). *Massively multiplayer online role-playing games: The people, the addiction and the playing experience.* Jefferson: McFarland & Company, Inc.

Kim, J. H. (1998, October). "The threefold model FAQ." *rec.games.frp.advocacy.* Retrieved September 1, 2009, from www.darkshire.net/~jhkim/rpg/theory/threefold/faq_v1.html#faq2.

_____. (2008, March 20). "The threefold model." http://www.darkshire.net/~jhkim/rpg/theory/threefold/. Retrieved September 1, 2009, from http://www.darkshire.net/~jhkim/rpg /theory/threefold/.

Kushner, D. (2003). *Masters of doom: How two guys created an empire and transformed pop culture*. New York: Random House.

Labov, W. (1972). "The transformation of experience in narrative syntax." In *Language in the inner city* (pp. 354–396). Philadelphia: University of Pennsylvania.

Lacy, K. N. (2006). *Narrative and identity in fantasy role-playing games*. (Doctoral dissertation, New York University.) Retrieved June 18, 2009, from home pages.nyu.edu/~knl201/diss.html.

Lewis, S., J. Trevett, and R. Dansky (2004, July 23). Panel presentation at Trinoc*coN, Raleigh, NC.

Lowery, L. (1983). *Spell Of the winter wizard: Endless quest book #11*. Lake Geneva: TSR.

Mackay, D. (2001). *The fantasy role-playing game: A new performing art*. Jefferson: McFarland & Company, Inc..

Mazzanoble, S. (2007). *Confessions of a part-time sorceress: A girl's guide to the D&D game*. Renton: Wizards of the Coast.

Miller, C. (1984). Genre as social action. *Quarterly Journal of Speech, 70*, 151–167.

Miller, C., and D. Shepherd (2004). "Blogging as social action: A genre analysis of the weblog." *Into The Blogosphere*. Retrieved October 22, 2004, from blog.lib.umn.edu/blogosphere/ blogging_as_social_action.html.

_____. (in press 2009). "Questions for Genre Theory from the Blogosphere. "In J. Giltrow and D. Stein (eds.) *Theories of genre and their application to internet communication*. Amsterdam: John Benjamins.

Mona, E., and J. Jacobs (2004, November). The 30 greatest *D&D* adventures of all time. *Dungeon, 116*, 68–81.

Montfort, N. (2003). *Twisty little passages: An approach to interactive fiction*. Cambridge: The MIT Press.

Murray, J. H. (1998). *Hamlet on the holodeck: The future of narrative in cyberspace*. New York: The MIT Press.

Nephew, M. (2006). "Playing with identity: Unconscious desire and role-playing games." In J. P. Williams, S. Q. Hendricks, and W. K. Winkler (eds.) *Gaming as culture* (pp. 120–139). Jefferson: McFarland & Company, Inc.

Ochs, E., and L. Capps (2001). "A dimensional approach to narrative." In *Living narrative* (pp. 1–57). Cambridge: Harvard University Press.

Park, A., and E. Chin (1999). History of advanced *Dungeons and Dragons. Gamespot*. Retrieved September 13, 2009, from au.gamespot.com/features/ history_add/index.html.

Pearson, R. (2007). "Bachies, bardies, trekkies, and Sherlockians." In J. Gray, C. Sandvoss, and C. L. Harrington (eds.) *Fandom: Identities and communities in a mediated world* (pp. 98–109). New York: New York University Press.

Prince, G. (2003). *A Dictionary of Narratology* (Revised.) Lincoln and London: University of Nebraska Press.

Punday, D. (2005). "Creative accounting: Role-playing games, possible-world theory, and the agency of imagination." *Poetics Today, 26*(1), 113–139. doi: 10.1215/03335372–26–1–113.

Rausch, A. (2004, August 15). "A history of *D&D* video games." *GameSpy*. Retrieved September 13, 2009, from pc. gamespy.com/articles/538/538865p1. html.

Reid, T. M. (2001). *The temple of elemental Evil*. Renton: Wizards of the Coast.

Reynolds, S. K. (2003, January 26). "Breakdown of RPG players." Retrieved September 1, 2009, from www.seankreynolds.com/rpgfiles/gam ing/BreakdownOfRPGPlayers.html.

Rilstone, A. (1994). "Role-playing games: An overview." *Inter*Action*. Retrieved October 10, 2003, from 216.239. 41.104/search?q=cache:zQjD3kHc5x QJ:www.rpg.net/oracle/essays/rpgov erview.html+narrative+%22role+play ing+games%22&hl=en&ie=UTF-8.

Rimmon-Kenan, S. (2002). *Narrative fiction: Contemporary poetics* (2nd ed.) London and New York: Routledge.

Russell, D. (1997). "Rethinking genre in school and society: An activity theory analysis." *Written Communication, 14*(4), 504–555.

Ryan, M. L. (1991). *Possible worlds, artificial intelligence, and narrative theory.* Bloomington and Indianapolis: Indiana University Press.

_____. (2003). *Narrative as virtual reality: Immersion and interactivity in literature and electronic media.* Baltimore: The Johns Hopkins University Press.

_____. (2004). *Narrative across media: The languages of storytelling.* Lincoln: University of Nebraska Press.

_____. (2005a). "Media and narrative." In D. Herman, M. Jahn, and M. L. Ryan (eds.) *Encyclopedia of Narrative Theory* (pp. 288–292). London and New York: Routledge.

_____. (2005b). "Narrative." In D. Herman, M. Jahn, and M. L. Ryan (eds.) *Routledge Encyclopedia of Narrative Theory* (pp. 344–348). London and New York: Routledge.

_____. (2006). *Avatars of story.* Minneapolis and London: University of Minnesota Press.

Stahl, G. (2003). "Tastefully renovating subcultural theory: Making space for a new model." In D. Muggleton and R. Weinzierl (eds.) *The Post-Subcultures Reader* (pp. 27–40). Oxford: Berg.

Sternberg, M. (1981). "Ordering the unordered: Time, space, and descriptive coherence." *Yale French Studies, 61,* 60–88.

Swales, J. (1990). *Genre analysis: English in academic and research settings.* Cambridge: Cambridge University Press.

Temple of Elemental Evil: A Classic Greyhawk Adventure. (2003). Video Game. Atari.

Toolan, M. (2001). *Narrative: A critical linguistic introduction* (2nd ed.) London and New York: Routledge.

Tulach, C. (2008, July 30). "Part 5: Living *Forgotten Realms.*" *Dragon, 365.* Retrieved July 29, 2009, from www.wizards.com/default.asp?x=dnd/drrep/20080730.

Tweet, J., M. Cook, and S. Williams (2003). *Player's handbook, Version 3.5* (3rd ed.) Renton: Wizards of the Coast.

Walsh, R. (2007). *The rhetoric of fictionality: Narrative theory and the idea of fiction.* Columbus: The Ohio State University Press.

Waters, D. (2004, April 26). "What happened to *Dungeons and Dragons?*" *BBC.* Retrieved August 31, 2009, from news.bbc.co.uk/2/hi/uk_news/magazine/3655627.stm.

Weinzierl, R., and D. Muggleton (2003). "What is 'Post-subcultural studies' anyway?" In D. Muggleton and R. Weinzierl (eds.) *The Post-Subcultures Reader* (pp. 3–26). Oxford: Berg.

Whedon, J. (2008). *Dr. Horrible's Sing-Along Blog.* DVD, Mutant Enemy, INC., from www.drhorrible.com/.

Wittgenstein, L. A. G. (1953). *Philosophical Investigations* (G.E.M Anscombe, trans.). The MacMillan Company, New York.

Williams, J. P., S. Q. Hendricks, and W. K. Winkler (2006). *Gaming as culture: Essays on reality, identity and experience in fantasy games.* Jefferson: McFarland & Company, Inc.

Winkler, W. K. (2006). "The business and the culture of gaming." In J. P. Williams, S. Q. Hendricks, and W. K. Winkler (eds.) *Gaming as culture* (pp. 140–153). Jefferson: McFarland & Company, Inc.

Wizards of the Coast. Retrieved July 2009, from http://wizards.com/.

Wyatt, J. (2001). *The Speaker in Dreams.* Renton: Wizards of the Coast.

Index